MIKHAIL KIZILOV

KARAITES THROUGH THE TRAVELERS' EYES:

ETHNIC HISTORY, TRADITIONAL CULTURE AND
EVERYDAY LIFE OF THE CRIMEAN KARAITES
ACCORDING TO THE DESCRIPTIONS OF THE TRAVELERS

*A Publication of the al-Qirqisani
Center for the Promotion of Karaite Studies*

New York
2003

Library of Congress Card Number: (pending)

ISBN 0-9700775-6-4

To my dear homeland, the troubled southern land of the Crimea, its warm sea, shadowy valleys, and high mountains.

Моей дорогой родине, неспокойной земле крымского полуострова, ее теплому морю, тенистым долинам и высоким горам.

Table of Contents

LIST OF ABBREVIATIONS

AAN MWRiOP	*Archiwum Akt Nowych, Ministerstwo Wyznań Religijnych i Oświęcenia Publicznego*
AFP	*Archivum Fratrum Praedicatorum*
AGAD AKW	*Archiwum Główne Akt Dawnych, Archiwum Koronne Warszawskie*
AGAD ASK	*Archiwum Główne Akt Dawnych, Archiwum Skarbu Koronnego*
AOASH	*Acta Orientalia Academiae Scientiarum Hungaricae*
BEK	*Bulletin d'Études Karaïtes*
EJ	*Encyclopaedia Judaica*
GAARK Krym	*Gosudarstvennyi Arkhiv Avtonomnoy Respubliki*
HUS	*Harvard Ukrainian Studies*
ITOIAE	*Izvestiia Tavricheskogo Obschestva Istorii, Arkheologii i Etnografii*
ITUAK	*Izvestiia Tavricheskoi Uchenoi Arkhivnoi Komissii*
JE	*Jewish Encyclopedia*
JEx	*Jewish Expositor*
JJoS	*Jewish Journal of Sociology*
JJS	*Journal of Jewish Studies*
JQR	*Jewish Quarterly Review*
KZh	*Karaimskaia Zhizn'*
KV	*Karaimskie Vesti*

MS LLAS	*Library of Lithuanian Academy of Sciences*
MAIET	*Materialy po Arkheologii, Istorii i Etnografii Tavriki*
MK	*Myśl Karaimska*
PSB	*Polski Słownik Biograficzny*
RGADA	*Rossiiskii Gosudarstvennyi Arkhiv Davnikh Aktov*
RM	*Rocznik Muzułmański*
ZhMNP	*Zhurnal Ministerstva Narodnogo Prosvescheniia*
ZOOID	*Zapiski Odesskogo Obshtchestva Istorii i Drevnostei*

Pronunciation Guide

Many names in this volume are of Turkic origin, and the Turkic spelling of the names has been preserved. In order to facilitate their correct pronunciation, the following guide is herein presented.

a	like a Patah in Hebrew
b	like a b in English
c	like a j in English
ç	like a ch in English
d	like a d in English
e	like a Seghol or Sere in Hebrew
f	like an f in English
g	like a hard g in English
ğ	like a Gimel Rafah in Hebrew/Ghayn in Arabic (but in modern Istanbul pronunciation [due to Greek influence] is more like a palatalized y)
h	like a Heh or a Het in Hebrew/He or Ha in Arabic
i	like a Hireq in Hebrew
ı	like ы in Russian or the î in Romanian
j	like the j in French
k	like a Kaf in Hebrew/Kaf in Arabic/k in English
kh	like a Kaf Rafah in Hebrew/Kha in Arabic
l	like the Lamed in Hebrew/Lam in Arabic
m	like an m in English
n	like an n in English
ng	like the ng in the English word long
o	like a Holam in Hebrew
ö	like ö in German
p	like a p in English, but not as hard at the end of a word
q	like a Qof in Hebrew/Qaf in Arabic
r	like a Resh in Hebrew/Ra in Arabic/R in Spanish or Italian, but, in Istanbul pronunciation palatalized similar to a r with a hacek above in Czech when occurring at the end of a word
s	like a Samekh in Hebrew/Sin in Arabic
ş	like an sh in English/Shin in Hebrew/Shin in Arabic
t	like a Taw in Hebrew/Ta in Arabic, but at the end of a word it is softer like a Taw Rafah in Hebrew
u	like a Shuruq in Hebrew
ü	like ü in German
v	between a v and w in English
w	like a w in English

y	like a Yod in Hebrew/Ya in Arabic
z	like a z in English

The digraphs of a vowel followed by a y are:

ay	like a Patah-Yod in Hebrew/Fatha-Ya in Arabic
ey	like a Seghol-Yod in Hebrew
oy	like a Holam-Yod in Hebrew

Luck	pronounced "Lutsk"

Image Index

Acknowledgements

Hereby the author would like to express his most sincere gratitude and thankfulness to all persons and institutions without whose academic, financial, and personal support this book hardly could have ever been published.

To my dear teachers and academic advisors, Dr. A.G.Gertsen (Simferopol'), Professor Gerhard Jaritz (Budapest), Professor Daniel Frank (Oxford), and Professor Jerzy Tomaszewski (Warsaw).

To Dr. Philip Miller (New York), whose unparalleled dedication to the history of the Crimean Karaites inspired me to attempt my own research in this field.

To Dr. Dan Shapira (Jerusalem), for friendly support and numerous advices related to various historical and linguistical problems this book is dealing with.

To Mr. Artem Fedorchouk (Moscow), for years of friendship and academic assistance.

To Mrs. Golda Akhiezer (Jerusalem), for many valuable remarks concerning the contents of this study.

To Mr. Brad Sabin Hill (Oxford-New York), for permission to consult his Karaitica collection in Oxford.

To Mr. O.B.Belyi (Sevastopol') and V.G.Zarubin (Simferopol').

To Mr. Vidas Alvikas, assistant of the Trakai History Museum, Karaim ethnographic section (Trakai, Lithuania).

To Mr. Leonid Berestovskiy (Simferopol') for providing me with some of his excellent photos of the Crimean Karaite monuments.

To Tatiana Velichko and Mikhail Tiaglyi – to Tania for the permission to consult her Karaite materials.

To Sergei Borisov, for his constant willingness to participate in our numerous and lengthy field trips to the Crimean mountains, and help in the investigation of the Crimean Karaite monuments *de visu*.

To the library of the Crimean Museum of Local Lore "Taurica" ("Таврика") in Simferopol', its director N.N.Kolesnikova, and T.V.Shubina, for their help in my research and permission to use materials of the library.

To the Çorefs, a Karaite family residing in Bakhçesaray, and especially to Mr. Mikhail Çoref, for the permission to consult his private family collection of the material objects of Karaite history and culture.

To my parents, Boris and Natalya, for their patience, care, and understanding.

To the institutions whose financial and academic support helped the author to carry out his research in the field of Karaite Studies:

To Mr. George Soros and the Open Society Foundation (Budapest) for many years of financial support in my studies beyond the borders of the former Soviet Union.

To the department of Mediæval Studies of the Central European University (Budapest) and, personally, to one of its senior members, Professor Janos Bak.

To the Oxford Center for Hebrew and Jewish Studies (Yarnton, Oxford).

To the Graduate School for Social Research (Warsaw) and its dean, Professor Stefan Amsterdamski, for supporting my studies in Poland, and field-trips to Lithuania and its archival collections.

To the Center for Studying and Teaching of Jewish Civilization "Sefer" (Moscow), and to Dr. V.V.Mochalova and Dr. R.M.Kaplanov.

To the Crimean department of the Institute of Oriental Studies (Simferopol'), and its director, Professor A.I.Aibabin.

To the Simon Dubnow Institute for Jewish History and Culture (Leipzig), its director, Professor Dan Diner, and Dr. Stefan Wendehorst.

And, finally, to the institution who is responsible for the book you are holding now in your hands, the al-Qirqisani Center for the Promotion of Karaite Studies (New York), and specifically, to the project team who worked on this volume: Avraham Ben-Raḥamiël Qanaï, Ana Yaron, and Yosef Yaron, for their self-sacrificing work on the editing and proofreading of my manuscript, and Ana Yaron for her jacket design, and for proofreading the final copy of this work.

Foreword

In spite of the fact that the bibliography of publications related to the history of the Crimean Karaites is quite large, consisting of several hundred items written in various European and Oriental languages, this topic is far from exhausted. There are several schools of thought relating to the history of this highly interesting ethno-confessional group, which seem (sometimes deliberately, sometimes accidentally) to ignore each other. They exist, so to say, in different dimensions, and operate using different terms, methodologies, definitions, and approaches. One of these schools is represented by scholarship in Russian. This school is distinguished by its good orientation in local understanding of the issues, and visual acquaintance with Karaite architectural and archæological monuments; however, simultaneously, they possess scarce and superficial knowledge of Western scholarship (the sources in Hebrew and European languages).[1] The other school is represented by West-European, American, and Israeli academic literature, which – despite its very profound infiltration into the world of the Crimean Karaism, and emphasis upon the in-depth analysis of sources in Hebrew and Karaim – has its shortcomings, namely, a superficial knowledge of rare nineteenth – twentieth century publications in Russian and Polish. Furthermore, they possess only a second-hand acquaintance with the Crimea's everyday reality. This is the aftermath of the iron curtain, which did not allow Western scholars to travel abroad and work in the libraries and archives of the Soviet Union.[2] The third approach is represented by Karaite scholarship, which tends to be much more biased and tendentious than the aforementioned schools, emphasizing only the Khazar-Turkic roots of Karaism, and often denying any

---

[1] *E.g.* A.G.Gertsen and Y.M. Mogarichev, *Krepost' Dragotsennostei. Chufut-Kale. Kyrk-Or* [The fortress of treasures: Çufut-Qalé, Kyrk-Or] (Simferopol', 1993); O.B.Belyi, "Karaimskaia obshchina Chufut-Kale (obzor istochnikov i istoriografii)" [The Karaite community of Çufut-Qalé: a review of sources and historiography], in *Problemy istorii "peshchernykh gorodov" v Krymu* [The problems of the history of the "cave-towns" in the Crimea] (Simferopol', 1992), 151-163; I.N.Belaia and O.B.Belyi, "K voprosu o nazvanii i samonazvanii vostochnoevropeiskikh karaimov v XIII-nachale XIX vekov" [On the question of the external appellation and self-appelation of the Eastern-European Karaites in the 13th to early 19th centuries], in *MAIET* 5 (1996), 271-278; V.L.Vikhnovich, *Karaim Avraam Firkovich: Evreiskie rukopisi, istoriia, puteshestviia* [The Karaite Abraham Firkovich: Jewish manuscripts, history, travels] (St.Petersburg, 1997) et alia.

[2] It is only in the 1990s that Western scholars received a chance to undertake a serious study of the Karaitica collections of the Russian libraries and archives.

relationship between the Eastern European Karaites, Judaism, and Jewish civilization in general.[3]

In this book, I would like to disprove Rudyard Kipling's famous "*East is East, and West is West, and never the twain shall meet,*" and attempt to combine the knowledge I received in the West with my first-hand acquaintance with local Crimean material, and Karaite scholarship in Russian and Polish. This book, a result of long-term research in many European libraries,[4] was originally intended as a term paper; it later grew into the draft for a doctoral dissertation, and only then, some years later, it was transformed into a separate monograph.

Antoine Roquentin, the main character of J.P.Sartre's "Nausée", complained that, while compiling a historical essay on the biography of the Marquise de Rolbone, he was often on the verge of loosing the feeling of reality surrounding the historical matters he was studying. I, however, while reading the well-worn pages of the travelers' notes, used as the main sources for this book, never had this feeling of historicity vanishing in the library's air. On the contrary, when raising my head from the books I was reading, I could clearly see before my eyes the noble faces of my authors, whose travel diaries I have been so diligently studying in the course of my several years' work. I could see E.Clarke mounting the inaccessible mountain of Mangoup, a settlement with the remains of an abandoned Karaite colony, Xavier Hommaire de Hell dying of fever in Persia, Russian writer E.Markov observing with astonishment the figure of Avraham Firkovich approaching him amidst the picturesque ruins of Çufut-Qalé – John Webster, a young British aristocrat who died soon after his journey to the Crimea – Poland's most famous poet A. Mickiewicz

---

[3] A full bibliography is too vast to be given here; see the latest publications: Simon Szyszman, *Les Karaites d'Europe* (Uppsala, 1989); E.I.Lebedeva *Ocherki po istorii krymskih karaimov-tiurkov* [Sketches on the history of the Crimean Karaims-Turks] (Simferopol', 2000); Y.A.Polkanov, *Karai – Krymskie karaimy-tiurki. Karais – the Crimean Karaites-Turks* (Simferopol', 1997); *Legendy i predaniia karaev (krymskikh karaimov-tiurkov)* [Legends and traditions of the Karais (Crimean Karaite Turks)], ed. by Y.A.Polkanov (Simferopol', 1995); *Karai (Krymskie karaimy): Istoriya, kultura, sviatyni* [Karais (Crimean Karaites): History, culture, shrines] (Simferopol', 2000).

[4] "Taurica" and University libraries in Simferopol' (Crimea), Russian National Library (RNB) in St.Petersburg, Bodleian and Oriental Institute libraries in Oxford, National Library in Warsaw (Poland), National Library in Budapest (Hungary), Library of Lithuanian Academy of Sciences (Vilnius/Wilno, Lithuania) Hebrew University Library in Jerusalem (Israel), Deutsche Bücherei and University Library in Leipzig (Germany), Bibliotheque nationale de France in Paris, private Karaitica collections, to mention some of them.

20

having a dinner in the house of Simḥah Babovich – E.Henderson's vain attempts to decipher the Hebrew letters on the most ancient Karaite tombstones in the cemetery in the Yehoshafat Valley, worn by the hand of time – and many, many other men of letters, scholars, travelers, and tourists from various countries and epochs, who dedicated their time and attention to the description of the mysterious *Benei Miqra'* community: The Karaites of the Crimea.

However, when I start reading the travelers' notes again, their faces fade away. They are replaced by the picturesque, Biblical countenances of the subjects of their travel diaries. These are Crimean Karaites, dressed in Oriental Tatar attire, speaking the guttural Turkic language of their Muslim neighbours, raising their prayers and litanies to God in the mountainous synagogues of Mangoup and Çufut-Qalé, engraving eloquent Hebrew epitaphs on the tombstones of their fathers in the local Karaite cemeteries. I see young Shelomoh Beim, while shy of the wrath of the community's elders, satisfying the inquisitiveness of European visitors to Çufut-Qalé. I see the patriarchal face of A.Firkovich met by Wł.Syrokomla in Troki, far from the atrocities of the Crimean War. There is Yehudah Qazas conversing with A.Demidov while carving the next page in "the stone book of Yehoshafat," as he euphemistically called the cemetery in the Yehoshafat Valley near Çufut-Qalé. I feel the unbearable summer heat of Evpatoria's crooked, narrow streets. I see the dilapidated stones of the ruined Çufut-Qalé, the despair of the old Karaite Simḥah – expelled, together with other members of the community, from their ancient seat on the top of the mountainous Mangoup...

Drawing my look back to the pages of my book, I would like to ask these travelers, whose notes I am using as the main foci of my sources, those Crimean Karaites, to pardon me for any possible mistakes, that might have occurred in my attempts to interpret their words, ideas, feelings, deeds, and emotions.

My dear readers you are now about to start your journey to the remote realm of the Crimean Karaim. It is remote both in terms of time and distance. Please, be aware: much of what you will find here might seem strange, unusual or even outrageous. However, as Goethe said in one of his poems:

Wer den Dichter will verstehen
Muss in Dichter's Lande gehen...

CHAPTER 1
INTRODUCTION: HISTORICAL BACKGROUND AND REVIEW OF THE SOURCES

Travelers' notes concerning the Crimean Karaites, in spite of their unquestionable value and importance, have been rather superficially investigated by students of Karaism.[5] Although many

---

[5]   It seems that the only accounts analyzed in detail are from the time of the Crimean War (1853-1856), *i.e.*: Moshe Gammer, "The Karaites of the Crimea during the Crimean War: A French Report," in *Turkish-Jewish Encounters*, ed. M.Tütüncü (Haarlem, 2001), 65-78; Emanuela Trevisan Semi, "The Crimean Karaites in the French Jewish Press," in *Proceedings of the Eleventh World Congress of Jewish Studies*, div.B, vol.III (Jerusalem, 1994), 9-16; as a very good (though rather brief) example of the usage of travel accounts as important source for the history of the Crimean Karaites see Philip Miller, *Karaite Separatism in Nineteenth-Century Russia: Joseph Solomon Lucki's Epistle of Israel's Deliverance* (Cincinnatti, 1993), 21-29. See William Harris Rule, *History of the Karaite Jews* (London, 1870), 173-199, as a "good" example of superficial and inaccurate treatment of travelers' reports. Highly significant is the interest in the travel accounts on the Karaites of the last political East European Karaite *Ḥakham* (or *Ḥakhan*, as he called himself) Seraja Szapszal. See numerous quotations from the travel reports on the Karaites among his private papers in MS LLAS, F.143 (Szapszal's collection): 917, 918. In the nineteenth century travel accounts appeared in the focus of academic interests of another famous Karaite leader, Avraham Firkovich (Dan Shapira, private communication based on the materials found by him in Firkovich's collection in St.Petersburg). Travelers data on the Crimean Karaites had also been analyzed in several articles by the author of this study: Mikhail Kizilov, "Krymskie karaimy 16-19 vekov po opisaniyam puteshestvennikov" [The Crimean Karaites in the sixteenth-nineteenth centuries according to descriptions of European Travelers], in *Piligrimy Kryma* (Simferopol', 1999), 119-124; the same, "Svidetel'stva puteshestvennikov kak istochnik svedeniy po izucheniyu etnicheskoy istorii, traditsionnoy kul'tury i byta krymskikh karaimov" [The travelers' information as a source of data on the ethnic history, traditional culture, and way of life of the Crimean Karaites], in *Materialy Sed'moy Ezhegodnoy Mezhdunarodnoy Mezhdistsiplinarnoy Konferentsii po Iudaike. Tezisy* (Moscow, 2000), 172-174; the same, "Svidetel'stva puteshestvennikov XVIII – XIX vv. kak istochnik svedeniy o formirovanii natsionalnoy samoidentifikatsii i stanovlenii kontseptsiy etnicheskoy istorii u krymskikh karaimov" [Travel Accounts of the eighteenth – nineteenth centuries as a source of data on the forming of the Crimean Karaites' national self-identification and creation of concepts of their ethnic history], in *Materialy Sed'moy Ezhegodnoy Mezhdunarodnoy Mezhdistsuplinarnoy Konferentsii po Iudaike*, pt.1 (Moscow, 2000), 306-315; the same, "Karaimskie necropoli Chufut-Kale i Mangupa po opisaniyam puteshestvennikov 18 – 19 vekov" [Karaite cemeteries of Çufut-Qalé and Mangoup according to description of the eighteenth – nineteenth century travelers], in *Materialy Vos'moy Mezhdunarodnoy Konferentsii po Iudaike* (Moscow, 2002), 191-205; the same, "Karaimskaya obshtchina g.Gezleva (Evpatoria) v 18 – 19 vv. po opisaniyam ochevidstev" [Karaite community of Gözlöw (Evpatoriya) according to descriptions of eyewitnesses], in *Tirosh. Trudy po*

scholars have used some of the most well-known travel reports in their studies, travel accounts have rarely been analyzed as literary texts, which have their own rules and conventions. Moreover, many of the interesting and important travel accounts related to the history of the Crimean Karaites, examined herein, seem to escape the attention of a scholarly audience. What has been missing is a comprehensive picture of Crimean Karaite life, thus demonstrating the importance of the travel accounts, which provide this, as a source for the history of this ethnic group. An analysis and overview of the most important travel accounts, written from the twelfth to the nineteenth centuries, and further attempts to reveal common topics and patterns in the travel descriptions of the Karaites – including various aspects of their social, political, ethnic, and administrative life, as presented in these texts – (long overdue) is herein contained. Special attention has been given to the evaluation of the veracity and importance of travel accounts as a historical source.

In addition to historical matters of the thirteenth-nineteenth centuries, frequent digressions related to twentieth century Crimean Karaites' perception of their history, which often deny almost everything so carefully nourished and preserved by their forefathers, were also requried.[6]

Overview: The first chapter provides necessary (though rather brief) information about the background, and main historical stages and tendencies, of the problems surrounding the topic at hand. The second chapter is dedicated to such problems as: the ethnogenesis of the Karaites as determined by the travelers – their contacts and relations with the Karaites' closest ethnic neighbours, the Rabbanites and Crimean Tatars – and the legal status of the community in the Crimean Khanate and Russian Empire. Furthermore, chapter two seeks to draw the attention of the audience to the travelers' vivid and emotional descriptions of their contacts with such outstanding Karaite

---

Iudaike 5 (Moscow, 2002), 245-256; the same, "Krymskie 'peshtchernye goroda' po opisaniyu E.Skirmunt (Pojata)" [Crimean 'cave towns' according to description of E.Skirmunt (Pojata)], *MAIET* 9 (2002): 543-548; the same, "Batei 'olamin qarai'm shel Qerim," in *Studies in a Karaite Community*, ed. Dan Shapira (Jerusalem) (forthcoming); the same, "Crimean Karaites According to the Data from Travel Accounts," in *Karaite Judaism: Introduction to Karaite Studies*, ed. M.Polliack (Leiden, 2003) (forthcoming).

6 Apart from some specially indicated cases, all quoted sources and scholarship in Hebrew, Latin, Polish, Russian, German, and French will be given in the author's translation into English. The names of the Polish authors and travelers will remain unchanged (*e.g.* Czacki, Chojecki, Hlebnicki-Jozefowicz), whereas most of the Polish placenames will be Anglicized (Luck, Halich, Derazhnia, Kukizov etc.)

personalities as: Yiṣḥaq Ben-Shelomoh, Avraham Firkovich, Shelomoh Beim, and Simḥah Babovich. The third chapter analyzes the traditional culture and everyday life of the Crimean Karaite community. The history of the main Karaite colonies and quarters in larger Crimean towns is analyzed in the fifth chapter. In the final chapter, the most important features of the travel accounts as valuable written sources on the history of the Karaites are discussed. The reasons why the travel reports depict such positive images of the Karaites are also discussed therein. In closing, there is an analysis of the general tendencies that influenced the process of the formation of the Karaites' ethnic self-conciousness, as well as a look at the historical consciousness of East-European Karaites in the nineteenth through twentieth centuries.

1.1. Karaites and Karaism: an historical outline.[7]

The Karaites are members of an independent religious movement within Judaism that formally emerged in the eighth century in Babylon, and spread from there to the countries of The Middle East, Byzantium, North Africa, the Iberian Peninsula, and Europe. The Karaites derive their name from the Hebrew word for Scripture (*Qara'im, Benei Miqra', Ba'alei Miqra'*). The first of these terms, *Qara'im* (sing. *Qara'i*) should be translated as "readers", in the sense "those who read the Scripture"; the terms "*Benei Miqra'*," and "*Ba'alei Miqra'*" might be translated as "Sons/Disciples of the Scripture" or "Masters of the Scripture."[8] The name reflects the main

---

[7]   Readers are reminded that this is just a brief overview of the history of Karaism, with special emphasis put on the history of Eastern European Karaites, the main focus of this work. For more details concerning the history of Polish, Lithuanian, and Crimean Karaites readers are advised to consult such chrestomatical works as Jacob Mann, *Texts and Studies in Jewish History and Literature.* Vol.2: *Karaitica* (Philadelphia, 1935); Philip Miller, *Karaite Separatism in Nineteenth-Century Russia: Joseph Solomon Lucki's Epistle of Israel's Deliverance* (Cincinnatti, 1993); Meir Balaban, "Karaici w Polsce," in his *Studia Historyczne* (Warszawa, 1927), 1-92; concerning Byzantine and Turkish Karaites see Zvi Ankori, *Karaites in Byzantium: the Formative Years, 970-1100* (New York-Jerusalem, 1959); Abraham Danon, "The Karaites in European Turkey," *JQR* 3 (1925): 285-360; on the Egyptian Karaites see *The Karaite Jews of Egypt,* by Mourad El-Qodsi (Rochester, 1990); on the Polish-Lithuanian Karaites see Golda Akhiezer and Dan Shapira, "Qara'im BeLitah UVeVohlin-Galiṣiyah 'Ad HaMe'ah Ha-18" [The Karaites in Lithuania and Wohlynia-Galicia until the eighteenth century], *Pe'amim* 89 (2002), 19-60; Mikhail Kizilov, "The Arrival of the Karaites (Karaims) to Poland and Lithuania: A Survey of Sources and Critical Analysis of Existing Theories," *Archivum Eurasiae Medii Aevi* 12 (2003) (forthcoming).

[8]   Some scholars also connect this name with Hebrew *Qore',* i.e. a "caller" or "propagandist" in the sense of the Arabic-Persian word *da'āwatkar* by which the

25

characteristic of the sect, viz. the recognition of the *TaNaKh* (a.k.a. Old Testament) as the sole and direct source of religious law, with the rejection of the "Oral Law" (a.k.a. the Talmud). To over simplify the issue, the Karaite objection to the Oral Law lay in its introduction into Judaism of many regulations composed by the Rabbis not found in the *TaNaKh*. Due to the prominence of the Rabbanites in Jewish life, much Karaite literature was directed specifically against the doctrine the Rabbanites.[9]

'Anan Ben-Dawid, who carried out his religious and propagandistic activity in the second half of the eighth century c.e., is traditionally considered the founder of Karaism.[10] Followers of 'Anan's movement (initially called 'Ananites) absorbed many elements of older, non-talmudic Jewish traditions.[11] In the ninth-twelfth centuries (this period might be called the time of consolidation) Karaism developed as a separate religious movement within Judaism, taking into itself other schisms. During this period, the Karaites engaged in an active proselytization of the Rabbanite Jews. This age saw the rise of such famous Karaites scholars and exegetes as Binyamin Ben-Mosheh al-

---

Shiites designated propagandists on behalf of 'Ali. See Leon Nemoy, *Karaite Anthology* (New Haven, 1952), xvii; Natan Schur, *The Karaite Encyclopedia* (Wien,1995), 214.

[9] These two features – the rejection of the Talmud, and a bitter rivalry with the more numerous Rabbanite Jews – were two features that attracted the close attention of Christian missionaries and theologians, the antisemitic Nineteenth-century Russian administration, scholars, travelers, and men of letters to the otherwise rather scanty, insignificant communities of the East European Karaites.

[10] According to some of the Karaite sources, however, the origins of their movements go to much more ancient times, to the period of the king Yerav'am [Jeroboam] (cf. al-Qirqisani); according to these sources, the true understanding of Torah was preserved by the Ṣaddoqites and their leader Ṣaddoq, whereas 'Anan merely revived the true understanding of the doctrine.

Rabbanite sources, however, ascribe the beginning of the Karaite schizm to the personal ambitions of 'Anan, whose younger brother Ḥananyaḥ was appointed exilarch in his stead (Leon Nemoy, "Karaites," EJ 10, 764-765). [*ed.* The Rabbanite story was a pure fabrication. There is no record of such a dispute, nor an Exilarch named Ḥananyaḥ (the Exilarch at the time was Shelomoh Ben-Ḥisdai II, who was succeeded by his son Yiṣḥaq Iskoy. For more information read, Leon Nemoy, "Early Karaism, the need for a new Approach", in *JQR* 40;307-315) and Daniel Lasker "Islamic Influences on Karaite Origins," *Studies in Islamic and Judaic Traditions II*, 23-47.]

[11] In the opinion of Zvi Ankori, Karaism in general should be understood and analysed as a "product of Jewish experience under mediæval Islam" (Ankori, *Karaites*, 3). Consolidation of the 'Ananites and early Karaites, who actually represented different movements, took place in the first half of the eleventh century (Haggai Ben-Shammai, "Between 'Ananites and Karaites," in *Studies in Muslim-Jewish Relations* 1 (Oxford, 1993), 24-25.

26

Nahawendi, Dani'el Ben-Mosheh al-Qumisi, Ya'aqov al-Qirqisani, and others.

Until the end of the eleventh century, the Karaites' spiritual center was in Jerusalem. After the First Crusade destroyed Jerusalem and the Jewish community there (1099), however, it shifted to Europe (predominantly to Byzantium).[12] Eventually, the following main historical seats of Karaism developed in the world: Byzantium and Turkey, Egypt, North Africa, the Near East, Jerusalem, Spain, and Eastern Europe.

1.1.1. Byzantium and Turkey.

Constantinople became a main spiritual center of Karaism at the beginning of the twelfth century. Zvi Ankori, who analyzed several "romantic" theories explaining the appearance of the Karaites in Byzantium (called by the author "Crimean," "Khazarian," and "Missionary"), came to the conclusion that the main factors for the ascension of the Karaites in Byzantium were practical, namely: the Byzantine annexation of new areas in which a native Karaite population was already established, and a further Karaite immigration inland.[13]

After 1492, when the Jews who had been expelled from Spain were granted asylum in Turkey, there was a tendency for rapprochement between the Karaite and Rabbanite Jews. According to some scholars, this led to the gradual decline of the Byzantine-Turkish Karaites into a state of "spiritual lethargy."[14] In spite of this, Byzantium produced such important Karaite scholars as Kalev Afendopolo, Eliyahu and Mosheh Başyaçı, Ya'aqov Ben-Re'uven, the Beği family of Karaite scholars, and many others.

The devastating conflagrations, which often gutted the community from the eighteenth to the beginning of the twentieth centuries, forced it to leave its traditional settlement in the Hasköy quarter of Constantinople (Istanbul) between the 1660s-70s. The local community, with some of its members still speaking their peculiar Græco-Karaite dialect, amounted to 350 persons in the mid-50s. However, by the end of the 80s – according to Polish Karaite A.Sulimowicz, who visited the community at this time – it had

---

[12] The troops of Godfrey de Buollion, who entered Jerusalem on July 15th, 1099, forced a large part of the Jewish population of the city to the main synagogue and burned it (Danon, "Karaites," 291).

[13] See Ankori, *Karaites*, 86. Ankori's concept received a severe critique from the Karaite author, Simon Szyszman: "Les Karaites des Byzance," *BEK* 3 (1993): 58-62.

[14] Nemoy, "Karaites," 771.

dwindled to only ninety persons, with the synagogue sometimes closed even on Saturdays. From the old Karaite quarters of Hasköy, only a few old houses remained on a small avenue called Karaim Çıkmazı (Karaite blind-alley).[15]

1.1.2. Egypt, North Africa, Near East, Jerusalem, Spain.

The origins of the Karaite community in Egypt are quite ancient; however, their origin is not known. Some Karaites left Jerusalem in the 1060s, a short while before the First Crusade, and settled down in Fustat (Cairo).[16] Until the end of the twelfth century, the local community outnumbered Rabbanites. According to S.Szyszman, in 1186/1187 – 1313, the community possessed the so-called Codex Allepensis, one of the most ancient and complete copies of the Bible.[17]

The Egyptian community, the second largest Karaite community in the twentieth century,[18] came to a rapid end, due to the political and social impact of the Arab-Israeli wars. Most of the Egyptian Karaites emigrated to Israel, France, and the USA, leaving only twenty-four Karaites in Egypt in 1984.[19] In addition to Egypt, the Karaites settled in other North African communities. Some epigraphic and archival sources testify to the presence of the Karaites, in the twelfth century, in Algeria and the Maghreb.[20]

Between the tenth and the twelfth centuries, the Karaites spread their activities as far as Spain, where they established a thriving intellectual community. The community existed until 1178, when they were expelled by the edict of king Alfonso VIII of Castille (1158-1214), as a result of a quarrel with the local Rabbanites.[21] [22]

---

[15]   Anna Sulimowicz, "Karaimi znad Złotego Rogu." *Awazymyz* 1 (1989): 9-10.

[16]   Ankori, *Karaites*, 453. The local Karaites claim pre-"Anan origins for their community, referring to the document given to the community by the first Islamic governor of Egypt, 'Amr ibn al-'Āṣ in 641 A.D (cited in *at-Tahdhib*, no. 38, Cairo 5 September, 1902, p. 158; *Ash-Shubban Al-Qarra'in*, no. 4, Cairo June 2nd, 1937, p. 8; Mourad El-Qodsi, *The Karaite Jews of Egypt*, Lyons, NY, 1987 and *The Karaite Communities in Poland, Lithuania, Russia and Crimea* (Lyons, 1993), 4).

[17]   Simon Szyszman, "La communauté karaïte égyptienne: une fin tragique," *BEK* 3 (1993): 81.

[18]   According to Karaite sources, in the 1920s the local community numbered 700 families (around 3.500-5.000 souls): *MK* 1:3 (1926): 30.

[19]   This according to Szyszman, "Communaute," 83-84. The author also accused the community's last president, Elias-Khidr Massouda, of an irresponsible and casual attitude concerning the destiny and cultural heritage of the community (*ibid.*, 83-86).

[20]   Adrian Schenker, "Karaer im Maghreb," *BEK* 3 (1993): 9-13; Mann, Texts, 139; according to A.E.Mourant, Ada C.Kopec, and Kazimiera Domaniewska-Sobczk, *The Genetics of the Jews* (Oxford, 1978) p.33.

[21]   Schur, *Encyclopedia*, 267-268; see also Daniel J.Lasker, "Karaism in Twelfth-

One of the most ancient Karaite communities – that of Hit (Iraq), which existed since early mediæval times – preserved a number of conservative Karaite prescriptions and customs, and, simultaneously, because of their separate and remote location – developed a number of specific, local rituals and traditions. A. Firkovich, who visited the community in the nineteenth century, recorded that the community contained sixty-seven people. In 1960, thirteen families of the Iraqi Karaites were airlifted to Israel, where they were settled in Be'ersheva'.[23]

Another early, mediæval Karaite community, that of Jerusalem, which had been very small and quite poor since the times of the First Crusade, has also survived until today. Twenty-seven Karaites lived there in 1641, when the community was visited by the Karaite pilgrim Shemu'el Ben-Dawid, and only ten (nine females and one male) in the 1920s.[24] The two Sinanis, the last caretakers of 'Anan's synagogue, were taken prisoner by the Arab Legion in 1948. In 1967, this part of the city was recaptured; in the 1970s, the synagogue was restored, and the Karaites settled in the old city of Jerusalem again [ed. others had been living in the new city since the 1940s.]. These Karaites mostly came from Egypt. They publish a small community periodical "*Biṭa'on Benei Miqra'* (*Biṭa'on HaYahdut HaQara'it Ha'Olamit BeYisra'el*) [Organ of the Benei Miqra' (Organ of Universal Karaite Judaism in Israel)]."

1.1.3. Eastern Europe: Crimea, Poland and Lithuania. Thirteenth century – the end of the eighteenth century: Crimean Khanate and Polish-Lithuanian Commonwealth.

It is in this period we first hear of the Karaites in Eastern Europe (thirteenth-fourteenth centuries). Unfortunately, there is not a single, reliable mediæval source to provide details regarding the nature

---

Century Spain," in *Jewish Thought and Philosophy*, vol.1, (1992): 179-195.

[22] [*ed.* Actually, it was the Rabbanites under the leadership of Yosef Ferrizuel, called "cidellus" [little El Cid], who sought and obtained permission from the Catholic king to persecute and drive the Karaites out of the kingdom. See, Encyclopaedia Judaica, vol. 6, p. 1236, the article "*Ferrizuel, Joseph Ha-Nasi*"; Yitzhak [sic!] Baer, *A History of the Jews in Christian Spain*, end of Chapter 1, vol. I, p. 77; *ibid.* Chapter II, vol. I, p. 95; Avraham Ibn Daud, *Sefer HaQabbalah* (with critical English translation by Gershon D.Cohen, published as *The Book of Tradition*, JPS, Philadelphia, 1967), pp. xxii, xlvi-l, 94-103. The whole of Ibn Daud's book is an anti-Karaite polemic. Cohen's critical analysis and notes are very well done.]

[23] Schur, *Encyclopedia*, 135-136; El-Qodsi, *Communities*, 7.
[24] See *MK* 1:3 (1926): 30.

and exact date of the Karaite settlement in Poland-Lithuania and the Crimea. According to a Karaite tradition, the Lithuanian prince Alexander Vytautas (Vitold) (b. ca.1350, grand Duke from 1392, d. 1430) moved several hundred Karaite families from the Crimea to the north and settled them in Troki, Luck, and Halicz). The only relevant source testifying to this historic event comes from very late Karaite traditions about Vitold, first documented and published by Polish scholar and statesman Tadeusz Czacki in 1807.[25] This tradition was repeated by Karaite sage Mordekhai Sultanski. According to him, in 4978 (1218 c.e.) Witold Jagello invaded the Crimea and took many prisoners there, including 483 Karaite families from Sulkhat (*i.e.* Eski-Qırım or Stary Krym). He settled 330 of these families in Troki, and 150 in Ponevezh. There, he provided them with land and privileges. However, in 1242 he made a new raid to the Crimea and carried another 380 Karaite families from Solkhat to Halicz.[26] The Karaites of Halicz have a different tradition that speaks about their arrival in the mid-thirteenth century as a consequence of the peace treaty between the Ruthenian prince Daniel of Halicz and Batu Khan of the Golden Horde.[27]

The problem of establishing an exact time for the advent of the arrival of the Karaite community in the Crimea is as controversial and complicated as that of their Polish-Lithuanian brethren. In spite of

---

[25] "A common tradition of all Karaite synagogues is the following: the Grand Prince of Lithuania Vitold brought 383 Karaite families from the Crimea to Troki, and in the next military raid, he transferred new colonies to Lutsk and Halich" However, Czacki himself was very sceptical about the veracity of the source of his information: "The notes written by them [the Karaites] or by certain "pólmędrek" [something like "pseudo-scholar"] contain strange historical controversies: *e.g.* Vitold lived in the XIIIth century; Ladislaus Yagello was the son of the queen Bona, which means that the grandfather was the son of his own grandson.» (my translation from Tadeusz Czacki, "Rozprawa o Karaitach," in his *Rozprawa o Zydach* (Wilno 1807), 263). On Czacki [see more in §1.3.2] (herafter, apart from some specially indicated cases, all quoted sources and scholarship in Polish, Russian, German, and French will be given in my translation into English – M.K.).

[26] Mordekhai Sultanski, *Zecher Caddikim* [*Zekher Ṣaddiqim*], ed.S.Poznanski (Warsaw, 1920), 107-109. The work was completed in 1838. Practically the same information, with small variations correcting the most obvious historical mistakes, was included by Araham Firkovich in his famous *Avnei Zikkaron* (Vilna, 1872), 251-253.

[27] See more about it in Jaroslav Stepaniv [Daszkiewicz J], *"L'époque de Danylo Romanovyc d'après une source Karaïte," HUS* 3:2 (1978), 334-373; Mikhail Kizilov, *"The Arrival of the Karaites (Karaims) to Poland and Lithuania: A Survey of Sources and Critical Analysis of Existing Theories"* (in print); Golda Akhiezer, Dan Shapira, *"Qara'im BeLita UVeWohlin-Galiṣiyah 'Ad HaMe'ah Ha-18,"* (Karaites in Lithuanian-Wohlynia-Galicia up to the 18th Century) *Pe'amim* 89 (2002), 19-60.

the fact that the above-mentioned Karaite traditions report the Crimean community as already well-established in at least the first half of the thirteenth century, the first reliable evidence of Karaite presence in the Crimea is a brief remark of Aharon Ben-Yosef concerning a dispute between the Karaite and Rabbanite Jews in Sulkhat in 1279.[28] Thus, until new testimonies and sources related to this problem are found, it is only possible to state that, in all probability, the Karaites migrated to the Crimean peninsula no earlier than the second half of the thirteenth century.

While the exact circumstances and precise date of their arrival is difficult to establish, it is very tempting to suppose that the migration of the Karaites to the Crimea went by two main routes: one that brought the earliest, most likely Turkic (Qıpçaq) speaking, Karaites together with the Tatar conquerors of the Crimea in the mid- 13th century, and the other, which was realized through the migration from the Karaite communities of Byzantium.[29]

In the thirteenth-fifteenth centuries, the main Karaite seats in Eastern Europe were Eski-Qırım, Kaffa, Qırq-Yer (later: Çufut-Qalé) and Mangoup in the Crimea, and Troki, Halicz, Lwow and Luck in the Polish-Lithuanian Commonwealth. In the sixteenth-eighteenth centuries, with the increase of the local Karaite population and the expanding of their activity to new places advantageous to their commercial activity, Karaite communities appeared in Gözlöw and Qarasubazar (Crimea), Kukizow, Derazhne, Poniewiez, Poswol, Nowe Miasto, and many other Polish and Lithuanian towns and villages.[30]

---

[28] See Schur, *Encyclopedia*, 13-14; Ankori, *Karaites*, 340-341; Danon, *"Karaites,"* 294-296; On Aharon Ben-Yosef HaRofe' the Elder, one of the most famous Karaite exegetes, who was, according to some suggestions, of Crimean origin; see also Daniel Frank, *"Ibn Ezra and the Karaite Exegetes Aharon Ben-Yosef and Aharon Ben-Eliyahu,"* in *Abraham Ibn Ezra and his Age: Proceedings of the International Symposium* (Madrid, 1990); Daniel J.Lasker, *"Aharon Ben-Yosef and the Transformation of Karaite Thought,"* in *Torah and Wisdom*, R.Link-Salinger (ed.) (NY: Shengold, 1972), 121- 128.

[29] Late nineteenth – early twentieth century Karaite scholarship, supported by the opinions of some non-Karaite scholars (mostly linguists), created a completely different vision of the problem, according to which the Crimean Karaites in fact represented the descendants of the Khazars, converted to the Karaite type of Judaism in the eighth century. This theory, which is still not refuted by the academic world (especially in Poland and Lithuania), however, has much less of a factual foundation than the theory that suggests the thirteenth century arrival of the Karaites (Akhiezer, Shapira, *"Qara'im BeLita UVeWohlin-Galişiyah 'Ad HaMe'ah Ha-18"*).

[30] The Karaite scholarship usually refers to the presence of the Karaite communities in 32 or 42 settlements of the Polish-Lithuanian Commonwealth (Abraham Szyszman, "Osadnictwo karaimskie i tatarskie na ziemiach W.Księstwa Litewskiego," *MK* 10 (1934), 29, ft.1). This data, undoubtedly, goes back to Firkovich's *Avnei Zikkaron*

It was in this period that the Crimea and Lithuania became the new centers of Karaite thought and learning. The history of the Crimean and Polish-Lithuanian communities seem to have developed in parallel: both produced prominent thinkers and exegets of their times, both had been actively involved in commercial actvity,[31] both often suffered from the tyranny of their non-Jewish rulers – and such drastic events as Cossack invasions, civil wars, epidemics, conflagrations, and natural disasters.[32]

In the seventeenth-eighteenth centuries that European Christian scholars began displaying an interest in studying the Karaites. Around this time, the first academic works dedicated to the history, manners, customs, and laws of East European Karaites and their settlements appeared.[33]

---

where the latter counted 32 Karaite settlements in Poland-Lithuania (p.252). This estimation, in spite of its seemingly exaggerated nature, when taking into consideration existence of tiny Karaite communities (2-3 families) living in small rural villages, seems rather feasible.

[31] It seems, however, that the Polish-Lithuanian Karaites were more involved in agricultural activity than their Crimean brethren; hence their less prosperous œconomic situation in comparison to the wealthy and influential status of the Karaite community of the Crimean Khanate.

[32] Polish Karaites were especially damaged by the Cossack pogromists: the Cossacks of Nalivaiko sacked the Karaite shops of Luck as early as 1595. In the mid-seventeenth century, Cossacks massacred a large part of the Karaite Volynian communities. In the eighteenth century (1768), the communities of this region (Luck, Kotow, and Deraźne) suffered from invasions of the Haidamaks. See D.I.Evarnitski, *Istoriya zaporozhskikh kozakov* [The history of Zaporozhian Cossacks], vol.2 (Kiev, 1990), 103; Sergjusz Rudkowski, *Krwawe echo Humania na Wołyniu. Podanie* (Luck, 1932). On the devastating raids of the Cossacks to the Crimea in the seventeenth century [see §4.2.1] of this book; one of the most tragic events in the history of the Lithuanian Karaites was an epidemic of plague, which considerably shrunk the population of Troki in 1710 (Abraham Szyszman, "*Osadnictwo karaimskie w Trokach za Wielkich Książąt Litewskich*," *MK* 11 (1936), 68, ft.71; Szyszman, *Karaites d'Europe*, 52); speaking about natural disasters, both Crimean, and Polish-Lithuanian communities often suffered from famine, bad harvests, and conflagrations, which frequently destroyed not only dwelling quarters, but also precious libraries and manuscripts (*e.g.* in 1765 the Karaites of Luck complained that the fire burned all the privileges that had been given to them by the Polish kings (AGAD ASK XLVI, s.18, k.12); devastating conflagrations seriously damaged Karaite dwelling quarters of Halicz in 1913; in 1830 they burned down the local wooden synagogue together with all the ancient manuscripts kept there (Balaban, "Karaici," 3, 23).

[33] See Gustav Peringer, *Epistola de Karaitarum Rebus in Lithuania* (1691); Jacob Trigland, *Diatribe de Secta Karaeorum* (1703); Johann Christoph Wolf, *Notitia Karaeorum* (1721); Simon Szyszman, "*Gustaf Peringers Mission bei den Karaern*," in *Zeitschrift der Deutschen Morgenländischen Geselschaft* 102:2 (1952), 215-228. Most likely, English millenarians were the first to turn their attention to the Karaites as perspective object for conversion to Christianity; according to some of their

It seems that, until the second half of the eighteenth century, because of close contact and competition with their Rabbanite neighbours, the Polish-Lithuanian community – which produced such outstanding scholars as Yiṣḥaq Ben-Avraham Troki, Mordekhai Ben-Nisan Kukizow, Simḥah Yiṣḥaq Lucki, Zeraḥ Ben-Natan, 'Ezra Ben-Nisan, et alia – was more learned and advanced than their Crimean brethren. In the eighteenth century, however, with a worsening of the œconomic situation within the community and the migration of its intellectual elite to the Crimea, the Lithuanian community became much less important, lagging behind from the rapidly growing and flourshing Crimean community. Thus, in the eighteenth century, the Crimea began to evolve into the spiritual and financial center of the Karaite movement across Euorpe and the world.

The end of eighteenth – beginning of the twentieth century: Russian Empire

After the annexation of the Crimea (1783) and the incorporation of some parts of the former Polish-Lithuanian Commonwealth into Russia (in 1772, 1793, and 1795), almost all European Karaites became subjects of the Russian Empire.[34] In the nineteenth century, the Karaites began to settle throughout the Russian Empire and Europe. By the end of the century, scattered Karaite communities were present in: St. Petersburg, Moscow, Odessa, Kharkov, Poltava, Nikolaev, Elisavetgrad, Ecaterinoslav, Berdiansk, Kishinev, Harbin, Vienna, Warsaw, &c. According to the estimations of M.S.Kupovetski, in 1783, the Karaite population of the Russian Empire consisted of 3,800 Karaites with 2,600 Karaites living in the Crimea.[35]

After the forced removal of the local Crimean Christian population (1777), and the mass migration of the Tatars, the Crimean Karaites found themselves in a very advantageous position. As a result of the migrations, they turned out to be the most influential commercial power of the depopulated, but still highly important, new southern

---

thinkers, the Karaites were supposed to play a special, decisive role during the battle of Armageddon (R.H.Popkin, *"The Lost Tribes, the Caraites and the English Millenarians," JJS* 37 (1986), 213-227).

[34] The only exception represented the Karaite community of Halicz, which became subject to the Austro-Hungarian Empire. See Balaban, "Karaici," 17-25; Schur, *Encyclopedia*, 36-37.

[35] M.S.Kupovetski, "Dinamika chislennosti i rasselenie karaimov i krymchakov za poslednie dvesti let" [Dynamics of the population and settlement of the Karaites and Qrimchaks during the last 200 years] in *Geografiia i kul'tura etnograficheskikh grupp tatar v SSSR* (Moscow: Nauka, 1983), 77.

region of Russia.[36] Moreover, at the end of the eighteenth century, the Karaites started to receive perferential legal treatment: in 1795 they were relieved of the double tax imposed upon the Jews, and in 1827 they were exempted (unlike the Rabbanites) from obligatory military service in the Russian army.[37] Until these meaures were taken, despite all the polemics and quarrels, the history of the Karaite and Rabbanite Jews was similar; thus, clearly, this moment is a turning point in the history of the East European Karaites. As time passed, the distance between the privileged Karaites and their Rabbanire brethren grew, reaching its climax in 1863, when the Karaites were accorded full rights of citizenship in the Russian Empire, and were integrated into society, serving in the Tsar's army, and in the government.[38]

It seems that, largely due to the aforementioned securing of its œconomic prosperity, and stable position in the society, the Karaite population of the Empire grew dramatically. From 3,800 Karaites in 1783, the population grew to 12,894 (6,372 – males; 6,522 – females) in 1897.[39]

---

[36] 'Azaryah Ben-Eliyah mentioned that, "Besides Karaites and Jews living in Karasubazar, there were not any other ra'īya [=non-Muslim subjects] left in the Crimea" ('Azaryah Ben-Eliyah, "Sobytiia sluchivshiiesia v Krymu v tsarstvovanie Shagin-Girey-khana," transl. by A.Firkovich [Events happened in the Crimea during the rule of Shahin Girey Khan], *KZh* 5-6 (1911), 76). The complete Hebrew original of this highly interesting source is being prepared for publication by G.Akhiezer (Israel); see also her M.A. dissertation submitted to the Hebrew University of Jerusalem in 1999: *Events that happened in the Crimea during the rule of Shahin Girey Khan: Historical Chronicle from the 18th century by the Karaite 'Azaryah Ben-Eliyah* (in Hebrew).

[37] See detailed analysis of these events in Miller, *Separatism*. At the same time, the Rabbanite Jews were severely oppressed and humiliated while being forcibly recruited into the army, paying a heavy double taxation, not allowed to enter institutions of higher education, etc.

[38] *Sbornik starinnykh gramot i uzakonenii Rossiiskoi imperii kasatelno prav i sostoianiia russko-poddannykh karaimov* [Collection of the old charters and statutes of the Russian Empire regarding the rights and status of the Russian subjects, Karaites], Z.A. Firkovich (ed.) (St. Petersburg 1890), 89. Zaria Avra'amovich (Zeraḥ Ben-Avraham) Firkovich, the son of Avraham Firkovich, the editor of this collection of the Karaite charters, was correctly rebuked by Yuliy Gessen for his non-objective and inconsistent treatment of these documents (Yuliy Gessen, "Bor'ba karaimov g.Trok s evreyami" [The struggle between the Troki Karaites and Jews], Evreyskaia starina 4:3 (1910), 579, ft.1).

[39] *I.e.* it became more than three times larger! According to the census of 1897 there were 6,166 Karaites in Tavricheskaya guberniya, 1,383 in Poland-Lithuania, 5,345 in other parts of Russia (including Siberia and Central Asia). The largest were the communities of the following towns: Evpatoria – 1,505; Feodosia – 1,233, Odessa – 1,049, Sevastopol' – 813, Simferopol' – 709, Nikolaev – 554, Troki – 377, Wilna – 155. According to the data of Tavricheskoe gubernskoe zemstvo (a kind of local government) in 1907 there were already 8,683 Karaites in Tavricheskaya guberniya

The nineteenth century also marked the appearance of a number of theories related to the origins and history of the Karaites, popularized both by Karaite leaders and non-Karaite scholars. According to some, the Karaites had come to the Crimea before the time of Christ. Consequently, they were the only true, ancient Israelites, the descendants of the Ten Lost Tribes of Israel;[40] moreover, it was Karaite missionaries who converted the nomadic, Turkic Khazars to Karaite Judaism. Later, at the end of the nineteenth – first half of the twentieth century, East European Karaite authors created a completely different version of their ethnic history, which denied all links to the Jewish people, and stressed their origins from Turkic Khazar proselytes, converted to Karaism in the eighth century.[41]

Twentieth century: Soviet Union, Poland and Lithuania.

After World War I, when Poland again became an independent state, and the Russian Empire was transformed into the atheistic Soviet Union, the fate of the Rabbanite and Karaite communities differed further still. In interwar Poland, with its less than one-thousand Karaite inhabitants, the Karaites started to be called "najmniejsza mniejszość narodowa" (*i.e.* "the most minor ethnic minority") and were treated by the goverment with great caution and care.[42] The ascension of S.M.Szapszal, whose Khazar and Turkic sentiments were public as early as 1896,[43] to the office of the Karaite Ḥakham in Poland (1927), symbolized the final stage of the process of

---

(Veniamin Sinani, "K statistike karaimov (po perepisi 1897 g.)" in *KZh* 1 (1911): 30-31, 36).

[40] It followed from this statement that the Karaites could not be blamed for the Crucifixion, or participation in the composition of the Talmud: a defensive mechanism that had often been employed by small Jewish communities at the time of Christian persecutions [see more in Conclusion].

[41] More about the Khazars see in D.M.Dunlop, *The History of the Jewish Khazars* (Princeton: Princeton University, 1954); on the Karaite theories concerning their Khazar origin see Ananiasz Zajączkowski, *Karaims in Poland* (La Haye-Paris-Warsaw, 1961).

[42] Official Karaite circles stated that there was about 1,500 Karaites in Poland (AAN MWRiOP 1464, k.22). However, archival documents would report a much smaller number of Polish Karaite citizens in the 1920s: Luck – about sixty-five Karaites, Halicz – 150, Troki – 203, Wilno – 127, *i.e.* 552 altogether. See AAN MWRiOP 1466, k.28-29, 118, 167. Even when taking into consideration that, during the 1920s, some of the local Karaites were still migrating to Poland from Russia, and adding a small Lithuanian community of Poniewiez (around sixty persons), we would hardly get more than 700 – 900 Karaites.

[43] See S.Szapszal, *Karaimy i Chufut-Kale v Krymu* [Karaites and Çufut-Qalé in the Crimea] (Simferopol' 1993, reprint of St.Petersburg edition of 1896), 11.

"endogenous dejudaization",[44] which resulted in the forming of the completely separate self-identification of the East European Karaites, wherein they deny all links to Judaism or the Jews whatsoever.

The Karaites of the Soviet Union, where all religious cults were "unwelcome", were forced to abandon their religious practices and assimilate into the monolithic, atheistic surroundings. As a consequence, the loss of the religious and national traditions of the Crimean Karaites is much stronger than that of their Polish-Lithuanian brethren.[45] Between the two world wars, 9,000 Karaites lived in the Soviet Union, mostly in the Crimea (6,500). A few families lived in Ponieviezh (at that moment Lithuania), in Berlin (18), in France (250), and in Italy (a few score).[46]

Their "dejudaizing" tendency spared many Karaites lives during the Holocaust; they were surveyed by the Reich Agency for the Investigation of Families and, after some examination, were recognized as a non-Jewish population.[47] In spite of a number of publications related to this issue, the role which was played by the Karaite population during World War II is at best murky. On the one hand, some of the Karaites participated in the war as the soldiers of the Red Army and in resistance movements,[48] on the other, some of them were known to collaborate with the German administration in the occupied territories and even serve in the Waffen SS.[49]

After the war, the number of Karaites in Eastern Europe considerably decreased.[50] In 1959, there were 5,727 Karaites, mostly in

---

[44] The term very successfully coined by Roman Freund in his "Karaites and Dejudaization," in *Acta Universitas Stockholmiensis*. 1991. – №30.

[45] I heard Polish-Lithuanian Karaites often grudging about the pagan practices and the so-called "cult of sacred oaks" practiced by the Crimean Karaites in the Yehoshafat Valley [see below ft.56].

[46] Schur, *Encyclopedia*, 77.

[47] YIVO archives, Berlin Collection, Occ E, 3, Box 100, letter dated January 5th, 1939

[48] A.Fuki, *Karaimy – synovia i docheri Rosii* [Karaites – sons and daughters of Russia] (Moscow, 1995), 57-146.

[49] See Warren P Green, "The Nazi Racial Policy toward the Karaites", *Soviet Jewish Affairs*, vol.8 (1978): 36-44; Philip Friedman, "The Karaites Under Nazi Rule", in *On the Track of Tyranny* by Max Beloff (London, 1960), 97-123; Schur, *Encyclopedia*, 137-138; Emanuela Trevisan Semi, "L'oscillation ethnique: le cas des Caraites pendant la seconde guerre mondiale", *Revue de l'Histoire des Religions* 206 (1989): 377-398; the same, "The Image of the Karaites in Nazi and Vichy France Documents". *JJoS* 32:2 (1990), 81-93; R.H. Weisberg *Vichy Law and the Holocaust in France* (New York, 1996), 68-75 *et alia*. Detailed analysis of this problem will be carried out by Mikhail Kizilov in his Ph.D. dissertation on the history of the Polish-Lithuanian Karaites in the 20th century (Graduate School for Social Research, Warsaw).

[50] Some of the Karaites left Russia with the retreating German armies in 1944 (Schur,

the Crimea, Lithuania and in the Western Ukraine. A few hundred still lived in Germany, France, and several hundred in the United States.[51] The Karaite population of the former Polish lands was then divided between Poland itself, and the Lithuanian (Troki, Vilna, Ponieviez) and Ukrainian Soviet Socialist Republics (Luck, Halicz). The Soviet authorities allowed the Karaites of the former Eastern Polish lands (Volynia and Galicia) to emigrate to Poland on the basis of their former Polish citizenship;[52] these emigrants, joined by some scattered groups of the Karaites who lived in central Poland before, and Karaite refugees from Lithuania, organized several new communities in Wroclaw, Warsaw, and Silesia (Gdansk, Gdynia, Sopot). On the other hand, the Soviet administration did not grant a permission to emigrate to Poland for inhabitants of Lithuania.[53]

The post war period is characterized as a period of stagnation in the religious and cultural life of the East European Karaites: practically all synagogues (keneseler) were closed; "Myśl Karaimska," perhaps the most ambitious Karaite periodical, was transformed into "Przegląd Orientalistyczny", an Oriental journal. The rite of circumcision stopped being practiced; the knowledge of Hebrew, Karaim, and Tatar languages rapidly deteriorated, as there was nobody to take care of the religious education of the youth.[54] These circumstances continued until the end of the 1980s-beginning of the

---

Encyclopedia, 137-138). Some died during the drastic events of the war ("Pamięci tych, co odeszli," *MK* s.n.1 (1946): 139-141). Several tens of the Karaites are said to have been deported from the Crimea in May, 1944, together with a number of other ethnic groups that inhabited the Crimean peninsula who were falsely accused of collaboration with the Nazis: Lebedeva, *Ocherki*, the page of the book cover which follows page 116; this page is absent in the recent re-edition of the book.

51 See Schur, *Encyclopedia*, 77, 89.

52 In 1945, according to the agreement between the Poland and USSR, the Polish population of the former Polish lands was allowed to emigrate to Poland; see more about the emigration of the Luck community in Anna Dubińska, "Garść danych o Karaimach z Łucka." *Awazymyz* 2 (3) (1999): 9-11.

53 According to Karaite sources, the Soviet officials were unwilling to do this because of the fact that the Karaites had been settled down there a long time ago, by Grand Duke Vitold. In fact, however, the Lithuanian Karaites were not allowed to emigrate because local administration knew them to be Karaites, not Poles. For more about the Polish-Lithuanian Karaites in the post war period see in Anna Sulimowicz, "Życie społeczności karaimskiej w Polsce." in *RM* 3:2 (1994): 47-50; Bogusław Firkowicz, "Ogniska karaimskie po latach". in *RM* 4:3 (1995): 87-89.

54 The Wroclaw Karaites gathered for the services in one of the private houses under the guidance of Rafał Abkowicz, called sometimes "Ostatni Ḥazzan" ("the last Ḥazzan"). See "Wspomnienie." Awazymyz. 1 (2) (1999): 4-5; Boltryk, M. "Ostatni Ḥazzan." Kontrasty 5 (May, 1986): 6-9). In Troki, similarly, for a certain period, the Karaites would secretly perform services in the local synagogue, but then stronger measures were taken against them, and they ceased.

1990s. With the fall of the totalitarian communist system, which oppressed all manifestations of national feelings and sentiments, a revival of Karaite religious and cultural traditions sprouted in the lands of the former Soviet Union. A number of periodicals and books were published,[55] two functioning synagogues (keneseler) were opened (one in Troki and the other in Evpatoria), there was also a renewed interest in the study and use of the Karaim language.[56]

According to Mourad El-Qodsi, who visited the Karaite communities of Eastern Europe in 1991, there were 154 Karaites in Poland (fifty in Warsaw, fifty in Gdansk, fifty-four in Wroclaw and its vicinity), 280 in Lithuania (150 in Wilno, fifty in Poniewiez, eighty in Troki), fifteen in Halicz, more than a hundred in Moscow, and 800 in the Crimea (250 in Simferopol', ninety in Evpatoria, seventy in Feodosia, fifty in Sevastopol', fifty in Bakhçeseray, thirty in Yalta and some other minor towns).[57, 58] At the writing of this text, ten years after El-Qodsi's visit, due to a considerable emigration of Crimean Karaites to Israel, the situation has changed, and the local Karaite population has

---

[55] From numerous publications, I will restrict myself only to mentioning the most important periodicals: *Coś* (An underground periodical of Polish Karaites. Published in 1979; only two issues. Editor Marek Firkowicz. Computer editing, restricted number of copies); *Awazymyz* (Computer edited periodical of Polish Karaites, restricted number of copies. Four issues (1 – 1989; 2, 3, 4 – 1999-2000). Ed. board A.Sulimowicz, M.Firkowicz, M.Abkowicz); *Karaimskie Vesti* (Newspaper of the Russian Karaites), and *Karaimskaia Entsiklopedia* (Published with the money of the French Karaite apostate to Christianity M.S.Sarach, a series of books on the history of the Karaites, denying all Jewish links and "proving" the ancient Altai and Mongol-Turkic roots of the East European Karaites).

[56] In spite of such optimistic news, a careful observer can not help noticing the consequences of the endogenous dejudaizatory processes the East European Karaites had come to: all links to Judaism and Jewish civilization are denied, there is hardly any tendency to revive the knowledge of Hebrew (which their ancestors had been so excellent and prolific in); moreover, some of the Crimean Karaites tend to substitute the religion of their forefathers with pagan practices and the cult of the Turkic deity Tengri Khan. Of interest is that Alexei/Avraham Kefeli (a Karaite of Crimean origin, present-day *Ḥazzan* in the Ashdod community) while visiting the Crimea in the Summer of 2002, together with two other Israeli Karaites, distributed a pamphlet entitled *"Karaimy. Razjasnitelnaya broshura"* (Ashdod, 2002), which challenged all the East European Karaites not to believe in pseudo-theories promoting their Turkic origins and return to their roots, both religious, cultural and ethnic – a revolutionary statement, which had not been said by any East European Karaites since Szapszal's times [see more in §5.3].

[57] El-Qodsi, *Communities*, 13-19.

[58] [*ed.* Of interest is a personal conversation held between the editor and Mr. El-Qodsi regarding his visit to the Eastern European communities. While he was there, Mr. El-Qodsi received several late night visitors at the different stops he made who, arriving under the cover of darkness, asked him under the promise of secrecy if they were really Jews.]

become even smaller.[59] According to the census of 1998, there were 265 Karaites in Lithuania (132 in Vilnius, sixty-five in Troki, and in some other towns). Mr. Szymon Pilecki, head of the Karaite Religious Union in Poland, informed me that the approximate number of Karaites living in Poland is 150. At the same time, he complained that this sort of estimation is quite imprecise because of a number of mixed marriages (private communication of October 17th, 1999).

Some of the East European Karaites (especially Lithuanian ones) preserve a tradition which forbids mixed marriages. When taking into consideration their small number, keeping up this traditional prescription does not promote their demographic growth.

There are considerable differences in the cultural and religious traditions of the Eastern European Karaites.[60] The Crimean Karaites have an association called the "Qırım-Qaraylar", which has branches in most of the large Ukrainian and Crimean cities.[61] The Polish Karaites established the "Karaite Religious Union in Poland" (their last statute was officially acknoweldged by the government in 1974). It seems, however, that there are only three Karaite communities in Eastern Europe strictly speaking (*i.e.* comparatively large groups of people with common ethnic origin, living in the same place, unified by adhering to the same cultural and religious tradition, and having from time to time common cultural events and festivities): Evpatoria, Troki, and Wilno.[62]

A logical question arises with regard to the future of Karaite culture, and Karaites as an ethnic entity in Eastern Europe. When I spoke with them, the representatives of the elder generation usually gave me pessimistic answers predicting the vanishing of the Karaites as a separate cultural and ethnic group during the first decades of the

---

[59] One of the recent publications, based on an oral report of Karaite informants, mentioned the number of 700 souls in the Crimea (A.Maschenko, "Edinstvennaia v SNG deistvuiushchaya kenasa" [The only functioning kenasa of the CIS], *Krymskoe vremia*. 8.02.2001). In our opinion, however, it is even smaller, less than five-six hundred souls.

[60] See above about the attempts to substitute traditional Karaite religious practices with a shamanistic Turkic-Mongol cult in the Crimea. Polish-Lithuanian Karaites, usually with deep regret, referred to these half-pagan views of their Crimean brethren.

[61] According to Alexei/Avraham Kefeli, in 2001 there also appeared an association "Qırım-Qaraylar" in Netaniah (Israel) (Kefeli, *Karaimy*, 2).

[62] Other communities seem to be too small and dispersed, devoid of places of worship. One of the Polish Karaites said to me that, in her opinion, the only thing that united Polish Karaites, was the Warsaw Karaite cemetery, the only place where they used to gather and perform religious rituals. One of the most the most interesting and traditional Karaite communities in Eastern Europe, that of Halicz (Western Ukraine), consists nowadays of only five elderly persons.

twenty-first century. The younger generation, however, often sounded more optimistic. They usually turned my attention to the revival of Karaite religious practice, and the Karaim language in Lithuania. Their general opinion was that, "they (*i.e.* scholars, journalists and public) say that we are dead since the beginning of the century; however, we are still alive up until now, and we do not have any wish to disappear."[63]

1.1.4. Karaites in the world today.

Due to the lack of exact statistical data, it is very hard to estimate the precise number of the Karaite community in the world at the time of this writing. However, it appears not to exceed more than 24,000 – 30,000 people. The largest communities are in Israel (where they have a *de facto* legal status which separates them from other Jews, synagogues, and religious courts)[64] and the USA (the largest centers being in San Francisco, Los Angeles, and Chicago). In addition to considerable communities in the Crimea, Poland, Lithuania, and Russia, there are also small commuities in Turkey, France, and some other countries. Of great interest for anthropologists is the varied nature of the national self-identification of the present-day Karaites: those of Israeli and Egyptian origin consider themselves Jewish, East European (Crimean, Lithuanian and Polish) and French Karaites (of non-Egyptian extraction) believe that they are of Turkic origin, whereas among the Karaites living in Turkey there are followers of both views.[65]

1.2. The Crimea: outline of its history in the twelfth-nineteenth centuries.

---

[63] One can compare the impressions that I received in the course of my contacts with Crimean, Polish and Lithuanian Karaites with the data retrieved by Iwona Koszewska, Waldemar Koszewski. *Karaimi Polscy. Struktura ekologiczna-społeczna mniejsości etnicznej i religijnej* (Warszawa, 1991), 59-61.

[64] Nehemia Meyers, "Israel's 30,000 Karaites follow Bible, not Talmud," in *Jewish Bulletin*. 10.12.1999, 1a, 49a; the number of 30,000 Israeli Karaites is said to be overestimated.

[65] More about the present-day state of the Karaite cominities in various countries of the world see Ross, *Acts of Faith*, 120-142; Schur, *Encyclopedia*, 77; Lasker D.J., "Karaites: Developments 1970-1988," *EJ Year Book*. – 1988/1989, 366-367, Emanuela Trevisan Semi, "The Pasha Karaite Meal and the Process of Transformation of Contemporary Lithuanian Karaism," *Nemzetiseg-Identitas* (Debrecen, 1991): 398-402; the same, "A Brief Survey of Present-Day Karaite Communities in Europe," *JJoS* 33:2 (1991): 97-106; El-Qodsi, *Communities*; Irena Jaroszyñska, "Skupiska karaimskie poza Polską," in *Karaimi. III Pieniężnieńskie spotkania z religiami (Materiały z sessii naukowej)*. Ed.A.Dubiński, Pieniężno: MMESDKW, 1987. – S.51-54.

In general, the history of the Crimea is characterized by an intensity of changes in the political, administrative, cultural, and socio-œconomic structure of the peninsula. Throughout the history of the region, different types of polities changed hands in the fight for predominance of the Crimean territory. At the end of the twelfth century, a short while before the supposed time of the arrival of the first Karaite settlers, the northern and central parts of the peninsula, together with the southern part of the present day Ukraine, were in the possession of the Kumans, while the maritime ports and towns were controlled by Byzantium. The traditional patronage of the Byzantine Empire over the peninsula began to weaken considerably after the conquest of Constantinople during the Fourth Crusade (1204). As a consequence, the largest Byzantine town, Kherson, situated in the western part of the Crimea, was gradually abandoned, until it ceased to exist by the middle of the fifteenth century.[66] The administrative, political, and œconomic center of the Crimea moved from the west to the eastern shore soon after the Genoese established their trading stations (Kaffa, Sudak) there in the thirteenth-fourteenth centuries. The Tatars, who first appeared and plundered the Crimea in 1223, settled in the northern part of the peninsula in the thirteenth century, and made the town of Sulkhat (Kırım, Eski-Kırım, Staryi Krym) their capital.[67] It seems that the appearance of the first Karaite communities should be connected with the arrival of the Tatars.[68]

The Genoese and Tatars coexisted, collaborated and, simultaneously, fought against the third important power on the Crimean territory, the Greek-Gothic principality of Theodoro (Mangoup) – which was situated in the mountainous area, and controlled a considerable part of the peninsula's west side.[69] From the end of the thirteenth century on, the Tatars' influence over the Crimean

---

[66] A.l. Romanchuk, *Khersones 12-14 vekov: istoricheskaya topographiia* [Chersonese from the twelfth to the fourteenth centuries: a historical topography] (Krasnoiarsk: KGU, 1986), 188.

[67] S.V. Bakhrushin, "Osnovnye momenty istorii Krymskogo Khanstva" [The main events in the history of the Crimean Khanate], *MAIET* 3 (1993): 323.

[68] See §1.1.3 above.

[69] The capital of this principality was Mangoup (Theodoro, Doros, Dorant); the history of the local Karaite community will be examined in §4.2. According to Yevgenii Veimarn, in this period the possessions of the principality of Theodoro stretched to the east, including Aluston and Funa, and to the west, including Chersonese and Kalamita (Inkerman), excluding the Genoese colony of Chembalo (Balaklava): "O dvukh nejasnykh voprosakh srednevekovia Jugo-Zapadnogo Kryma" [On two unclear questions of the south-western Crimea in the Middle Ages], in *Arkheologicheskie Issledovaniia Srednevekovogo Kryma* (Kiev: Naukova Dumka, 1968), 79.

territory began to increase; and, their power extended not only to the east and north, but also the central part of the peninsula. Another political power, the principality of Qırq-Yer, which had been inhabited by the Greek speaking Alanian and Gothic population, was seized by the Tatars during the reign of Canıbeğ, the Khan of the Golden Horde (1342-1357).[70]

However, after the Ottoman conquest in 1475, this situation completely changed. The peninsula was divided into two parts: Ottoman and Tatar. Those regions, ports, and towns that were most useful from a mercantile and administrative perspective came under Ottoman jurisdiction, while the rest of the Crimea, together with the southern part of contemporary Ukraine, was ruled by the Crimean Khan.[71] The Muslims (the Tatars and the Ottoman Turks) became the predominant ethnic group in the Crimean territory – while the Christians, even though still numerous in spite of their losses during the conquest, became their subjects. According to almost all written sources, the main income of the Crimean Khanate, at this stage, came from raids into the territories of adjacent countries (Poland, Russia, Georgia, Armenia, *et alia*), and the trade in slaves captured during these military campaigns.[72]

After the Ottoman conquest, the urban structure of the peninsula underwent considerable changes. Many old settlements (*e.g.* Mangoup, Qırq-Yer/Çufut-Qalé, Balaklava, and Sudak) started to lose their significance, while new towns (*e.g.* Bakhçesaray, Gözlöw

---

[70] Gertsen, Mogarichev, *Krepost'*, 56. Qirq-Yer, as well as a number of other Crimean towns first suffered from the invasion of the Tatars in 1299. See the chronicle of Rukh-ad-Din Bayjbar in *Sbornik Materialov Otnosiaschikhsia k Istorii Zolotoi Ordy* [The collection of the materials related to the history of the Golden Horde], ed. V. Tizengauzen, vol.1 (St. Petersburg, 1884), 112. The history of the Karaite community of Qırq-Yer (later Çufut-Qalé) will be examined in §4.1.

[71] See more details about the first years of the Ottoman rule in the Crimea in Alan Fisher, *The Crimean Tatars* (Stanford,1978), 8-16.

[72] Trade in slaves and captives was one of the most important (if not the most important) incomes of the Crimean Khanate in the sixteenth – eighteenth centuries. According to some estimates, in the first half of the seventeenth century, the number of captives taken to the Crimea was around 150,000 – 200,000 persons. About 100,000 were captured in the period from 1607-1617. See A.L. Yakobson, *Srednevekovyi Krym* [The Mediæval Crimea] (Moscow-Leningrad: Nauka, 1973), 141; A.A.Novoselski, *Bor'ba moskovskogo gosudarstva s tatarami v pervoy polovine XVII veka* (The struggle between the Moscow state and the Tatars in the first half of the seventeenth century) (Moscow-Leningrad, 1948), 436. On the role of the Jewish population in the Crimean slave trade see Mikhail Kizilov, "Jewish Population and the Trade in Slaves and Captives in the Crimean Khanate in the XVIIth century" (to be published in the Proceedings of the Thirteenth World Congress of Jewish Studies).

[Evpatoria], Qarasubazar, Ferakh-Kerman, Perekop, and Aqmeçit [Simferopol']) began to participate actively in the œconomic and political life of the region. Kaffa, often called by contemporary sources Küçük-İstanbul (Turkish "Small Istanbul"), the largest Crimean town in the fourteenth – fifteenth centuries, became a center of Kaffa Veyalet (Ottoman province) after 1475, which also included lands beyond the borders of the Crimea.[73]

With the decline of the Ottoman Empire in the seventeenth-eighteenth centuries, the military power of the Crimean Khanate also started to diminish.[74] At the end of the eighteenth century, the Russian Empire, which had for a long time wanted to expand to the South, finally annexed the Crimea in 1774-1783, after a series of successful military campaigns against Turkey. The territory of the former Crimean Khanate was first reorganized as Tavricheskaia Oblast' (i.e. the Tauridian district) and then was included in the structure of Novorossiiskaia Guberniia. After the annexation of the Crimea to Russia, the ethnographic situation in the peninsula changed once again. The territory, which was considerably depopulated because of the removal of the local Christian (Greek and Armenian) population in 1778 and the emigration of the Crimean Tatars,[75] was filled with Russian, Greek, German, Bulgarian, Jewish (Ashkenazic) and even Swiss colonists. A number of new European cities were built in the place of rather insignificant Tatar villages and settlements; many Tatar and Turkish names of the local settlements were substituted with new toponyms, mostly of Greek origin.[76] In the course of the nineteenth century, in spite of such tragic, devastating events as The Crimean War (1853-1856), the Crimea became a flourishing, prosperous part of the Russian Empire. From that moment on, the picturesque Crimea – with its varied, multinational population, a number of beautiful resorts, historic monuments, and sights – was internationally acknowledged as one of Europe's most attractive and interesting places.

---

[73] See Fisher, *Tatars*, 34-35.

[74] Alan Fisher supposed that one of the main reasons for worsening of the demographic and œconomic situation in the seventeenth century Crimea was the frequent, devastating raids of the Don and Zaporozhian Cossacks (A.Fisher, "The Ottoman Crimea in the Mid-Seventeenth Century," *HUS* (1979-1980): 216, 221.

[75] The Tatar emigration continued in the nineteenth century as well. It is estimated that around 80,000 left the Crimea before the end of the eighteenth century, 30,000 during the time of reorganization of the peninsula (1796-1802), less than 100,000 after the Crimean War in 1859; the gradual emigration also continued after the war with Turkey in 1877 (Fisher, *Tatars*, 88-89, 93).

[76] In this way Aqmeçit became Simferopol', the small Tatar village of Akhtiyar was transformed into the splendid Sevastopol', Gözlöw became Evpatoriia, Kaffa – Theodosiia etc.

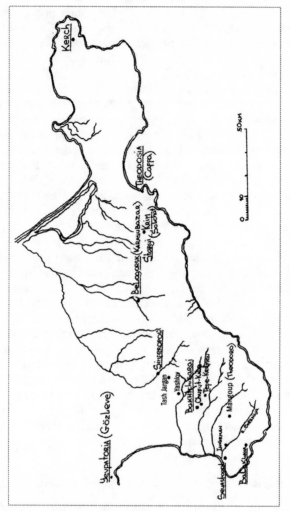

A map of the Crimean peninsula indicating the settlements of the Karaite communities in the thirteenth-nineteenth centuries.

44

1.3. The sources: travel accounts on the Crimean Karaites.
1.3.1. The value of travel accounts as a historical source.

"Visit, observe, and describe the places of pilgrimage – [graves] of the great saints... steppes and deserts, high mountains, unusual trees and rocks, towns, remarkable monuments, and fortresses. [Write] about their conquerors and builders, about the size [of the fortresses] and create a work, which you should name the "Book of Travels."
(instruction for a traveler, ascribed by the seventeenth century Ottoman voyager, Evliya Çelebi to his father)[77]

In spite of the fact that travel accounts[78] represent a very interesting and, to a certain extent, unique source, it is only in the last few decades that they have become accepted as important for understanding the history of mediæval and early-modern Europe.[79] In the Middle Ages, travel descriptions and accounts were one of the most important sources for contemporaries on remote and mysterious countries. In later periods, travelers promoted the spread of geographical lore when describing events, places, and phenomena, that they saw themselves, or of which they had heard from the descriptions of other eyewitnesses.

When analyzing travel accounts, one should assume that, in most cases, a traveler is a person who is thrown into strange and unfamiliar surroundings; the paradox of this is that a stranger may see everything more clearly. Usually, travel accounts tell us a lot about the differences between countries: contrasts between the home world and the one visited, different patterns of consumption and dress, strange

---

[77]   As quoted in Mikhail Kizilov, "Kniga i ee avtor" [The book and its author], afterward to *Kniga Puteshestviy* [The Book of Travels] by Evliya Çelebi (Simferopol', 1996), 184-190. These words might serve as the best guidelines for any traveler, both contemporary and mediæval.

[78]   There are several words in the English language which have approximately the same meaning as *travel account*: travelogue, itinerary, travel journal or travel notes, guide, etc. There are slight differences among these terms: for example, *account* usually describes a trip actually taken, while *itinerary* tends to give to a reader a verbal map and guide of a journey to a specific place of destination. See Linda Davidson and Mary Jane Dunn-Wood, *Pilgrimage in the Middle Ages: a research Guide* (New York-London, 1993), 14, 43.

[79]   It is possible to recommend several collections of recent articles for those interested in this topic: *Voyager a la Renaissance*, ed. Jean Ceard and Jean-Claude Margolin (Paris, 1987); *Der Reisebericht*, ed. Peter Brenner (Suhrkamp, 1989); *Reisen und Reiseliteratur im Mittelalter*, ed. Xenja von Ertzdorf and Dieter Neukirch (Amsterdam, 1992); *Travel and Travelers in the Middle Ages*, ed. Arthur Percival Newton (London, 1949); C. Raymond Beazley, *The Dawn of Modern Geography*, 3 vols (London, 1897-1903).

customs and landscape. All these influenced a traveler to record his impressions in writing. In style and content, travel descriptions are usually full of legends, marvels, dramatic experiences and personal impressions.[80]

It is this personal point of view that distinguishes travel accounts from other written sources. However, the subjectivity and emotionalism of travel accounts is at the same time a shortcoming; one has to treat information from travel accounts very carefully, because travelers were often inclined to exaggerate real facts and events. Besides, travelers often simply "described" strange phenomena, without "measuring" or evaluating them. Thus, having failed to understand foreign countries and people properly, travelers usually invented so-called "home-made yardsticks" for measuring and comprehending the unknown phenomena surrounding them.[81] On the other hand, one can extract very interesting and important information from a traveler's personal point of view and/or from various peculiar and specific details.

Travel descriptions possess another advantage: travelers frequently described historical and architectural monuments that have not survived. Sometimes, the description left by a traveler is the only information on the history of an architectural ensemble in a given city or town. Furthermore, one can compare data from travelers' accounts with archæological, ethnographic, and cartographic evidence as well as with data from other written sources.[82]

In addition to their historical value, travel accounts also represent precious examples of literary works. They are usually easy to read; and entering the world of a colorful, vivid and emotional travel account can be very rewarding.

---

[80] As regards the link between present and mediæval time, if a reader compares the contemporary travelogues of tourists to the Crimea with the mediæval travelers' descriptions of this region, he will not notice a marked difference. Excluding the style of narration and some modern details of a technical character, it is possible to find the same content: the difficult and hardly comprehensible language of the local inhabitants, strange and unknown customs, and descriptions of magnificent architectural and historical monuments (*e.g.* Sheila Paine, *The Golden Horde: Travels from the Himalaya to Karpathos* (London, 1997), 248-254; El-Qodsi, *Communities*, 18-21).

[81] Antoni Maczak, "Renaissance Travelers' Power of Measuring," in *Voyager à la Renaissance*, 246.

[82] A good example of such a comparative analysis is the work of Antony Bryer and David Winfield, where the authors attempt to reconstruct a history of the existence of a number of Byzantine architectural monuments: *The Byzantine Monuments and the Topography of the Pontos*, 2 vols. (Washington, 1985).

46

1.3.2. Revue of the sources[83]

Of the sources surveyed here, we may distinguish two main groups: accounts written prior to the Russian annexation of the Crimea (1783), and those composed after this date. Travel descriptions written before 1783 are very important for understanding the early history of the Karaites. Unfortunately, however, their number is not very large. Moreover, it is worth mentioning that the only travelers after 1475 who managed to enter the territory of the Crimean Khanate (which was hostile to Europeans) were members of diplomatic, missionary or military embassies. Their freedom of travel within the country was quite limited, and they were able to describe only what they were permitted to see.

Reviewing travel accounts written before 1783, it is notable that the travelogues of the mediæval and Renaissance periods are not as detailed and descriptive as those that followed. Travelers, even if they spent a long time in the Crimea, most often simply noted their presence there and/or gave brief information concerning the major towns and their inhabitants. However, these scarce notes are, to some extent, more important than the later descriptions, because they were written independently, without any borrowings from one another. In addition, they belong to a period that contains little other evidence.

As has been mentioned, the first indisputable evidence regarding the presence of the Karaites in the Crimea is the report of a conflict between the Rabbinic Jews and Karaite Jews in the town of Sulkhat in 1279 [see §1.1.3]. Some scholars suggest that the first reference to a possible Karaite presence in the vicinities of the Crimea might be found in the travel account of Rabbi Petaḥyah of Regensburg (between 1177-1187). According to his account, Petaḥyah embarked from Prague and, after visiting Poland and Russia, reached the "Land of Qedar." Most scholars identify the latter with the Southern Ukraine. For the Crimea, Petaḥyah used another term, *Khazaria*. In this "Qedar" he met certain Jewish *minim* (heretics) whose main distinctive feature was a strict observance of the Sabbath.[84] Some believe this part of

---

[83] The readers are reminded that this is just a brief introduction to the world of the travel accounts related to the Crimean Karaites, which outlines the most important tendencies, trends, authors, and their works. More details about other travelers and their accounts will be given further on.

[84] The original manuscript of his account has not survived. All that remains is an abridgement compiled by his traveling companion, Rabbi Yehudah Ben-Shemu'el HeḤasid. Petaḥyah did not record his purpose in travelling, but he may well have wished to visit his distant Jewish brethren and become acquainted with their fate. See Petaḥyah of Ratisbon, *Travels of Rabbi Petachia of Ratisbon, Who, in the Latter End of the Twelfth Century, Visited Poland, Russia, Little Tartary, the Crimea,*

Petaḥyah's narrative should be interpreted as the first direct testimony to the presence of a Karaite population. Others suggest that Petaḥyah was referring to the remnants of the Khazarian population rather than the Karaites. A modern Qrımçaqlar author has interpreted it as a reference to the early Rabbanite-Qrımçaqlar.[85]

The travelers of the late Middle Ages and Early Modern period (fifteenth-eighteenth centuries) did not pay much attention to the Karaites, and hardly differentiated them from the Rabbanites. The authors of this period left notes on the Karaites incidentally, because of their interest in the administrative and military significance of Kaffa, Mangoup, and Çufut-Qalé, the settlements where the Karaites lived. In their accounts, the Karaites are usually mentioned among other ethnic groups inhabiting these settlements. Sometimes, important (though rather brief) details are mentioned there as well [see the accounts of the fifteenth-sixteenth century travelers: J.Schiltberger,[86] M.Broniovius, [87] and Guilliaume de Beauplan].[88]

Armenia, Assiria, Syria, the Holy Land, and Greece, transl. Dr. A.Benisch (London, 1861), 6-9.

[85] See A.Benisch and W.F.Ainsworth, "Preparatory Remarks," in *ibid.* 5; Beazley, *Dawn*, 268; *Jewish Travelers*, E.Adler (ed.) (London, 1930), 64, 66; Ankori, *Karaites*, 61-64, f.19; Schur, *Encyclopedia*, 231; I.V. Achkinazi, *Krymchaki* [Qrımçaqlar] (Simferopol', 2000), 55. The author of this book is inclined to think that Petaḥyah's remark is too brief and too uncertain to come to any decisive conclusions concerning the ethnic identification of these Judaic "*minim*".

[86] Johann Schiltberger, *Hans Schiltberger Reisebuch* (Tubingen, 1885), 63. The German soldier Johannes (Hans) Schiltberger (1380-after 1438) spent about thirty years in Turkish captivity, and left a brief description of the countries he visited during this period. In his description of the largest Crimean port, Kaffa, Schiltberger mentioned that two kinds of the Jews lived there (*i.e.* probably Rabbanite and Karaite).

[87] Martinus Broniovius, *Martini Bronovii de Biezdzfedea bis in Tartariam nomine Stephani Primi Poloniae Regis Legati Tartariae Descriptio* (Cologne, 1595), 7. Martinus Broniovius (Marcin Broniewski), who was an ambassador of Stephan Bathory to the Crimean Khan Mehmed Giray in 1578-1579, described the majority of the towns and castles of the Crimea and the way of life of the Crimean Tatars in his *Tartariae Descriptio*. He mentioned that the Jews inhabited many Crimean ports and towns, but did not differentiate the Rabbinic Jews from Karaite Jews. The only direct reference to the Karaites is his remark about the Jews who composed a considerable part of the population of Mangoup.

[88] Guillaume Levasseur de Beauplan, *Opys Ukrainy* [Description of Ukraine], Ukrainian translation together with original text, (Kiev-Cambridge, 1990), vol.2, 32; vol.1, 51. The French cartographer and engineer Guillaume Levasseur de Beauplan (1600-1673) included much interesting information regarding the manners of the Crimean Tatars and a historical topography of the Crimea in his *Description d'Ukraine* (the second quarter of the seventeenth century). The author did not visit the Crimea, and got his information about this region either from the Ukrainian Cossacks, or from Dominican missionaries.

Accounts of the seventeenth-eighteenth centuries are much more numerous and informative than those of earlier periods. During this period, the attitude of a traveler towards his writing became substantially different. Travelers paid much more attention to the sources of their information, providing what statistical data was available to them, and writing in less exaggerated and prejudiced terms [see the accounts of the members of the Second Dominican mission in the Crimea: E.P. D'Ascoli, G. da Lucca[89]; see also Peyssonel].[90] In contrast to European travelers, who still failed to differentiate the Rabbanite Jews from the Karaite Jews, the Ottoman traveler Evliya Çelebi (1665-1666), clearly differentiated representatives of the Karaite community from the Rabbanites, and pointed out numerous differences in traditional dress, outer appearance, and the religious doctrines of the Karaites and Rabbanites. When describing the Crimean towns of Mangoup, Çufut-Qalé, and Qarasubazar, Evliya devoted much of his time and interest to the description of the Karaites, and their rites and manners. It is very likely that he had come

---

[89]   The activity of this mission and the accounts of its members were analyzed in Ambrosius Eszer, "Neue Forschungen zur Geschichte der II. Krim-Mission der Dominikaner (1635-1665)," *AFP* 41 (1971): 181-240. One of the members of the mission, Giovanni da Lucca in the 20-30s of the seventeenth century visited several countries of the Black sea area (Crimea, Georgia, Mingrelia, Abkhazia etc.). The account of his stay in these countries, which was composed around 1634, contains much valuable data on the history of the Rabbanite and Karaite inhabitants of the Crimea. See Giovanni da Lucca, "Opisanie Perekopskikh i Nogaiskikh Tatar, Cherkesov, Mingrelov i Gruzin" [The description of the Perekop and Nogay Tatars, Circassians, Mingrels, and Georgians]. *ZOOID* 11 (1879): 473-493; Giovanni da Lucca, "*Fatta da me Fra Giovanni da Lucca Dominicano circa il modo di vivere colle particolarita de costumi delli Tartari Percopiti, Nogai, Circassi, Abbaza etc. Mangrilli e Giorgiani.*" In *Bibliogaphia Critica delle Antiche Reciproche Corrispondenze* by Sebastiano Ciampi, 52-72. Firenze, 1834; on da Lucca and his biography see Ambrosius Eszer, "Giovanni Giuliani da Lucca O.P.: Forschungen zu Seinem Leben und zu Seinen Schriften." *AFP* 37 (1967): 353-468. Emidio Portelli D'Ascoli, the head of the Dominican mission in Kaffa, also left an account of his stay in the Crimea, where he supplied much valuable information on the history of the Jewish population of the Crimean peninsula in the seventeenth century. See Ambrosius Eszer, "Die *Beschreibung des schwarzen Meeres und der Tartarei* des Emidio Portelli D'Ascoli." *AFP* 42 (1972), 233-234; on a biography of the author see Ambrosius Eszer, "Emidio Portelli D'Ascoli und die II. Krim-Mission der Dominikaner (1624-1635)." *AFP* 38 (1965): 165-258. "*Dortelli D'Ascoli*" was a widespread variant of his name among Russian-speaking scholars, which appeared due to the error of the nineteenth century Kievan publisher of his account (cf. the title of the first publication of this account: Emiddio *Dortelli* D'Ascoli, "Descrittione del Mare Negro e della Tartaria 1634." In *Cztenia 5 Istoricheskogo Obshtchestva Nestora Letopisca.* Vol.5. Kiev, 1891).

[90]   Claude Charles de Peyssonel, *Traite sur le Commerce de la Mer Noire* (2 vols.) (Paris, 1787).

across Karaites prior to his visit to the Crimea, in Istanbul.[91]

After the annexation of the Crimean Khanate – at the end of the eighteenth/beginning of the nineteenth century, attracted by the mystery of its formerly forbidden status and its exotic ethnic groups – many European and some Russian travelers began to visit the Crimea. Paradoxically, the accounts of the Russian voyagers are less numerous, and less interesting than the travelogues of the West-European travelers.[92]

In the wake of the enlightenment, travelers began to perceive the world outside of their purview in a much more objective way, forgetting many rudimentary, mediæval views and prejudices. All the same, many travelers based their accounts on hearsay, and unreliable legends and stories of the local population, which was rather ignorant regarding its own past. Another common shortcoming was the fact that travelers very often simply borrowed statistical data from their colleagues, instead of collecting data themselves. An interesting feature of the travel writings of this period is their emphatic stress upon the good nature and general (moral and physical) purity and cleanliness of the Karaites. A motif of the comparison of the "bad Jews" (*i.e.* the Rabbanites, perplexed by their "Talmudic ravings") to the "good Jews" (*i.e.* the Karaites, who were not corrupted by the Talmud) is common place in the accounts of the first half of the nineteenth century.

Travelers of this period had much more focused and specific interests; some of them looked forward to meeting the Karaites with "pleasing anticipations." They read academic and popular literature on

---

[91] The fragments of Evliya's travel account related to the history of the Crimea were translated only into Polish and Russian: Ewlija Czelebi, *Ksiega podróży Ewliji Czelebiego* [The book of travel of Evliya Çelebi], transl. Z.Abrahamowicz, A. Dubinski et alia (Warsaw, 1969). Hereafter, I will refer to the Russian translation, done from the Polish edition: *Kniga Puteshestvii* [The book of travels], transl. M.Kizilov (Simferopol', 1996).
Evliya Çelebi (1611-1683) left precious data on the history, ethnography, linguistics, and historical geography of the countries he saw in his ten volume travel account entitled *Seyahatname* (The Book of Travels). Regarding the Karaites, he left a very informative description of several Crimean Karaite communities, which he visited in 1665-1666. Evliya not only described the manners, appearance and everyday life of the Karaites of Mangoup, Çufut-Qalé, and Qarasubazar, but also supplied data regarding the number of their houses, and the size of the population. See more on Evliya Çelebi in Mikhail Kizilov, "Kniga i ee avtor" [The book and its author], afterward to *Kniga Puteshestviy* by Evliya Çelebi (Simferopol', 1996), 184-190; Dan Shapira, "Evliya Çelebi 'Al Yehudei Qerim" (forthcoming); Mikhail Kizilov, *Kniga Puteshestvij Evlii Çelebi kak istochnik svedenij o byte Krymskikh tatar" [The Book of Travels* by Evliya Çelebi as a source on the Crimean Tatars' way of life], *MAIET* 3 (1993): 273-275.

[92] As has been noted before, a stranger may often see things more clearly.

50

them, while preparing themselves for a journey to the Crimea. In this period, a time of fast development in the natural sciences, the travelers often combined their traveling interests – which inspired them to cast an inquisitive glance upon ethnic groups such as the Karaites, which they perceived as enigmatic and exotic – with serious, scholarly historical, ethnographic, and anthropological observations. Travelers of this period not only clearly differentiated Karaite from Rabbanite Jews, but also noted features of their manners and customs, and described some of their ideological principles and historical perceptions. A very good example of this part tourist/part scholarly travel account is the work of P.S.Pallas (1793-1794) who, perhaps, was the first to attempt an academic description of the Crimean Karaites, their way of life and the peculiarities of their religious practices.[93] Edward Clarke's account (1800) of his visit to "the Jewish colony of Dschoufout Kale" is another good example of this attitude of travelers towards their writings. A serious and scrupulous scholar, professor Clarke described not only the main historical monuments and external appearance of the settlement, but also the manners, and the religious, ideological and historical views of these people. He paid much attention to such everyday details as quality of their food, and the style of their dress and houses.[94] Anatoli Demidov (1837), on the other hand,

---

[93]   Peter Simon Pallas (1741-1811), a German scholar who spent half of his life in Russia, left a very detailed and scrupulous description of his travel to Southern Russia and the Crimea in 1793-1794. His account was first published in German, French, and English, and only much later, in the second half of the nineteenth century, a considerably abridged Russian translation of his travels appeared. See P.S.Pallas, *Bemerkungen auf einer Reise in die suedlichen Statth8alterschaften des Russischen Reichs in den Jahren 1793 und 1794* (Leipzig, 1801), vol.2; P.S.Pallas, *Travels through the Southern Provinces of the Russian Empire, in the years 1793 and 1794*, transl. from German, vol.2 (London: A.Strahan, 1802); P.S.Pallas, "Puteshestvie po Krymu akademika Pallasa v 1793 i 1794 godakh" [The travel of the academic Pallas in the Crimea in 1793 and 1794], *ZOOID* 12 (1881): 62-208.
Many British and West European scholars and travelers praised the academic and individual qualities of Pallas: "Pallas was one of the most distinguished scholars the Russians have produced:" Henry H.Howorth, *History of the Mongols*, pt.1 (London, 1876), xxvi. The English traveler Edward Clarke wrote in a letter to his friend W. Oter: "He [Pallas] became more than father to me; he received me into his house; became my physician, my friend, my instructor:" William Oter, *The Life and Remains of Edward Daniel Clarke* (London, 1825), 62.

[94]   Edward Daniel Clarke, *Travels in Various Countries of Europe, Asia, and Africa. Part 1: Russia, Tahtary, and Turkey*, vol. 1 (London, 1816), 185-195. The English traveler and scholar Edward Daniel Clarke (1769-1822) who, due to certain political circumstances, was forced to stay in the territory of Russia much longer than he wished, left a detailed description of his stay in the Crimea as well. This work, because of its anti-Tsarist and anti-Russian bias, was not welcomed in Russia and, hitherto, has been used by Russian scholars very superficially.

was very personal and emotional in his description of *Tchioufout-Kaleh*, and his visit to the house of a local "Rabbi"; he also added scholarly, dry, scientific essays, written by other members of his expedition, to the first edition of his memoirs.[95] Dubois de Montpereux (1838), was, perhaps, too dry and academic in his description of the Crimean Karaites. He paid more attention to the analysis of data from written sources than to his own personal impressions.[96]

A drawing by the French painter Auguste Raffet who accompanied the Russian traveler Anatoli Demidov through his journey in the Crimea in 1837: the travelers are entering Çufut-Qalé from its Eastern side, close to the Yehoshafat Valley. Following them is the gang of local Gypsies who used to molest the strangers with unbearably bad music and noise in order to get some money from them.

In addition to such scholarly accounts, a number of travelogues depict a character of travel memoirs revealing nineteenth century tourists eager to express in writing their personal impressions and emotions from visiting remote countries. Travelers of this "non-scholarly" type fixed their interest more on: their personal contacts with the Karaites, funny misunderstandings that happened to them while visiting the Karaites, the behavior and appearance of Karaite

[95] Anatoli Demidov (1813-1870), was a representative of a noble and wealthy Russian family, who visited the Crimea in 1837 as a member of a scientific expedition there. His memoirs were written in French, and only later translated into Russian and English. See Anatoli Demidov, *Voyage dans Russie Meridionale et la Crimée par la Hongrie, la Valachie et la Moldavie execute en 1837* , 4 vols (Paris, 1840); *ibid. Travels in Southern Russia, and the Crimea*, 2 vols (London, 1853).

[96] Frederic Dubois de Montpereux, *Voyage autour du Caucase*, vol. 6 (Paris: de Gide, 1843), 338-349.

women, everyday Karaite life, etc. Travel accounts of this type, despite their rather belletristic and poetic character, also supply important and valuable data on the Karaites; moreover, they allow us to feel the atmosphere of that time and place.[97]

While analyzing travel accounts, it is worth mentioning the name of the Polish author, scholar and statesman Tadeusz Czacki (pronounced: *Chatski*). His *Rozprawa o Karaitach* (Essay on the Karaites), which concentrated on the Polish Karaites, was published in 1807. It greatly influenced not only the writings of many Polish and Russian travelers, but practically all academic scholarship related to the field of Karaite Studies published in the course of the nineteenth century.[98] Though prone to error and inaccuracy, in the context of its own time, this essay was one of the earliest scholarly attempts to investigate the intricate and mysterious history of the Karaite Jews. The Karaites also paid great attention to this work: Yosef Shelomoh Lucki testified in his itinerary that, in 1827, he gave Czacki's book to the Baroness S.Diebitsch for translation.[99]

The essay aroused the interest of many Polish, Russian, and Western scholars, and travelers to the Karaites. It greatly stimulated their eagerness to visit Karaite sites and monuments in the Crimea. Nevertheless, the aftermath was not always positive. Many travelers who lacked Czacki's academic training and erudition did not exert themselves in collecting historical data, nor in venturing their independent theories. Rather, they were satisfied in adapting Czacki's work, or offering direct quotations from it.[100]

---

[97] *E.g.* accounts of the Russian traveler to the Crimea Pavel Sumarokov: *Dosugi Krymskogo Sudii* [Leasure time of the Crimean judge], vol. 1-2 (St.Petersburg, 1803-1805); the same: *Puteshestvie po vsemu Krymu i Bessarabii v 1799 godu* [Travel through the whole Crimea and Bessarabia in 1799] (Moscow, 1800). Olimpiada Shishkina, *Zametki i vospominaniia russkoi puteshestvennitsy po Rossii v 1845 godu* [Notes and memoirs of a Russian traveler through Russia in 1845]. Vol. 2 (St.Petersburg, 1848), 109-120. Olimpiada Shishkina (1791-1854) – a Russian traveler and writer, in a very romantic and unfortunately rather imprecise manner described her visit to Çufut-Qalé and Mangoup in 1845. I.M.Muraviev-Apostol, *Puteshestvie po Tavride v 1820 godu* [Travel to Taurida in 1820] (St.Petersburg 1823), 128.

[98] T.Czacki, "Rozprawa o Karaitach," in T.Czacki, *Rozprawa o Zydach,* Wilno 1807, 246-272. The only known translation to European languages is the nineteenth century Russian translation: T.Czacki, "Issledovanie o evreiach karaitach," [Essay on the Jews-Karaites], *Severnyi Archiv* 6 (1827), 97-111.

[99] Miller, *Separatism*, 144.

[100] Some travelers did not even refer to Czacki's book as the source for their information: Edmund Chojecki, *Wspomnienia z podróży po Krymie* (Warsaw 1845), 213-216; Antoni Nowosielski [A.Marcinkowski], *Stepy, morze i góry. Szkice i wspomnienia z podróży*, vol.2 (Vilno, 1854), 195-199. K.Kaczkowski inserted into

In the nineteenth century, the Karaites, perceived as the Jews who rejected the Talmud, were often looked upon by Christians as a prospective target for missionary propaganda. One of the travel accounts most valuable for our topic, *Biblical Researches and Travels in Russia*, was written by the British missionary Ebenezer Henderson, who visited the Russian Empire in 1821-1822 with the aim of studying the Jewish population of the country, and spreading Christianity among them. Henderson not only documented his conversations with Crimean Karaite leaders, and reflected his impressions of *Djufut-Kale*, but also drew serious, analytical conclusions about the language and ethnic history of these people. Of great importance is his description of Karaite public worship in Luck and the local Karaite community.[101] In 1838, two other missionaries, Scottsmen Andrew Bonar and Robert McCheyne, visited and left some notes on the communities of the Crimea and Constantinople.[102]

The Crimean War (1853-1856) stimulated a great interest in the history, geography, and œconomy of the Russian Empire in general, and in the Crimea in particular. In order to satisfy the desire of the public to learn about the historical and geographic information of this area, a number of books dedicated to the Crimea and its history was published in many European languages in 1854-1856. Many of these publications supplied important details concerning the local Karaite population.[103]

---

the speech of the Karaite rabbi of Çufut-Qalé not the rabbi's own words, but a practically unchanged quotation from Czacki (cf. Karol Kaczkowski, *Dziennik podróży do Krymu, odbytej w roku 1825*, pt.4 (Warsaw, 1829), 101-102 and Czacki, "Rozprawa," 258-259). Karol Kaczkowski (1797-1867) was an author of many scientific works, and famous Polish physician.

[101] See Ebenezer Henderson, *Biblical Researches and Travels in Russia* (London, 1826), 306-339. Ebenezer Henderson (1784-1858) was a member of the British Bible Society, a scholar with a knowledge of several old and modern languages, and academic literature. In 1825 he was sent out of Russia because the local Russian orthodox authorities disapproved of his missionary activities. For more about the missionary activity of Henderson and his colleagues among the Karaites of Luck see "Extract of a Letter from the Rev. Drs. Paterson and Henderson," *JEx* 6 (1821), 469-470; "Interesting Communication of Dr. Pinkerton, Respecting the Jews in Poland, " in *JEx* 6 (1821), 444-445; "Extract of a Letter from the same [W.Ferd.Becker]", in *JEx* 7 (1822), 74.

[102] Their first-hand description of the Constantinople community is really impressive, whereas information concerning the Crimean Karaites should not be considered reliable because of the fact that the travelers did not visit the Crimea themselves, basing their data on the oral report of a certain "young American tourist" (Andrew A. Bonar and Robert Murray McCheyne, *Narrative of a Mission of Inquiry to the Jews from the Church of Scotland in 1838* (Edinburgh, 1842), 441).

[103] Nicolai Berg, *Bakhçesaray* (N.p., 1856), 19. The Russian officer Nicolai Berg resided in Bakhçeseray during the Crimean War and witnessed the vain attempts of

54

The interest of the travelers of the middle and second half of the nineteenth century was greatly stimulated by the conspicuous activity of Avraham Firkovich and his archæological and palæographic discoveries. Evgeni Markov left an especially detailed account of his contact with Firkovich in his *Sketches of the Crimea* (1860s).[104] Completely different was the account of Ephraim Deinard who, in a bitter and sarcastic tone, criticized Firkovich's activity.[105] In addition – because of the mass migration of the Karaites from the town of Çufut-Qalé in the second half of the nineteenth century, which was subsequently perceived as an abandoned, mystical, enigmatic, mediæval fortress – travelers were attracted to Çufut-Qalé by its projected eerie atmosphere.[106]

Travel accounts, as a literary genre, at the end of the nineteenth century, became less fashionable than they had been before.

Shelomoh Beim to rescue from complete abandonment the "hardly breathing", "half-legendary" town of Çufut-Qalé. See also S.Steinhard (as quoted in Pojata [H.Skirmuntowa], "Szkice z Krymu," *Tygodnik Ilustrowany* 8:201 (1871): 219, 222). Highly important accounts of the French travelers who visited Çufut-Qalé at the time of the Crimean War were analyzed in Moshe Gammer, "Karaites," 65-78; Emmanuela Trevisan Semi, "The Crimean Karaites in the French Jewish Press," 9-16.

[104] Evgeni Markov, *Ocherki Kryma* [Sketches of the Crimea] (Simferopol', 1995), 84-90, 452-461. Evgeni Markov (1835-1903) – Russian traveler and writer; his *Sketches* were one of the most popular books on the Crimea's history in nineteenth century Russia.

[105] Ephraim Deinard, *Sefer Massa' Qerim*, Warsaw, 1878; the same, *Toledot Firkovich*, Warsaw 1875. Ephraim Deinard (1846-1930) – a Rabbanite Jew born in Latvia, who worked as Firkovich's secretary over the course of seven years, in the 1860s. In addition to *Sefer Massa' Qeirim* and *Toledot Firkovich*, Deinard also wrote and published a number of other books and articles. The historical value of his works and the very controversial personality of their author, who was called by Emmanuela Trevisan Semi "Firkovich's alter ego", was discussed in many academic publications. See Vikhnovich, *Firkovich*, 70, 170; Schur, *Encyclopedia*, 86; Emanuela Trevisan Semi, "Le "Sefer Massa Qrim" de Deinard: but parodique ou polemique?" *Revue des Études Juives* 157:1-2 (1998), 57-67; Brad Sabin Hill, "Ephraim Deinard on the Shapira Affair" in *The Book Collector. Special Number for the 150th Anniversary of Bernard Quaritch* (1997), 167-179. See esp. M.A. dissertation by Simcha Berkowitz, *Ephraim Deinard (1846-1930). A Transitional Figure*. Columbia University, 1964. A special word of thanks goes to Brad Sabin Hill (YIVO) who gave me access to the copy of Berkowitz's dissertation, which was in his possession.

[106] *E.g.* Berg, *Bakhchisaray*, 19; Markov, *Ocherki*, 84-90, 452-461. Markov's description of Çufut-Qalé is lengthy and expressive, with a special emphasis on portraying the general atmosphere of the dying town and its historical and architectural monuments. See also Pojata, "Szkice," 8:201 (1871): 222; F.Remy, *Die Krim in ethnografischer, landshaftlicher und hygienischer Beziehung* (Odessa-Leispig, 1872), 94-95; [L.Hlebnicki-Józefowicz], "Wspomnienia Krymu," *Kłosy* 25:637 (1877): 165.

From the second half of the nineteenth century, travel accounts gradually lost their centrality as historical sources, and newly developed scientific disciplines, such as archæology, ethnography, anthropology and linguistics, were applied in historical study. Thus, the chronological frames surrounding valuable travel accounts are limited to the analysis of those accounts that were composed not later than the end of the nineteenth century. In terms of the typology of these sources, it is possible to distinguish the following groups:

1. *Travel relations* – travel notes of participants in diplomatic missions, usually written in the form of an official account about their activities in the visited countries. As a rule, because of their official character, they tend to be less open and more tendentious than non-official travelogues (*e.g.* M.Broniovius (1578), V.Tiapkin (1681), Savelov (1626)).

2. *Scholarly travel accounts* – travel notes written by representatives of academic circles with the aim of attempting to compose a scientific essay concerning events, nations, plants, animals, etc. seen while journeying in foreign countries (*e.g.* P.S.Pallas (1793-1794), Dubois de Montpereux (1838), J.Kohl (1838), A.Demidov (1837)).

3. *Travel diaries (itineraries)* – travel notes constructed like a journal, composed either while traveling, or a short while afterwards. Such accounts are usually characterized by their precise day-by-day structure, and detailed (though usually rather succinct) descriptions of everything the author had seen while traveling. It is possible to distinguish two types of these accounts: private travel diaries, and those composed with the aim of further publication (*e.g.* Evliya Çelebi (1665-1666), A.S.Griboedov (1825), V.A.Zhukovskiy (1837)).

4. *Travel memoirs* – travel notes usually composed some time after completion of a journey. Most of them have a very personal, emotional, belletristic character. Their authors usually put emphasis upon their private feelings rather than upon concrete historical and ethnographic data (*e.g.* F.Remy (1871), R.Lyall (1822), A.Nowosielski (1850), A.Neilson (1855), E.Markov (1860s), P.Sumarokov (1800, 1803-1805)).

5. *Travel accounts of epistolary genre (letters)* – common during the nineteenth century, these documents were frequently published in the form of a collection of letters sent by the traveling author to some close friend or relative at home (*e.g.* Muraviev-Apostol (1820), V.Izmailov (1799), D.B. (1816), M.Guthrie (1796), N.Kleeman (1769)).

6. *Accounts of missionaries* – travel notes composed by missionaries forming an account of the representatives of other religions visited by them while carrying out their proselytization; in spite of their very detailed character, they tend to be rather biased and insincere (*e.g.* E.Henderson (1821-1822); A.Bonar and R.McCheyne (1838)).

7. *"Captivity accounts"*[107] – travel notes left by reluctant "travelers" – *i.e.* those who were taken prisoners in military campaigns. They tend to describe the sufferings and misfortune of their authors in captivity (*e.g.* J.Schiltberger (beginning of the fifteenth century); notes of Polish soldier in the book of N.Witsen).[108]

8. *Literary works* – poetic or prosaic writings that also contain the travel impressions of their authors (*e.g.* poems of S.Bobrov (1804), A.Mickiewicz (1825) and A.K.Tolstoy (1855); monk Matthew (1395)).

9. *Miscellanea* – marginal notes, commentaries of travelers about writings of other voyagers, quotations from lost travel accounts, references to oral reports of other travelers, *et alia*.

---

[107] This term was suggested by Michael Harbsmeier in his "Elementary Structure of Otherness: an Analysis of Sixteenth-Century German Travel Accounts," in *Voyager a la Renaissance*, 342-343.

[108] Nicolaas Witsen, *Noord en Oost Tartarye* (Amsterdam, 1705), 577.

CHAPTER 2
KARAITES AS SEEN BY TRAVELERS: ETHNIC HISTORY, RELATIONS WITH THE NEIGHBOURS, IMPORTANT PERSONALITIES, AND LEGAL STATUS OF THE COMMUNITY

2.1. Ethnonyms

Travelers of the fifteenth-seventeenth centuries did not differentiate between Karaite and Rabbanite Jews, and referred to them in the same manner: *Giudei, Juifs, Juden* or *Judaei.*[109] The only exception we are aware of is Evliya Çelebi who, already in the mid-seventeenth century, called them "Karaites" or "the Jews of the Karaite confession." Çelebi noted that they were hated by other Jews, and compared their status in the Jewish community to that of the *qızıl-baş,* (*i.e.* the Shiites) among the *Sunni* Muslims.[110] However, neither he nor any other traveler of this period ventured to suggest any theories regarding the ethnic origin of the Karaites.

The French ambassador Claude Charles de Peyssonel (1753) called the Karaites "Juifs Karaites" (or simply "Juifs") and noted that, in the Crimean Khanate, they are much more numerous than the Rabbanite Jews.[111] De Peyssonel attached distinctive confessional meaning to the term "Karaites," indicating by this term the adherence of the Karaites to a specific religious stream within Judaism.[112]

Many travelers of the eighteenth-nineteenth centuries erroneously thought the origin of the term Karaite (or Qaraite – transliterating the Hebrew Qof with a "Q") was not Hebrew, but Turkic and, accordingly, translated it as the "*Black Jews*" (from the Turkish "qara" – "black"). Thus, the Austrian traveler Nicholas Kleeman (1769) called them "*Karai Yaodi oder Schwarze Juden*" (Germ.

---

[109] E. D'Ascoli in Eszer, " *Beschreibung,*" 234, 236; Lucca, "Fatta da me," 56; Schiltberger, *Reisebuch,* 63; Broniovius, *Descriptio,* 7.

[110] Evliya Çelebi, *Kniga,* 990.

[111] According to the estimations of M.S.Kupovetski, by 1783 the Karaites constitued approximately 75% of the Jewish population of the Crimean Khanate (Kupovetski, "Dinamika," 87).

[112] Peyssonel, *Traite,* vol.2, 320. The French ambassador Claude Charles de Peyssonel (1727-1790) was sent to the court of the Crimean Khan Arslan Giray (1748-1756) in 1753. This well-educated French diplomat left many references to the Karaites in his historical-œconomic treatises, which were published in the second half of the eighteenth century. He supplied important information on the life of the Karaite communities of Mangoup and *Tchifout-Kalessi* (*i.e.* Çufut-Qalé), and recorded a very interesting legend about the origin of the privileged status of the Karaites in the Crimean Khanate.

"*Karai Yaodi* or *Black Jews*").[113] The term "*Yaodi*" (sing.) – and its plural form "*Yaodilare*", often used by travelers of this period – is a corruption of the Turkish "yahudi" and "yahudiler," *i.e.* the "Jews." An anonymous French traveler, the author of *Lettres sur la Crimee* (1808), called the Karaites "*Karay Yardi ou Juifs noirs*" (French "*Karai Yaodi* or *Black Jews*").[114] Maria Guthrie mentioned that the *Karai Yaodi* called themselves "*Black Jews*" in order to be distinguished from their Jewish brethren in Poland and Turkey.[115]

Many of the authors of this period were not mistaken by the seemingly Oriental appearance of the term "Qara'im," and tried to find its derivation in the field of Biblical or Hebrew lore. Thus, I.M.Muraviev-Apostol (1820) supposed that the term "Karaites" should be translated as "Scripturalists" (Russ. "pis'mennye") from the word "Qara'", *i.e.* "Scripture" (Russ. "pisanie").[116] A.Demidov was of the opinion that the term "Qara'" came from the word "Scripture," but in an earlier stage of its development the movement had been called "Societe des fils de Judee."[117] E.Henderson mentioned the three most widespread Hebrew terms used for the designation of the Karaites: "*Benei-Miqra'* " (sons or disciples of the Scripture), "*Ba'alei-Miqra'* " (masters or possessors of the Scripture), and "*Qara'im*" (Scripturalists).[118]

Official Tatar documents at this time referred to the Karaites and other Jewish subjects using the word *yahudi*.[119] As can be seen

---

[113] Nikolaus Ernst Kleeman, *Reisen* (Wien: Chelenschen Buchhandlung, 1773), 74.

[114] *Pis'ma o Kryme, ob Odesse i Azovskom more / Lettres sur la Crimee, Odessa et la Mer d'Azof*, in French and Russian (Moscow, 1810), 68. This account, originally written in French, was first published in *Bibliotheque Britannique* in 1808. Its author, a French officer, visited and described the Crimea in 1808 while travelling in the peninsula with a French General. Strangely enough, in Russian scholarship this travel account is very often attributed as belonging to Maria Guthrie.

[115] Maria Guthrie, *A Tour, Performed in the Years 1795-6 through the Taurida or Crimea* (London: T.Cadell, 1802), 84. Mrs. Maria Guthrie, an English tourist who wished to improve her health, visited the Crimea in 1795-1796; "Alas! of little avail," her former husband sorrowfully remarked in the introduction: Guthrie, *Tour*, v. Her description of Mangoup is very misleading (the traveler mixed Mangoup with the Cloister of Dormition near Çufut-Qalé), but information about Çufut-Qalé, and the manners the Karaites are very detailed and interesting.

[116] Muraviev-Apostol I.M., *Puteshestvie po Tavride v 1820 godu* [Travel to Taurida in 1820] (St.Petersburg 1823), 128. Ivan Matveevich Muraviev-Apostol (1765-1851) – Russian traveler and writer, who visited the Crimea in 1820 and left very picturesque and romantic descriptions of Çufut-Qalé and Mangoup.

[117] Demidov, *Voyage*, vol.II, 736.

[118] Henderson, *Researches*, 320.

[119] See *Sbornik starinnykh gramot i uzakonenii Rossijskoi imperii kasatelno prav i sostoianiia russko-poddannykh karaimov* [Collection of the old charters and statutes of the Russian Empire regarding the rights and status of the Russian subjects,

from other written sources, the Crimean Tatars commonly called the Karaites *Çufut (Çufutlar)*; the Karaites themselves deliberately and consistently, up to the present day, avoid using this word because of its pejorative meaning, which is similar to the Russian "*zhid.*" P.S.Pallas tried to analyze the etymology of the term "*çufut*," and supposed that it was of Genoese origin. In his opinion, the Crimean Tatars had borrowed this term from the Genoese merchants who had used it as pejorative for the Jews in Italy. However, *Çufut* is generally believed to be of Turkish origin.[120] According to Johann Kohl (1838), those Karaites, who were aware of the derogatory meaning of the word, applied the term "Dschufutt" with regard to the Talmudic Jews.[121]

Sometimes one finds humorous misunderstandings about the name of the Karaites. Some travelers and local inhabitants called them "Karaibes" (*i.e.* Caraïbes). August von Haxthausen (1843) was very amused by this misunderstanding, and even asked one of the locals whether these "pseudo-Caraïbes" were used to eating human flesh.[122]

Karaites], Z.A. Firkovich (ed.), St. Petersburg 1890, 62-93. In the official documents of the Khans' administration of the seventeenth – eighteenth centuries the Karaites were usually called *Karay Yahudi*", *i.e.* the "Karaite Jews." In the everyday spoken language of the Crimean Tatars the Karaites were usually called "*zülüfsüz çufutlar*" (*i.e.* "the Jews without earlocks"), whereas the Qrımçaqlar – " *zülüflü çufutlar*", *i.e.* "the Jews with earlocks."

[120] Pallas, *Travels*, 356-357; the same; *Bemerkungen*, 362; Miller, *Separatism*, 55, footnote 32. [*ed.* It is more likely of Iranian or Caucasian origin, since in the language of the Alanians (the original inhabitants of the Crimea and part of the Caucasus), which was similar to modern Ossetic, the word for Jew was *Çufut* and the Rabbanite Jews of Daghestan are called *Daǧ Çurfut/Çufut* ("mountain Jews") and call their Iranian Judæo-Tat dialect "*Çurfuti/Çufuti/Dzhurfuti/Dzhufuti*" (depending on the local sub-dialect).]

[121] Johann Georg Kohl, *Reisen in Suedrussland*, vol.2 (Dresden-Leipsig, 1841), 266. Johann Georg Kohl (1808-1878) – a famous German traveler, geographer and writer. In 1838 he visited the Crimea and Southern Russia; of especial interest for our topic is his essay "Nachtraegliches ueber die Karaiten" published in the second volume of his memoires (Kohl, *Reisen*, vol.2, 257-266). In spite of the fact that this essay was composed by the author mostly on the basis of his socializing with the Karaites of Odessa, readers will find many important references to the Crimean Karaites there as well. Kohl's notes on the Karaites were very popular in Germany and were published several times, with insignificant variations, before the appearance of his book: the same, "Die jüdische Sekte der Karaiten in Süd-Rußland," *Allgemeine Zeitung des Judenthums* 3 (1839): 399-400, 410-412, 439; the same, "Die Karaiten in der Krim," *Der Israelitische Volkslehrer* 5 (1855): 17-22, 62-67, 100-104; the same in *Magazin für die Literatur des Auslandes* 67-68 (1839). See also, the critical evaluation of Kohl's report on the Karaites by Isaak Markus Jost in his "Neuere Berichte über die Karaiten und deren Geschichte," *Israelitische Annalen* 1 (1839): 217-220.

[122] August von Haxthausen, *Studien ueber die innern Zustaende, das Volksleben und insbesondere die Laendlichen Einrichtungen Russlands*, vol.2 (Hannover 1847),

On the basis of the testimonies of the travelers, it is possible to come to the conclusion that the term "Karaites" identifying a specific religio-ethnic group became important in the eyes of the non-Jewish world in the eighteenth – nineteenth centuries. Travelers of the nineteenth century, more conscious about the history of the Karaites, usually called these people *Jews-Karaites* (*Karaims*) or simply *Karaites* (*Karaims*). Most of the eighteenth – nineteenth centuries' travelers contended that the term "Karaite" had exclusively confessional meaning, and did not imply any ethnic connotation. It is only in the second half of the nineteenth century that the term "Karaite" started to have a distinctive ethnic dimension. It is interesting to note that the pejorative terms "*zhid*" and "*çufut*" were applied to all Jews (Rabbanite and Karaite) of the Crimean peninsula.

2.2. Ethnogenesis and historical past.

As mentioned, in the end of the eighteenth/beginning of the nineteenth century, the Karaites received special juridical status that legally separated them from the Rabbanite Jews. In the 1830s, the Karaite leaders felt the necessity to "justify" the receipt of this profitable and advantageous status to the Tsarist administration. They felt they had to prove they were worthy of being exempted from the double tax imposed on the Rabbanites. In spite of the fact that this special status had already been secured for the Karaites, in 1839 general-governor M.S.Vorontsov sent an official inquiry to the Karaite Spiritual Assembly in Taurida. In it he demanded that the Karaites give him sufficient historical information regarding their origin, the time of their arrival to the Crimea, the reasons for their separation from other Jews, &c.[123] It seems that this moment was one of the crucial stages in the forming of the Karaites' self-identification and re-

---

261; see also abridged English translation: August von Haxthausen, *The Russian Empire, Its People, Institutions, and Resourses*, tr.R. Farie, vol.2 (London 1856). The traveler was so amused because, in fact, the Caraïbes were primitive tribes living in the South America, *i.e.* quite faraway from the Crimea; they were widely known for their cannibal practices. The German scholar August Franz von Haxthausen (1792-1866) visited the Russian Empire in 1843-1844, because of his interest in the history and œconomy of the country. The account of his travel to the Crimea, despite its undoubtful value, contains numerous "borrowings" from the aforementioned work by J.Kohl; another shortcoming of the author's information regarding the Karaites is his blind belief in all the "discoveries" of A.S.Firkovich.

[123] A full text of this enquiry was published by O.Belyi in his "Obzor arkhivnykh dokumentov po istorii karaimskoi obshchiny Kryma v pervoi polovine XIX veka" [A Survey of the archival documents related to the history of the Crimean Karaite community in the first half of the nineteenth century] *Krymskii muzei* 1995-1996, 114.

development of their ethnic history. The task of giving an answer to the official inquiry, and finding "evidence" regarding their ancient settlement in the Crimea was given to A.S.Firkovich. It was Firkovich, Shelomoh Beim, and, later, Seraya Szapszal who published a number of historical treatises and essays where they fabricated a new vision of the history of the Crimean Karaites, which they based on feeble columns of emotions, a biased interpretation of historical sources, guess-work, and even forgeries.[124]

The travel accounts of this period represent a very important source, which supply valuable data on the Karaites' views of their ethnic origins and history in the period preceding the aforementioned dejudaizing activity of the Crimean Karaite leadership. The travelers wrote down a number of interesting legends, traditions, and stories regarding the history of the Karaites in the Crimea, their severance from the Rabbanites, the nature of their privileged status in the Crimean Khanate, &c.

One of the earliest travelers to supply information of this kind was the French ambassador Claude Charles de Peyssonel (1753), who recorded some very interesting oral traditions, which circulated in the Crimean Karaite communities of that time. He relates that, according to the Karaites' claims, they came from Bokhara (Middle Asia) together with the Tatar conquerors of the Crimea; moreover, their privileged status in the Khanate and exemption from public services were explained by certain services that they had rendered to the Khan-conquerors of the Crimea. However, Peyssonel did not believe this story.

He recorded another tradition (more reliable in his opinion), according to which the Karaites were exempted from many administrative and agricultural services for the Khan because a certain Karaite physician cured *Ulukhanım* ("great lady"), the sister of Haci Selim Giray Khan.[125] E.Henderson attributed this event to the beginning of the eighteenth century (*i.e.* to the reign of Selim Giray Khan [1702-1704]).[126] According to Avraham Firkovich, this event happened much earlier, in the beginning of the sixteenth century, and the name of the physician was Sinan Ben-Yosef, a Karaite from Persia.

---

[124] See Avraham Ben-Shemu'el Firkovich, *Avnei Zikkaron* (Vilna, 1872); Shelomoh Beim, *Pamiat' o Chufut-Kale* [Memories about Çufut-Qalé]. Odessa, 1862; S.Szapszal, *Karaimy i Chufut-Kale v Krymu* [Karaites and Çufut-Qalé in the Crimea] (Simferopol' 1993, reprint of St.Petersburg edition of 1896.).

[125] Peyssonel, *Traite*, vol.2, 320-321.

[126] Henderson, *Researches*, 315.

In Firkovich's version, however, he cured the daughter of a Khan.[127] The Karaite communities of Turkey and Poland possessed similar oral traditions regarding the privileges granted to the Karaites because of medical services they provided in royal courts.[128]

Completely different information regarding the origin of the privileged status of the Karaites in Muslim countries was written down by J.Kohl (1838) and A.F. von Haxthausen (1843). According to their travel accounts, the most ancient privileges were given by the prophet Mohammed.[129] Karaite *Ḥazzan* Shelomoh Beim informed A.F. von Haxthausen that "there is a tradition that Mohammed's teacher was a Karaite; this is why Mohammed granted to the Karaites a privilege..." As a consequence, Haxthausen came to the conclusion that the Muslims in general are nothing but a Karaite sect.[130]

Despite the number of inaccuracies and unrealistic details, many of the legends and stories written down by the travelers preserve grains of historical events. The analysis of the travelers' testimonies allows one to suppose that the Karaites of the "pre-Firkovich" period believed they arrived in the Crimea at the time of the Tatars' settling in the Crimean peninsula in the thirteenth – fourteenth centuries.[131] For example, E.Henderson noted that the Crimean Karaites, whom he visited at the beginning of the nineteenth century, did not maintain that they originated from the Bukharian Jews mentioned by Peyssonel in 1753: "...the only traditional account current among them is, that their

---

[127]   Miller, *Separatism* , 9-10.

[128]   The Turkish Karaites were of the opinion that the piece of land in the Hasköy quarter in Constantinople had been given to them because of the miraculous healing of the Sultan Abdul-Aziz from eye-disease by an old Karaite lady (Anna Sulimowicz, "Karaimi znad Zlotego Rogu," *Awazymyz* 1 (1989), 9; Jaroszynska, «Skupiska", 52); the Karaites of Troki informed T.Czacki that the Karaite physician Ezra Nisanowicz (*i.e.* 'Ezra Ben-Nisan Ha-Rofe') cured the wife of Jan III Sobieski and received a village as the King's gift; according to other data, he cured the daughter of the King Jan Casimir (Czacki, "Rozprawa," 265; Grzegorz Pelczynski, *Najmniejsza mniejszosc. Rzecz o Karaimach polskich* (Warsaw, 1995), 16; Mikhail Kizilov, "Karaite Physician Ezra Ben-Nisan ha-Rofe of Troki (1595-1666): Legend and History" (forthcoming)). Cf. also the travel account of Binyamin of Tudela, containing a very similar story about Rabbi Shelomoh HaMiṣri, a king physician in Constantinople, through whom the Jews enjoyed considerable alleviation of their oppression: *Jewish Travelers*, E.Adler (ed.), London 1930, 39.

[129]   Kohl, *Reisen*, vol.2, 258; Haxthausen, *Studien*, 399. Cf. tradition of the Cairo Karaites that the local community had a document given to them in 641 by the Muslim governor of Egypt '*Amr ibn al-'As* (El-Qodsi, *Communities*, 4).

[130]   Haxthausen, *Studien*, 401.

[131]   Most scholars consider the thirteenth – fourteenth centuries to be the most probable time for the Karaites' settling in the Crimea (*e.g.* Schur, *Encyclopedia*, 75; Miller, *Separatism*, 9; Ankori, *Karaites*, 60 [see also §1.1.3].

64

ancestors came from Damascus, and settled here about 500 years ago, under the protection of the Khans of the Crimea".[132] D.B. was informed by an "aged Karaite Rabbi" that the Karaites had arrived in the Crimea during the reign of the Crimean Khans from Smyrna, Damascus, and some other towns, whereas the town of Çufut-Qalé had been given to them after the expulsion of the Genoese builders and masters of the town.[133] According to the supposedly ancient tradition narrated to Karaite sage Mordekhai Sultanski by three elderly inhabitants of the former Mangoup community, the Karaites migrated to the Crimea together with the Tatars from Persia, Bukhara, and Circassia.[134] Similar information regarding the arrival of the Karaites to the Crimea in the thirteenth – fourteenth centuries had been mentioned by many other nineteenth century travelers as well.[135]

Testimonies of the travelers also give evidence that the Karaites of the "pre-Firkovich" period believed that the earliest Karaite graves in the Crimean Karaite cemeteries belonged to the thirteenth - fourteenth centuries. Karaite guides, who showed the travelers sights of Çufut-Qalé, unanimously pointed out the tombstones of the thirteenth – fourteenth centuries as the most ancient and venerated.[136] Only from the 1840s, as a result of Firkovich's activity, did the Karaites start to inform the travelers that the oldest tombstones of the cemetery of Çufut-Qalé dated to the first millennium c.e.[137]

The travelers paid a great attention to the ethnic origin and history of the Karaites. In spite of this, the analysis of their data suggests that neither the Karaites, nor the scholars and travelers of the first half of the nineteenth century, possessed a clear, unified understanding of the history of the development of Karaite Jewish settlement in the Crimea.

---

[132] Henderson, *Researches*, 315.
[133] D.B., [D.N.Bantysh-Kamenskiy?], "Otryvok iz puteshestviya po Krymu" [A fragment from the travel to the Crimea], *Syn Otechestva 36:8 (1817):* 48-49. In our opinion, D.N.Bantysh-Kamenskiy, a son of the famous Russian historian N.N. Bantysh-Kamenskiy, might have concealed his name by the initials "D.B."
[134] P.I.Koeppen, *O Drevnostiakh Juzhnago Berega Kryma i Gor Tavricheskikh. Krymskii Sbornik* [On the antiquities of the Southern coast of the Crimea and the Tauridian mountains: Crimean collection] (St. Petersburg, 1837), 289-290.
[135] Demidov, *Voyage,* vol.2, 736; Kohl, *Reisen,* vol.2, 258; Montpereux, *Voyage,* 339-340.
[136] Henderson supplied the date of 1346, whereas von Haxthausen and Dubois were told that the most ancient grave dated to 1249: A.D.Henderson, *Researches,* 312-314; Haxthausen, *Empire,* 111; Montpereux, *Voyage,* 347. See also Demidov, *Voyage,* vol.1, 372; Jean De Reuilly, *Voyage en Crimée et sur les bords de la Mer Noire, pendant l'année 1803* (Paris: Bossange, 1806), 133.
[137] Markov, *Ocherki,* 431; Shishkina, *Zametki,* 109; Remy, *Krim,* 98.

The account of Johann Kohl (1838), regarding his visits to the communities of the Crimean and Odessa Karaites, is quite significant in this respect. One of his informants, "gelehrte Rabbi Ussuff"[138] of "Dschuffut-Kale," when comparing the status of the Karaites within Judaism with the status of Protestants in Christianity or Shiites in Islam, added that establishing the exact dates of Karaite separation from other Jews and the development of their religious doctrine was very difficult. As a consequence, Kohl came to the conclusion that "they themselves do not possess any history of their sect".[139] Special attention to the ethnic history of the Karaites was given by E.Henderson (1821). While rejecting a number of what he supposed were inaccurate theories (such as the theory of Karaite origin from the Bukharian Jews, Sadducees etc.), Henderson came to the conclusion that the Karaites represented a Turkic speaking ethnic group of Jewish origin, which came to the Crimea in the fourteenth century. Henderson also regarded Peyssonel's story regarding the origins of the privileged status of the Crimean Karaites as veracious.[140] Maria Guthrie (1795-1796), who was a very romantic traveler, keen to hear and write down various fanciful stories, supposed that the "*Black Jews*" or *Karai Yaodi* (*i.e.* the Karaites) were descendants of the Scythian tribe of Melanchlanoi (*Μελανχλανοι*), who were distinguished by wearing black garments.[141]

In spite of the appearance of a number of theories regarding the origin of the Karaites in the second half of the nineteenth century, the general public was still in a state of confusion. Travelers of this period seem to be puzzled by the pretentious academic tone of the works of Avraham Firkovich on the one hand, and the obvious impossibility of his theories on the other. The sources of this period usually refrain from evaluating information received from Firkovich or his disciples.[142] Firkovich's secretary, a Rabbanite Jew named Ephraim Deinard, sarcastically remarked on the confusion within the Karaite community itself regarding its own origins and history. In his opinion, such contradictory concepts as the origin of the Karaites from 'Anan

---

[138] Unfortunately, we could not establish the full name and identity of this "venerable elder", Rabbi Ussuff/Youssouf/Yosef, who welcomed several visitors to Çufut-Qalé in the 1830s. See also Spenser, *Travels*, vol.1, 373; Kohl, *Reisen*, vol.2, 257.

[139] Kohl, *Reisen*, vol.2, 257-258.

[140] Henderson, *Researches*, 315-319.

[141] Guthrie, *Tour*, 84.

[142] *E.g.* Markov, *Ocherki*, 431, 455; Władysław Syrokomla [L.Kondratowicz], *Wycieczki po Litwie w promieniach od Wilna* (Vilna, 1857), 57-88; Shishkina, *Zametki*, 109; Nikolay Kostomarov, *Avtobiographiya. Bunt Sten'ki Razina* [Autobiography. Sten'ka Razin's rebellion] (Kiev, 1992), 291.

Ben-Dawid, Yehudah Ben-Tabbai, Ṣaddoq and the Boethusians, Khazars and Mongols changed hands in the fight for predominance over Karaites' minds in the second half of the nineteenth century.[143]

The creation of a unified and persuasive picture of the Karaites' historical past, which would provide solid grounds for a governmental recognition of non-Jewish status, became one of the most important ideological tasks for the Karaite national movement of the late 1830s through the second half of the nineteenth century. It was especially important in this process to prove that the Karaites dissociated themselves from other Jews during the time of the destruction of the First temple and the subsequent Babylonian captivity, *i.e.* a long time before the Crucifixion of Christ and the compiling of the Talmud. They had to demonstrate to the Russian government that they, unlike other Jews, did not have any relation to the Crucifixion and the "vicious and corrupt" Talmud.

This idea was reflected in many travel accounts of the nineteenth century. Karaite *Ḥazzan* Shelomoh Beim informed August von Haxthausen in 1843 that "the Karaites had not been witnesses of the religious revolution effected by Jesus in Palestine, nor had [they] become acquainted with the Christians until a later period: they entertained therefore no hereditary animosity against Christianity." Another Karaite sage, "Rabbi Rebbi Jeschuah Dawidowitch Koen" (Yehoshu'aʻ Ben-Dawid HaKohen)[144] of Feodosia told von Haxthausen that the Crimean Karaites were the descendants of those Israelites who had been carried into captivity by *Nabuchodonosor* (Nebuchadnezzar). According to him, they did not return to the Promised Land, but were brought to Armenia. Koen contended that, about 2,100 years ago (*i.e.* around the third century B.C.), part of these captured Israelites (numbering roughly 6000 males) migrated to the Taman region, and from there further on to the Crimean towns of Kerch, Feodosia [Kaffa], Mangoup, Stary Krym [Eski Qırım / Sulkhat] and Çufut-Qalé.[145]

---

[143] Deinard, *Sefer Massa Qrim*, 60.

[144] Yehoshu'aʻ Kohen is mentioned in a letter from Yosef Shelomoh Lucki of 19 November, 1835. Lucki asks Yehoshu'aʻ to translate into Russian a poem in Hebrew written in honor of the Taurida archbishop Gavriil. According to Dan Shapira, who is indebted to Maksim Zaverjajev for this information, Yehoshu'aʻ Kohen was also a leader of the party among the Crimean Karaites, who opposed the religious innovations brought to the Crimea by the Luck Karaites (Dan Shapira, *Avraham Firkowicz in Istanbul (1830-1832). Paving the Way for Turkic Nationalism* (Ankara: KaraM, 2003), 58, ft.102).

[145] Haxthausen, *Empire*, 111; Haxthausen, *Studien*, 390-391, 401, 408.

E.Deinard was of the opinion that the theory of Karaite descent from the Ten Lost Tribes of Israel came from Firkovich himself.[146]

Apparently, the Karaites often narrated similar stories and legends about their origins. E.Clarke (1800) remarked that the schism between the Karaites and Rabbanites "is said to be as old as the return from the Babylonish captivity."[147] A.Demidov (1837) was told by the Karaites that this event had happened before the destruction of the first Temple,[148] whereas the marquise de Castelnau was very much impressed by the fact that the Karaite sect appeared in early antiquity, "when ten tribes had been taken to the captivity by Salmanazzar".[149] Xavier Hommaire de Hell mentioned that there are two points of view concerning the time of the separation of the Karaites from other Jews. According to one of them, this event happened before the birth of Jesus, according to the other, it happened much later, in 750 C.E.[150] A.Nowosielski (1850) mentioned a general confusion in both academic and Karaite circles regarding the Karaites' past. Nowosielski, who was puzzled himself, contemplated whether the Karaites could have taken part in the movements of Pharisees and Sadducees. He thought that the Karaites represented the descendants of the Ten Lost Tribes of Israel.[151]

In his memoirs, Wł.Syrokomla related the history of the development of the Karaite Jews according to information he had received from Firkovich. In short, it is as follows: the Karaites were captives of the Assyrian king *Shalmanazar,* who arrived in the Crimea during the time of *Cambyses,* son of *Cyrus.* Around 750, the Karaites converted the Khazars to Judaism, which was proved by the tombstone of Yiṣḥaq Sangari found by Firkovich. In 980, they tried to convert the

---

[146] Deinard, *Sefer Massa' Qerim,* 60.
[147] Clarke, *Travels,* 193.
[148] Demidov, *Voyage,* vol.2, 736.
[149] Gabriel de Castelnau, *Essai sur l'histoire ancienne et moderne de la nouvelle Russie,* vol.3 (Paris, 1820) 181. The Marquis de Castelnau spent many years in Southern Russia, and published quite an interesting and profound essay, for the beginning of the nineteenth century, in three volumes dedicated to its history; the third volume is dedicated to the Crimea and Odessa.
[150] Xavier Hommaire de Hell, *Travels in the Steppes of the Caspian Sea, the Crimea, the Caucasus* (London, 1847), 364. Xavier Hommaire de Hell (1812-1848) – De Hell was a French traveler and scientist who spent most of his life in travels; he visited the Crimea together with his wife in the 1840s.
[151] A.Nowosielski [Marcinkowski] *Stepy, morze i góry. Szkice i wspomnienia z podróży* (Wilno 1854), vol.2, 193, 202. A Polish journalist, writer and foklorist Antoni Albert Marcinkowski (1823-1880), who published his works under the pseudonames A.Nowosielski, Albertus Parvus, A.N. etc., visited the Crimea in 1850 and left a detailed account of his visit to Gözlöw (Euvpatoria), where he had a chance to get acquainted with the family of the Karaite *Ḥakham Rashi,* Simḥah Babovich.

Kievan prince Vladimir to the Mosaic faith. They were settled in Lithuania by Prince *Witold,* together with the Tatars in the fourteenth century. Witold's charter of 1388 was given exclusively to the Karaites of Luck.[152]

Many travelers noted that the Karaites were the best prospects within the Jewish community, in regard to their possible conversion to Christianity.[153] When speaking with the travelers regarding their past, nineteenth century Karaites always emphasized their mild and tolerant attitude towards Christians and Christianity. S.Beim, and some other Karaite informants of the first half of the nineteenth century, told travelers that, according to a local tradition, the Karaites had a common origin with Christ who was, as were the Karaites, from the tribe of Judah.[154]

The 1840s saw the appearance of the so-called "Khazar theory", which contended that the Karaites descended from the Khazars.[155] The Khazar theory, which became an integral part of official East European Karaite doctrine in the beginning of the twentieth century, was at first actively opposed by the Karaites. The

---

[152] Syrokomla, *Wycieczki,* 57-88. "Wladyslaw Syrokomla" is a pseudoname of Ludwik Kondratowicz, a famous Polish writer and poet of the nineteenth century. His information about Cambyses and prince Vladimir seems to originate from the Madgeliss document found by Firkovich in 1840. The supposed grave of Yiṣḥaq Sangari, later lost or destroyed, was considered to be a forgery even by many contemporaries of Firkovich (*e.g.* G.Karaulov, "Chufut-Kale i Evrei-Karaimy", *ZOOID* 13 (1893): 97); "Sangari's affair" is dealt with in detail in Dan Shapira, "Yitshaq Sangari, Sangarit, Becalel Stern, and Abraham Firkovich" (forthcoming)). Alexander Vitold (Vitautas) was the Grand Duke of Lithuania in 1392-1430; Czacki was the first to document the legends about the arrival of the Karaites to Lithuania during the reign of this ruler (Czacki, *Rozprawa,* 267). Vitold's charter of 1388, which was given to the Jews of Brest, was spread to all Jewish communities of the Grand Duchy of Lithuania, including the Rabbanites and less numerous Karaites as well (S.Lazutka, E.Gudavichus, *Privilegiya evreyam Vitautasa Velikogo 1388 goda* [The privilege of Vitautas the Great to the Jews in 1388] (Moscow-Jerusalem, 1993), 36).

[153] Henderson, *Researches,* 330-331; Bonar A.A., McCheyne R.M. *Narrative of a Mission of Inquiry to the Jews from the Church of Scotland in 1838* (Edinburgh, 1842), 488.

[154] Demidov,*Voyage,* vol.II, 736; Haxthausen, *Empire,* 110-111; Haxthausen, *Studien,* 401.

[155] See K.F.Neumann, *Die Voelker des Suedlichen Russlands in ihrer geschichtlichen Entwickelung* (Leipzig, 1857), 125; V.V.Grigoriev, *Rossiya i Aziya* [Russia and Asia] (St.Petersburg 1876), 435. Concerning the Khazar theory see also Samoilovich, A.N. "K voprosu o naslednikakh Khazar i ikh kultury" [On the question of the Khazars' descendants and their culture]. *Evreiskaia Starina* XI (1924): 200-210; Zajaczkowski, 'Ananjasz. *Ze studiów nad zagadnieniem Chazarskim* [From the studies on the Khazarian problem] (Krakow, 1947); the same, *Karaims.*

69

German traveler F.Remy (1872) mentioned how eagerly Karaite leaders, such as A.S.Firkovich, I.I.Qazas, and S.Beim, protested against what were, in their view, nuisances and fancies regarding the history of their people.[156] Unlike most of the present day East European Karaite authors,[157] none of the nineteenth century Karaites (with whom the travelers conversed) mentioned their allegedly Turkic or Khazar origin. Moreover, according to brief remark of A.S.Griboedov (1825), the Karaites had some idea about the Khazars, and considered the latter to be the descendants of the Crimean Goths.[158]

It seems that the theory of the descent of the Karaites from the Ten Lost Tribes of Israel, and the separation of the Karaites from Israelites at the time of the Babylonian captivity was formed in academic circles much earlier than the nineteenth century: Gustaf Peringer and English millenarians had written about it as early as the seventeenth century.[159] Not infrequently, the theory of the Karaites' descent from the Ten Lost Tribes appeared in many other dispersed Jewish communities as a kind of defensive mechanism against Christian oppression and the accusation of taking part in the Crucifixion of Jesus.[160] At present, we can not be certain whether the legends concerning the Ten Lost Tribes circulated among the nineteenth century Crimean Karaites, or whether they were formulated by their leaders in 1820-30s as "evidence" of their non-participation in The Crucifixion and the compilation of the Talmud. It is also interesting to note that – from the end of the nineteenth century on, with the disappearance of the necessity to prove their separation from the greater Jewish population – the thesis concerning the descent of the Karaites from the Ten Lost Tribes was practically abandoned by the Karaite leadership.

---

[156] Remy, *Krim*, 96.

[157] E.g. Fuki, *Karaimy*, 11-14; Lebedeva, *Ocherki*, 4-5; *Karai (Krymskie karaimy)*, 7-15.

[158] A.S.Griboedov, *Sochineniya* [Works] (Leningrad 1959), 441. Alexander Griboedov (1795-1829) was one of the most famous nineteenth century Russian writers and poets, who left a number of brief but very keen remarks concerning the Karaites and their history while travelling in the Crimea in 1825.

[159] Peringer's *Epistola de Karaitis* was published by S.Szyszman in his "Gustaf Peringers Mission," 215-228 and partially in Ananiasz Zajaczkowski, "Najstarsza wiadomosc o jezyku tureckim Karaimów w Polsce (z XVII w.)", *MK* 12 (1938): 90-99; on the Karaites and Millenarians see Popkin, "Lost Tribes," 213-227.

[160] Cf. claims of the mountain Jews of Daghestan, Ethiopian Jews, Spanish Jews, Egyptian Karaites and other Jewish groups in Itzhak David, *Istoriia evreev na Kavkaze* [The history of the Jews in the Caucasus] (Tel-Aviv 1989), vol.1, 498.; "Tribes, Lost Ten," *JE* XII: 249-253.

70

An analysis of the eighteenth – nineteenth century travel accounts allows the following conclusions. The ethnic self-identification of the Crimean Karaites of this period is Jewish, with an emphasis on the specific features of Karaite religious doctrine differentiating it as true Judaism. The Karaites' understanding of their ethnic past was quite vague. Nevertheless, the Karaite informants of this period considered their people a part of the Jewish nation, dated their earliest tombstones in the Crimea to the thirteenth – fourteenth centuries, and did not identify themselves with the Khazars or any other Turkic people. They considered the thirteenth – fourteenth centuries to be the most probable time for their arrival to the Crimean peninsula. Only from the 1840s, due to the activity of A.S.Firkovich and other Karaite leaders, did the self-identification and ideology of the Karaite Jews shift in the direction of separation from the other representatives of the Judaic faith in the Russian Empire.

2.3. Karaites and Their Neighbours.
2.3.1. Karaites and Rabbanites.

> *"Will there ever be a consent and friendship between you, Dschuffut and Karaites?" – To this question of mine none of them, irreconcilable [rivals], gave me an answer."*[161]

It is very difficult to characterize in one word the complex nature of the relations between the Karaite and Rabbanite Jews, which has been formed by the representatives of these two different trends of Judaism in the course of more than one-thousand years, from the emergence of the Karaite movement in the mid-eighth century until today. These relations, which balanced between such polar feelings as brotherly friendship and bitter animosity, were determined by an understanding of mutual belonging to one religious entity on the one hand, and by a hostile attitude towards their brethren's "heretical" interpretation of religious law, on the other. Over many centuries of the history of the contacts between the Karaites and Rabbanites, it is possible to come across such manifestations of these ambivalent feelings as: brotherly love, help and advice, and, simultaneously, spite, abhorrence, and even betrayal. Travel accounts also supply important data related to this phenomenon.

Travelers often compared the attitudes of the Karaites and the Rabbanites toward each other. Generally, they noted that the Karaites

---

[161] Kohl, *Reisen*, vol.2, 266.

were hated and despised by the Rabbanite Jews. The first to remark on this point was Evliya Çelebi (1665-1666), who noted that the Crimean Rabbanites believed they would ride upon the infidel-Karaites during the day of the Last Judgement. Apparently, it was the local Rabbanites who informed Evliya about unscrupulousness of the Karaites in the dietary laws.[162] E.Henderson (1821) described cases of extreme abhorrence and even harassment of the Karaites by the Rabbanites, "...if they (*i.e.* the Rabbanites – M.K.) saw a Christian in danger of being drowned, it would be their duty to make a bridge of a Karaite in order to rescue him.... they will not receive a Karaite into their communion until he has previously made a profession of the Mohammedan or Christian faith." According to the traveler, the Karaites, on the contrary, did not show any hostility towards the Rabbanites and called them *Aḥeinu HaRabbanim* (*i.e.* "our brethren, the Rabbanites").[163]

Wł.Syrokomla (1854), similarly, mentioned the hostility that the Karaites felt towards the Rabbanites:

> It is quite probable that they (*i.e.* Karaites – M.K.) brought their unfriendly attitude towards the Rabbanites from Persia... Zealous in preservation of the Bible and observing its corruption performed by the Rabbanites by the means of the Talmud and Commentaries, they had full rights to consider them to be apostates... Their natural simplemindedness shuddered witnessing the swindle, which they correctly ascribed to the corruption of the Divine Law by the Talmud. Moreover, unlike other Jews, they do not have in the commandments of their creed hateful intolerance with regard to other nations.[164]

M.Guthrie mentioned that the "*Karai Yaodi*" (*i.e.* Karaites) called themselves "*Black Jews*" in order to be distinguished from the Jews of Poland, Turkey, and other countries, whom they hated.[165]

Very ambivalent information concerning the relations between the Rabbanites and Karaites was left by Johann Kohl (1838). On the one hand, Kohl called the Talmudic and Karaite Jews "brethren," noticed their similitude in "Jewish trading character," and

---

[162] Evliya Çelebi, *Kniga*, 90-91.
[163] Henderson, *Researches*, 324. Moreover, the traveler also testified that the Karaites sometimes consulted the Talmud (*ibid.* 320).
[164] Syrokomla, *Wycieczki*, 67-68.
[165] Guthrie, *Tour*, 83-84.

wrote down a quite peaceful and friendly dialogue concerning the coming of the Messiah, which took place between an Odessa Karaite and a Rabbanite woman [see §3.2.1]. On the other, he often stressed the constant, historical fight going on between the representatives of the two communities: "In this struggle smarter, educated and untiring Talmudists always gained the upper hand over simple and, because of their similarity to the Turkic people, more primitive Karaites..."

Kohl also wrote down an answer of the Karaites to the reproaches of the Rabbanites concerning the fact that among the Karaites there were no well-educated, extremely rich and genial people: " 'In these tremendous polarities, which are so widespread in the Talmudic society, from richness to poverty, from illiteracy to excessive learnedness,' said one of the Karaites to me, 'one can see a lack of modesty and viciousness of their nature... amongst the Karaites everybody can read and write, and this manifests only the harmony and modesty – Talmudists would say "mediocrity" – of our soul."[166]

A very curious case of these relations was documented by August von Haxthausen: the Rabbanites became so jealous because of his visit to the Karaite synagogue in Feodosia [Kaffa] that they decided to invite him to their synagogue, saying that it was much more interesting, and older.[167]

Thus, it seems from the travelers' reports that the relations between the Karaites and the Rabbanites were very hostile; moreover, much aggression and disdain emanated from the Rabbanite community. As might be expected, the travelers, who based their writings mostly on information received from Karaite sources, depicted the problem of Karaite-Rabbanite relations solely from the Karaite perspective. Furthermore, because of their apparent Karaite inclinations, which are clearly indicated by the praises they bestowed upon the moral qualities of the Karaites eulogistically, they could not avoid being influenced by general, anti-Talmudic pre-conceptions against the Rabbanite Jews [see Conclusion].

Internal documents, written by representatives of the Karaite and Rabbanite communities, yield a picture that is quite different from the perspective of "external" observers, such as the travelers. On the basis of these documents, one may conclude that in the eighteenth – beginning of the nineteenth centuries, relations between the Crimean Karaites and Rabbanites (Qrımçaqlar) were quite peaceful, and certain long-term animosity did not come out of the frames of internal

---

[166] Kohl, *Reisen*, vol.2, 259, 261.
[167] Haxthausen, *Empire*, 104-105.

confessional differences and controversies. Moreover, many documents testify to mutual understandings and frequent assistance between these two groups.[168] This comparatively serene atmosphere started to worsen in the first half of the nineteenth century, after the propagandistic activity of Avraham Firkovich[169] and the grant of a special status by the Russian government to the Karaites, which completely separated them from the burdens and sufferings of other Jewish subjects in the Empire.

2.3.2. Karaites and Crimean Tatars.

The relations between the Karaites and their Muslim neighbours, the Tatars and Ottoman Turks, were also not uniform. On the one hand, being attracted by their knowledge of Turkic languages and a similitude in their way of life, the Crimean Tatars eagerly participated in trade with the Karaites, and found in them friendly companions whilst visiting coffee-houses, smoking pipes, and drinking

---

[168] The examples of such mutual understanding are very frequent. Just to give a few of them: nineteenth century Karaite leaders often called the Rabbanites "*Aḥeinu HaRabbanim*"; moreover, they usually designated representatives of both communities "*Benei Yisra'el*" ("sons of Israel"), thus stressing the common nature and origins of Karaites and Rabbanites (Miller, *Separatism*, 74, 78). One of the very first books published in the Karaite typography of Çufut-Qalé in 1734 was a Qrımçaqlar (Rabbanite) *siddur* (prayerbook) (Philip Miller, "Agenda in Karaite Printing in the Crimea During the Middle Third of the Nineteenth Century," in *Studies in Bibliography and Booklore* 20 (1998), 83). Several unpublished Qrımçaqlar documents of the Eighteenth century represent appeals of the Qrımçaqlar community to the Karaites. See the catalogue of the Krimchack documents in Achkinazi, *Qrımçaqlar*, 159-161, nr36, 32. According to the Karaite chronicler 'Azaryah Ben-Eliyahu, in 1777, during the drastic events of the civil war, the Karaite community was rescued by a generous meddling of the Qrımçaqlar, who testified to the Crimean Khan regarding the loyalty of the Karaites as the khans' subjects ('Azaryah Ben- Eliyahu, "Sobytija," 60-61). In the eighteenth century even the Hassidic *ṣaddiqim* asked the help from the Crimean Karaites (*Iggerot Ḥasidim MeEreṣ Yisra'el* (Jerusalem, 1980), 56-60). Moreover, the Karaite and Qrımçaqlar quarters of most of the Crimean towns (Kaffa, Qarasubazar, Gözlöw, Simferopol', et alia) were situated nearby, in the close vicinity to each other, thus forming mixed Karaite-Rabbanite disctricts. The same might be said concerning the close location of most of the Crimean Rabbanite and Karaite cemeteries.

[169] One of Firkovich's letters testifies that its author suggested the Russian officials move the Rabbanites to borderland territories in the West (1825) (Schur, *Encyclopedia*, 215). Firkovich also composed several bitter polemical treatises directed against the *Ḥasidim* (1834) and Rabbanites (1838). See his *Massa' UMerivah* (Gözlöw: M.Tırışhqan, 1838) and *ḥotam Tokhnit* (Ramlah, 1997); on *Massa' UMerivah* see Sara Frenkel, "*Sefer Massa' UMerival LeAvraham Firkovich: Senṣurah 'Aṣmit o Ziyyuf?*" in *Proceedings of the Eleventh World Congress in Jewish Studies*. Div.III.Pt.1, 236-242.

coffee.[170] Khans often distinguished the loyalty and acumen of the Karaites when placing them in important administrative posts of the Khanate, and granting them numerous privileges. However, written sources of the eighteenth – nineteenth centuries are full of references to oppressive measures of the Khan's administration towards the Karaites, and a rather pejorative attitude of the Tatars to the Karaites on an every-day level.

The hostile attitude of the Tatars to the Karaites in the seventeenth century was described by a Karaite pilgrim from Derazhno (at present, the village of Derazhnia in Western Ukraine), Yosef Ben-Yeshu'ah HaMashbir. His poem in Karaite Judæo-Tatar, *"Me'irat 'Einayim"* – and *"Ner Ṣaddiqim"*, written by his grandson Simḥah Yiṣḥaq Lucki in the mid-eighteenth century – tells about Yosef's Crimean imprisonment. According to both sources, Ben-Yeshu'ah came to the Crimea to collect alms for the community in the Holy Land in 1666. However, someone informed the Crimean Khan (*"Melekh Qedar"*) about this. The Khan confiscated the money he had collected and imprisoned Yosef for three months "in iron chains in the Khan's house" (that is, perhaps, in the prison in Bakhçeseray). Thanks to the help of the leaders of the local Karaite community, he was released; however, the money was not returned. Ben-Yeshu'ah spent the next three years in Çufut-Qalé, which he called "a city and mother in Israel," and then went back to Poland.[171]

At the end of the eighteenth century, the Khans often imposed additional taxation on the Karaites, which were not regulated by any legal norms at that time. P.S.Pallas (1793-1794) mentioned that the Crimean Khans, when they wanted to get a "present" from the Karaites or raise a "voluntary" contribution from them, used to threaten them with the extirpation of the sacred trees, which grew in the adjacent to Çufut-Qalé Valley of Yehoshafat.[172] The Karaite chronicler 'Azaryah Ben-Eliyahu described tensions between the Karaites and Crimean

---

[170] Nowosielski, *Stepy*, 29.

[171] Jan Grzegorzewski, "Caraimica. Język Łach-Karaitów," *Rocznik Orientalistyczny* 2:2 (1916-1918), 268-270, 274-270; M.Nosonovski, V.Shabarovski, "Karaimy v Derahzno: stikhotvorny rasskaz o razrushenii obschiny" [The Karaites in Derahzno: poem-narration about the destruction of the community], 6. http://www.coe.neu.edu/~mnosonov/kar/; Avraham Kefeli, "O stanovlenii i globalnoi roli karaimskoi uchenoi mysli v regione sovremennykh Zapadnoi Ukrainy i Litvy" [On the formation and global role of Karaite scholarly thought in the territory of present-day Western Ukraine and Lithuania] in *Karaimy Galicha: Istoriia ta Kul'tura/The Halych Karaims: History and Culture* (Lwow-Halicz: Spolom, 2002), 69-70.

[172] Pallas, *Travels*, 35; the same; *Bemerkungen*, 35.

Tatars, and the oppressions that the Karaites suffered during the last years before the Russian annexation of the Crimea. In 1777, the Karaites were forced to pay an enormous sum of money under the pretext that they allegedly found and concealed a certain vessel containing a hoard of gold.[173] Moreover, it seems that it was the Tatar landowner 'Adil Bey Balatuqov that expelled the Karaite community of Mangoup from its ancient seat in 1792-1793 [see more on this in §4.2.1; see there also the testimonies of the late Karaite sources quoted by E.Deinard].

Seventeenth-eighteenth century legal documents show that, in spite of the existence of the official term "*yahudi*", on the everyday level the Tatars preferred to use the pejorative "*çufut*" for the designation of the Jewish subjects of the Khanate (both Rabbanite and Karaite alike) [see §2.1]. It seems that this situation was preserved in the nineteenth century as well. A.Nowosielski (1850), who depicted a serene vision of mutual understanding and peaceful co-existence between all ethnic groups in Gözlöw, mentioned that the Tatars despised the Karaites and called them by the pejorative "czufut/çufut." Moreover, according to information that Nowosielski received from the local inhabitants in Gözlöw, under the Turkish and Tatar dominion, when they did not have the right of erecting houses of prayer on the ground, the Karaites had to establish their synagogues in underground caves. Besides, in his opinion, Çufut-Qalé was a ghetto where "the Karaite Jews had to be wary of attacks from the Tatars, a people who hated the Jews." Nowosielski was also informed that the towns of Mangoup, Çufut-Qalé and Gözlöw were often defended from the "brigand-Tatars" by the authority of the Karaite clan of Çelebiler. The oppression of the Tatar spiritual authorities was so bad at one point that the Karaites were nearly forced to convert to Islam during the time of Yiṣḥaq Çelebi.[174]

From the 1920s – with the ascension of S.Szapszal, known for his pro-Turkic sentiments, to the office of *Ḥakham Rashi*[175] – Eastern European Karaite scholarship represented Tatar-Karaite relations as

[173] This work is very important for understanding the character of the relations between the Karaites and the Crimean Tatars. This is according to A.Firkovich's translation of 'Azaryah Ben-Eliyahu, "Sobytiia," 74-75. Paradoxically, a big vessel with more than four thousand coins (!), some of them of gold and silver, similar to the hoard that allegedly had been found by the Karaites, was discovered in 2002 near the hidden underground well of Çufut-Qalé [see more in §4.1.2].

[174] Nowosielski, *Stepy*, 27, 36, 42, 190, 210, 212.

[175] [*ed.* Szapszal insisted he be called *Ulu Ḥakham* in Karaite Judæo-Tatar rather than in Hebrew.]

one of a "brotherly attitude and kind influence."[176] In the second half of the century, with the firm establishment of Szapszal's concept of the Khazar-Turkic origins of the East European Karaites, the Crimean Tatars became viewed as brothers-in-arms, who had common historical roots and ethnic origins.[177] Nevertheless, objective examination of the sources related to this problem, as has been shown above, yields a rather different picture.

2.4. Personalia.

While visiting the Crimea, the travelers often met Karaite leaders, who usually played the role of "guides" for them to the historic sites of the Karaites and their settlements. The travelers' data and their impressions from their communication with the Karaite leaders supply us very valuable emotional information concerning these outstanding Karaite personalities, their biographies, literary activity, religious views, family life, habits and many other details.

2.4.1. Reformer of the calendar system Yishaq Ben-Shelomoh (1754-1826).

Yiṣḥaq Ben-Shelomoh, who for many years was the head of the Karaite community of Çufut-Qalé, is especially known for his works in the field of the Karaite *halakhah*. He attempted one of the most radical reforms in the history of Karaism, notably including the introduction of a new system of calendation, invented by him in 1779 and published in 1872. Yiṣḥaq Ben-Shelomoh is also known for his innovations in the fields of: marriage laws, liturgical poems, and religious works. He was also one of the members of the Karaite embassy to Catherine II in 1796.[178]

E.Clarke, who visited Çufut-Qalé in 1800, had a conversation with the local "Rabbi", who might have been Yiṣḥaq Ben-Shelomoh. Clarke was told about Yiṣḥaq's mission to Catherine II in

---

[176] T.S. Lewi-Babowicz, "O stosunkach wzajemnych między Karaimami i Tatarami na Krymie," *MK* 1:4-5 (1928): 26; see also this most important work, which introduced this new concept: S.Szapszal: *Kırım Karai Türkleri*, Istanbul 1928, 43pp. See critical analysis of this book by Kowalski Tadeusz. "Turecka monografja o Karaimach krymskich." MK 2:1 (1929): 2-8 and, recently, by Dan Shapira, "A Jewish Pan-Turkist: Seraya Şapsaloğlu and his Book Qırım Qarai Türkleri (forthcoming).

[177] Cf. the titles of some of the latest Karaite publications: E.I.Lebedeva, *Ocherki po istorii krymskich karaimov-tiurkov* [Sketches of the history of the Crimean Karaite Turks] (Simferopol', 2000); Y.A.Polkanov, *Karai – Krymskie karaimy-tiurki. Karais – the Crimean Karaites-Turks* (Simferopol', 1997); *Karai (Krymskie karaimy): Istoriya, kultura, sviatyni* [Karais (Crimean Karaites): History, culture, shrines] (Simferopol', 2000).

[178] Schur, *Encyclopedia*, 145-146; Miller, *Separatism*, 13-19.

St.Petersburg (most likely due to the inexact translation of his guide, however, Clarke wrote that Yiṣḥaq went to St.Petersburg for passing "public examination").[179] In the Clarke's opinion, Yiṣḥaq was held in high esteem by his flock for his outstanding knowledge. After a conversation with Yiṣḥaq concerning the particulars of the Karaite creed, Clarke purchased one of the Hebrew manuscripts from Yiṣḥaq's library.[180]

It was Yiṣḥaq Ben-Shelomoh and Binyamin Aǧa[181] who received E.Henderson in Çufut-Qalé in 1821. Henderson remembered this event with gratitude: "... the chief Rabbi, a venerable old man of the name of Isaac, by whom we were received with great courtesy, and conducted to the residence of Rabbi Benjamin... The conversation was carried on in Turkish and Hebrew..." To his great surprize, Henderson found books of the Talmud on the bookshelves of Yiṣḥaq's reading room; Yiṣḥaq answered that the Karaites "do not admit that the Talmud has any binding authority... but should we, on this account, reject what [is] good in it...?"[182]

Because of the Sabbath a "Jewish rabbi" of Çufut-Qalé (undoubtedly, Yiṣḥaq Ben-Shelomoh) could not himself read the letter of recommendation which was brought by Robert Lyall in 1822; as a consequence he gave it to his secretary. Lyall characterized Yiṣḥaq as "a reverend-looking man; he is distinguished by his talents... He has published a work upon astronomy, in Hebrew, and he also showed us a calendar of his composition in the same language." Later, the traveler stole into the house of Ben-Shelomoh when he was away. The absence of latticed windows which half-veiled Yiṣḥaq's wife and his four daughters during Lyall's previous visit destroyed his illusions, which "fancied them beautiful as houris... they were clumsy, pock-marked, and even ugly. They were excessively shy..." [183]

---

[179] It seems that the traveler's mistake represents a reference to the six-month stay of Yiṣḥaq in St.Petersburg for studying astronomy (Miller, Separatism, 15).

[180] Clarke, *Travels*, 190-192.

[181] The house of Binyamin Aǧa, which had often been used as the reception house for important guests of the fortress, was situated somewhere near the Eastern gate of Çufut-Qalé; at present, nothing except for the foundation remains from this once luxurious and splendid estate of nineteenth century Çufut-Qalé. Its gate, with an inscription in Hebrew, used to be kept in the Karaite library "Karay bitikliği" in Euvpatoria (Seraya Szapszal, "Akchokrakly, O. "Novoe iz istorii Chufut-Kale" (Recenzja)," *MK* 2:1 (1929), 39-40).

[182] Henderson, *Researches*, 310, 320.

[183] Robert Lyall, Travels in Russia, the Krimea, the Caucasus, and Georgia, vol.1 (London, 1825), 266-267, 273-274.

2.4.2. *"Most well-educated and pleasant man"*:[184] *Shelomoh Ben-Avraham Beim (1817-1867).*

Shelomoh Ben-Avraham Beim (1817/1819-1867) is the author of several books and articles on the Karaites written in Russian.[185] After Avraham Firkovich, Beim was, undoubtedly, the most well-known nineteenth century Karaite leader to the European and Russian audience. According to his own words, Beim was born in *Bakhçeseray* (perhaps, here Çufut-Qalé is meant), where his family was still living in 1839, the year when he returned to the Crimea (from Odessa?).[186] In the same year (1839), year young Beim took part in Firkovich's Crimean expedition, which resulted in the discovery of so many sensational manuscript and archæological findings.[187] He fulfilled the duties of the main *Ḥazzan* in Çufut-Qalé and Bakhchisarai (from 1842 until 1861) and, later, in Odessa (1861-1867). After the death of Simḥah Ben-Shelomoh Babovitch, in 1855, he fulfilled the duties of *Ḥakham*, until the election to this office of Simḥah's brother, Naḥamu (1799-1882; *Ḥakham* in 1857-1679).[188] In 1866, the Ethnographic museum in St.Petersburg offers 300 rubles for Karaite manequins, and asks Beim to send them to the capital. The last document in the Moscow archival collection of materials related to Shelomoh Beim is a letter of Naḥamu Babovich, dated March, 1867, permitting Beim to leave the *Ḥazzan's* office in Odessa, and visit St.Petersburg for twenty-

---

[184] This characteristic was given to S.Beim by A.K.Tolstoy: *Sobranie sochineniy* [Collected works], vol.IV (Moscow 1969), 286.

[185] Shelomoh Beim, *Pamiat' o Çufut-Qalé* [Memories about Çufut-Qalé] (Odessa,1862); Shelomoh Beim, *Chufut-Kale i karaimy* [Çufut-Qalé and the Karaites] (St.Petersburg,1861). There is no doubt that Seraya Szapszal borrowed much data from these publications of Beim in his first book, *Karaimy i Chufut-Kale v Krymu* [Karaites and Çufut-Qalé in the Crimea] (St.Petersburg, 1896). Paradoxically, the first publication of young Beim was a German translation of his letter to I.Blumenfeld: "Aufgefundene Spuren zur karaitischen Geschichte," *Israelitische Annalen* 2 (1840): 197-198; 215-216. This publication contained a German translation of the"Schreiben des Karaiten Salomo Baum aus der Krimm an Herrn I.Blumenfeld in Odessa", originally written by Beim in Hebrew, together with commentaries by Isaak Solomon Reggio and Isaak Markus Jost.

[186] "Aufgefundene Spuren zur karaitischen Geschichte," *Israelitische Annalen* 2 (1840): 197.

[187] See his own report in a letter to I.Blumenfeld in *ibid.* 197-198, 215. We may very cautiously suppose that it was Firkovich who instructed Beim to write this letter, thus attracting the attention of the European audience to their expedition. See also his marginal notes on official documents in RGADA. F.188. Op.1. nr365: 1r. Several archival documents found by Dr. Dan Shapira and Oleg Belyi show that friendly relations between Beim and Firkovich soon turned into bitter enmity and the exchange of serious accusations in falsification.

[188] RGADA. F.188. Op.1. nr365:50, 76r.

79

eight days...[189] However, the young *Ḥazzan* was destined to remain in this city forever. The exact reasons and circumstances for his untimely death on the way to St.Petersburg, in 1867, are still unknown. In Çufut-Qalé, he also worked as the teacher in the local *Beit Midrash* (seminary). While working as a teacher, Beim tried to update some of the most conservative Karaite customs, but faced severe opposition from traditionalists.[190]

From travelers' reports, it seems that Beim – young and well educated in the European fashion,[191] who knew European languages, and was distinguished by his politeness, impartiality of thought, hospitality to strangers, and loyalty to the Russian government – induced more of the travelers' sympathy than any other Karaite leader. According to travelers' reports, it was usually Beim, who was entitled to show visitors the sights of Çufut-Qalé, meet and entertain them. Among his hobbies were included such eclectic activities as collecting fossils, and wood carving.[192] A number of interesting archive documents, which allow one to get a new perspective on Beim's personality, are being prepared for publication by O.B.Belyi.

While visiting Çufut-Qalé in 1843, E.Chojecki was entertained by the young and polite Karaite "Rabbi" of the town, who should be identified, most likely, as Shelomoh Ben-Avraham Beim: "The house of the Rabbi is situated on the eminence close to the Karaite prayer house; amongst miserable little huts of the abandoned fortress the astonished traveler enters a house with its floor covered with carpets and a ceiling with golden partitions. A few years ago, the old rabbi died,[193] and now his son fulfilled his duties." In spite of the general welcoming and hospitable atmosphere of the Beim's house, where Chojecki received some refreshments, he could not help

---

[189] *ibid.* 129-130.

[190] *E.g.* on the negative reaction of Karaite circles see the letter of Fr.Dombrovski to S.Beim (1860): RGADA F.188.Opis' 1. Delo 365: 97r-98r.

[191] His European manners could be seen even in this particular detail: some of his visitors were offered such European drinks as champagne (Haxthausen, *Studien*, 401).

[192] According to some sources, twelve wooden figures engraved by Beim showing Karaite ethnogpahic types were lost on his way to St.Petersburg because of his sudden death in 1867; according to others, they were delivered to the Royal museum in Moscow or to some other museum in St.Petersburg (Szymon Firkowicz, "O Karaimskim Muzeum Historyczno-Etnograficznym na Krymie i w Polsce," *MK* 12 (1938), 22). A number of interesting archival documents which allow one to get a new perspective on Beim's personality are being prepared for publication by Mr. O.B.Belyi (Sevastopol').

[193] The traveler is mistaken: at that time Avraham Beim, Shelomoh's father was still alive.

noticing Beim's jealousy and irritation when the strangers could incidentally see "the black eyes of the mistress of the house."[194] Shelomoh Beim invited Chojecki and his companions to his house, showed them the synagogue and some other main sights of the fortress. While bidding farewell to the travelers, Beim showed his exquisite politeness, which was so often noted by his visitors: "'Whenever destiny would take you to Çufut-Qalé, do not delay your visit to your old friends.' While saying this the Rabbi, in accordance with oriental customs, puts his hand upon his heart, bows and sees the travelers off beyond the gates of his premises..."[195]

August von Haxthausen, who socialized with young Beim almost at the same time as Chojecki (1843), characterized him in the following way: "Salomon Beim, smart and vivid young man of thirty, who received his education in Odessa, and possessed a considerable amount of knowledge, spoke eight languages; his father was a Rabbi in Odessa." S.Beim guided the traveler and his companions in their visit to Çufut-Qalé, showed them synagogue, the cemetery in the Yehoshafat Valley, and finally invited them to his house. When narrating to Haxthausen his rather disputable views on Karaite history, Beim mentioned to Haxthausen his passionate desire to travel to China "in order to study local Jews, who evidently seem to adhere to the same religion as the Karaites."[196] Beim mentioned that he was going to study Chinese in the course of the next three years and expressed the hope that the Russian government would support his project. Beim also expressed his disapproval of A.S.Firkovich's activity.[197] It is interesting to wonder whether Beim was really thinking about the trip to China. Other sources do not supply us any information in this regard; it is possible to suppose that by 1843 Beim had become bored by the

---

[194] Chojecki, *Wspomnienia*, 218. Edmund Chojecki (pseudoname: Charles Edmond) (1822-1899), a Polish writer and translator.

[195] Chojecki, *Wspomnienia*, 228.

[196] On the p.399 Haxthausen wrote down Beim's information concerning the Karaites who settled down as far as China as a result of their trade activity. Beim's information most probably echoes the data concerning the Jews of Kaifeng, who were similar to the Karaites in their religious views and were often proclaimed by the latter as their "brethren in faith" (Miller, *Separatism*, 53, ft.12). The Karaites continued to be interested in the history of the Kaifeng Jews in the twentieth century as well. See the article "Kitaiskie izrail'tiane" [Chinese Israelites] published in *KZh* 5-6 (1911): 88-89. Moreover, in 2000 I found a leaflet on the Kaifeng Jewish synagogue standing on the bookshelf of one of the Polish Karaites! [*ed.* It is also quite possible that he may have been referring to the Karaite community of Khotan in Chinese Turkestan, members of which left in 1881 to avoid the war of the eastward expansion of the Tsarist empire and moved to the Crimea.]

[197] Haxthausen, *Studien*, 398-403.

mediæval and forlorn Çufut-Qalé, and indeed wanted to leave it. However, later he seemed to abandon this project.

Russian traveler Olimpiada Shishkina (1845) characterized Beim[198] as "quite a learned man," who readily entertained her during her visit to Çufut-Qalé. Beim was very proud that A.S.Firkovich had recently (in 1840) found the grave of Yiṣḥaq Sangari, and wanted to show it to his visitors, but a sudden rain forced them to find shelter in Beim's house. Shishkina was very touched to see the patriotic Russian tendencies of the young *Ḥazzan,* who emphasized his loyalty to the Russian government: "'In Russia,' said Solomon, 'our brethren are much more numerous than in any other country: there is no other place where we are treated so kindly.'" Her admiration became even stronger when Beim showed her a composition he had made in imitation of the Russian hymn "Bozhe Tsaria hrani" ("God save the Tsar") in Hebrew.[199]

---

[198] The traveler misspelled his name as "Beish."
[199] Shishkina, *Zametki,* 109-120.

ГИМНЪ БОГУ.

1.

Во свѣтлости лица Царева жизнь. О Ты, Спаситель, живущій вовѣки, внемли воплю Израиля!

Ниспошли свѣтъ Твой, чудное спасеніе Твое, на славу Царя крѣпкаго и благочестиваго—славы силъ нашихъ!

2.

Призри съ высоты небесъ на народъ Твой, призывающій имя Твое во гласѣ молитвы и моленія своего!

Внемли, Отецъ небесный, молитвамъ его (твоего народа), которыя онъ возносить къ тебѣ въ своихъ собраніяхъ!

3.

Ты, Царю вселенной, ниспосылаешь Монархамъ спасеніе, на которое они уповаютъ. Благослови и споспѣшествуй пути Царя правосуднаго, неоцѣненнаго, чтущаго Тебя (Боже), дивный и праведный!

4.

Великій Государь! Крѣпость и утвержденіе наше! Счастіе его постоянно увеличивается; имя его преславно, и какъ благъ совѣтъ его!

1.

בְּאוֹר פְּנֵי מֶלֶךְ חַיִּים
שׁוֹכֵן עַד הַגּוֹאֵל ·· פֶּה לֹא אֵל
שׁוּעַת יִשְׂרָאֵל
שְׁלַח אוֹרְךָ ·· הַפְלֵא עֶזְרָךְ
עַל הַדּוֹר
אַדִּיר מֶלֶךְ ·· יֶקֶר חֵילֵךְ
גָּאוֹן עֻזֵּנוּ

2.

הַבֵּט מִשָּׁמַיִךְ ·· עַל עַמָּךְ
קֹרְאִים שְׁמָךְ
בְּקוֹל רַחַם ·· וּבְהִתְחַנְּנָם
הַקְשֵׁיב
לְרֹב שִׂיחָתָם ·· בְּמַקְהֲלוֹתָם
אַתָּה אָבִינוּ

3.

נִיחָן לַמְּלָכִים ·· יֶשַׁע חוֹסִים
מַשִׁיל פְּלָכִים
אָנָּא תְבָרֵךְ ·· תַּצְלִיחַ דַּרְכּוֹ
תָּמִים
מֶלֶךְ יָקִירְךָ ·· אֵין לוֹ עֶרֶךְ
אַדִּיר צִדְקֵנוּ

4.

אַמְפְּרַאטוֹר גָּדוֹל ·· עַד וּמִגְדּוֹל
טוֹבוֹ לֹא יֶחְדָּל
מַכְבִּיד שְׁמוֹ ·· וּמַה טּוֹב טַעֲמוֹ

Ч. II

An imitation of the Russian hymn "Bozhe Tsaria khrani" (Russ. "God save the Tsar") composed by Beim in Hebrew. Hebrew original and a rather inadequate Russian translation (from Shishkina, Zametki, 109-120) [see the full poem in the Appendix].

S.Beim was especially polite and hospitable to A.Koshliakov, who visited Çufut-Qalé around 1847-1848. He not only met Koshliakov, but invited him to his house, showed him the main sights of the town ("Karaite family houses", mausoleum of Canike-Khanım (Janike-Khanym), cemetery in the Yehoshafat Valley), introduced him to all the details of Karaite history, and even accompanied Koshliakov on his way back to Bakhçeseray : "Sheleme Abramovich Beghim (*i.e.* distorted Shelomoh Ben-Avraham Beim")… showed us Çufut-Qalé, told us about the antiquity of this settlement, which had been existing for about 2,000 years [sic!][200], and invited us to his place... even now I vividly feel all what we experienced while being the guests of this kind Karaite; I am sending him regards from me and from our vagrant society which had so hospitably been received by him."[201]

In 1851 Beim got acquainted with A.Kunik, a famous Russian orientalist, and later a fierce opponent of Firkovich's theories. Although A.Kunik had a good impression of Beim from socializing with him, he could not help noticing shortcomings of his approach towards Karaite history: "The rabbi, who was quite young at that time, used to produce a very pleasant impression by his simple-heartedness... however, his academic education was very weak... he considered all Firkovich's discoveries to be genuine, and, in addition, he distorted them because of his lack of knowledge."[202]

Beim's position became especially important during the events of the Crimean War [see below on the secret tasks fulfilled by him for the Russian military command]. It was he, and not Firkovich (who at that moment left the Crimea for Wilno), who introduced Çufut-Qalé to the French officers in 1855. Historical notes in Russian, which were given by Beim to the officers, together with their personal observations, served as the basis for numerous publications on the Crimean Karaites, which appeared in the French-Jewish press in the 1850s.[203]

---

[200] This would take us approximately to the second century B.C.E., to the time when, undoubtedly, there was no settlement in this part of the Crimea whatsoever. In his *Pamiat' o Chufut-Kale* (p.26) Beim stated that Çufut-Qalé- Şela' HaYehudim – Qırq-Yer – had been founded by the Karaites about 400 years before the birth of Christ.

[201] [A.Koshliakov], *Desiatidnevnaya poezdka na yuzhnyi bereg Kryma* [10-day trip to the Southern coast of the Crimea] (Odessa, 1848), 37-40.

[202] A.Kunik, "Toktamish i Firkovich" [Toqtamiş and Firkovich] in *Prilozhenie k 27 tomu Zapisok Imperatorskoy akademii nauk* 3 (1876), 7.

[203] Analyzed by Trevisan Semi, "Crimean Karaites," 9-16. The full Russian text of Beim's report, together with the French translation by Perrotin was published in *les Archives Israelite* in August, 1856 – January, 1857 (Gammer, "Karaites," 65, ft.4; Moshe Gammer also published an early report by the French officer Beaudoin (1855), who, as it seems, is often referring to Beim's report as well: *ibid.* 65-78). Just a few weeks before submitting this book to the editor, I received a copy of a highly interesting manuscript in French entitled *"Extraits d'une traduction d'une notice sur Tchufut-Kaleh et le Secte des Juifs Karaïmes par S.Beym, Rabin des Karaïmes"* kept in the Archives de Guerres, Pays Étrangers, Russie (1856-1860). MR. 1497. Pièce 24bis (a courtesy of Pascale Hassoun-Lestienne, who graciously sent me a copy). The manuscript represents an early variant of Beim's *Pamiat' o Chufut-Kale* (Odessa,1862), with some very interesting variations. All the aforementioned are rare French publications, a highly important source on the history of the Crimean Karaites. They are almost inaccessible outside of France. Undoubtedly, they need to be grouped together with these manuscript documents, and re-published for a wider scholarly audience.

About the same time, in 1856, S.Beim evoked great interest in one of the most famous Russian writers and poets of the nineteenth century, Alexei Konstantinovich Tolstoy (1817-1875). In one of his letters to N.M.Zhemchuzhnikov the poet characterized Beim as "a most well-educated and pleasant man" and asked Zhemchuzhnikov to publish Beim's book on the history of the Karaites in the Petersburg university library.[204] According to some scholars, one of Tolstoy's Crimean poems was dedicated to Beim.[205] However, the main character of this poem, a jealous old man, a "grey-headed rabbi", "the enemy of the Talmud and Qabbalah," did not correspond to the Europeanized, 40-year old Beim. It seems that the poem was dedicated either to A.Firkovich, or to some other elderly member of the Çufut-Qalé Karaite community.

In addition to religious and community activity, Beim was engaged in the scientific investigation of the vicinities of Bakhçeseray and Çufut-Qalé. Charles (Karl) Kessler (1858) mentioned, "He visited a Karaite rabbi and found at his disposal quite a considerable collection of fossils from the adjacent mountains."[206] Similar information was left by N.Zhukov, who visited Çufut-Qalé approximately at the same time: "There are many shells in the apartment of the rabbi, which had been found here, on the mountain... I took one shell whose form proves its antiquity."[207]

It is very interesting to compare travelers' data with the image of S.Beim presented in the pages of Shemu'el Pigit's *Iggeret Nidḥei Shemu'el* – which represents, as it were, the "internal community" perspective on this interesting Karaite figure. On the one hand, Pigit, who was a very small boy at the time of the drastic events described by him, referred to Beim with great veneration, and characterized him as a man of great learnedness, an owner of a "pure heart." He mentioned

---

[204] A.K.Tolstoy, *Sobranie sochineniy* [Collected works], vol.IV (Moscow 1969), 286. It seems that Shelomoh Beim's first work, *Chufut-Kale i karaimy* [Çufut-Qalé and the Karaites] (St.Petersburg, 1861) indeed was published due to the help of Tolstoy and Zhemchuzhnikov.

[205] A.K.Tolstoy, *Sobranie sochineniy* [Collected works], vol.I (Moscow 1969), 109, 611.

[206] Karl Kessler, *Puteshestvie s zoologicheskoy tselju* [A travel undertaken with zoological intention] (Kiev, 1860), 161. Karl Kessler (1815-1881) was a Russian scientsist of German origin who undertook a "zoological" trip to Southern Russia and the Crimea in 1858. His notes on the Crimea bear not only scientific, but also ethnographic character.

[207] N.Zhukov, "Zametki v puti na yuzhnyi bereg Kryma" [Notes on the way to the Southern coast of the Crimea] in *Brega Tavridy* 1 (1995), 284. Several archival documents testify that Beim's collection of fossils indeed was interesting and valuable: RGADA. F.188. Op.1. nr365: 84-85.

that Beim knew both European (Russian, German, and French) and Oriental languages perfectly. He also wrote that the Russian generals Menshikov and Gorchakov considered Beim their friend, and often consulted him in complicated situations related to the military events of the Crimean War.

On the other hand, Pigit and the elderly Karaite sages were greatly annoyed and even insulted by Beim's European manners, and his close contacts with the Russian commanders. Pigit mentioned the great shock of the community when, during Yom HaKippurim, Beim interrupted his prayers and left Çufut-Qalé with a Russian soldier who brought an urgent order from the Russian officials.[208] Pigit also wrote about the conflict between *shammash* Mosheh Koylu, the representative of the Karaite conservative circles, and Beim. According to Pigit, Beim left Çufut-Qalé in 1861 in order to take the office of Odessa *Ḥazzan*.[209] In August, 1861, however, he was in the Crimea again, welcoming royal Russian visitors.[210]

A visitor to Çufut-Qalé can still see the ruins of Beim's house in the southern part of the so-called *New Town* of the fortress (one should not be mistaken by the misleading tourist sign which attributes to Beim the house of Çalbörü, one of the rare, still standing Karaite houses of Çufut-Qalé situated close to A.Firkovich's house) [see map §4.1].[211] O.Shishkina (1845) mentioned that "the house is standing on the edge of the steep mountain; windows from the three sides... [display a] beautiful landscape."[212] Not much has remained from the once very impressive Beim house: a door aperture walled with stones, a basement and the ruins of the walls.

In 1888, at the entrance to the cemetery in the Yehoshafat Valley, on its right side, Beim's sons Simḥah and Dawid erected a

---

[208] This order has been preserved in archive. The order of 23.09.1855 requested Beim immediately contact prince Mikhail Dmitrievich Dolgoruki, the chief commander of the Southern army in the Crimea. At the bottom of this order Beim later added a small note in Russian, probably as a sort of justification of his leave from the synagogue during the prayers: "Thus, I was invited by the authorities to the Second chief commander, who also charged me to take care for the benefit of the country..." (RGADA. F.188. Op.1. nr365: 44r). In 1854-1855 S.Beim also received a number of other secret letters and some monetary support for carrying out secret tasks for the Russian government, among others, collecting information about "secret gatherings of the Tatars" (RGADA. F.188. Op.1. nr365: 42-71).

[209] Samuel Pigit, *Iggeret Nidḥei Shemu'el* (St.Petersburg, 1894), 1-3, 10, 12. The author is greatful to Dr. Philip Miller for his help in the work with this source.

[210] Beim, *Pamiat'*, 49.

[211] For the location of the house see O.Akchokrakly, "Novoe iz istorii Chufut-Kale" [New informaion about the history of Çufut-Qalé]. *ITOIAE* 72 (1928): 161.

[212] Shishkina, *Zametki*, 110.

monument-cenotaph dedicated to "the chief Karaite rabbi of Çufut-Qalé and Odessa, Shelomoh Avraamovich Beim," who was buried, according to the Russian text of the epitaph, on 8.04.1867 on the Volkhovskoe cemetery in St.Petersburg. The Hebrew epitaph conveys some details that are not mentioned in other written sources. According to its text, Beim was born in Çufut-Qalé, and died during *Ḥagh HaMaṣṣot* (*Pesaḥ*). The bilingual Russian-Hebrew inscription on the other side of the monument relates that Beim's wife was buried there – "Yevva Moiseevna Beim, born Azarievich. [Ḥawaḥ Bat-Mosheḥ Ben-'Azaryaḥ]" The monument is still standing at the time of this writing.

Present day view of the forsaken Çufut-Qalé. On the right you can see the walled aperture of the Beim's house (photo by M.Kizilov)

2.4.3. The Karaite last of the Mohicans: patriarch of Çufut-Qalé Avraham Ben-Shemu'el Firkovich (1787-1874)

Avraham Firkovich: Photo courtesy of Trakai History Museum, Karaim Ethnographic section (published for the first time, all rights of reproduction belong to the Trakai History Museum).

"Archæologist is seen in all his views and deeds."
Markov, Ocherki, 461.

Avraham Firkovich (or Firkowicz) is, undoubtedly, one of the most prominent and controvercial figures in the history of Karaism.

Born in Luck, Poland (presently in Western Ukraine) in 1787, Firkovich moved to Evpatoria (Gözlöw) in the 1820s, and later to Çufut-Qalé, where he died in 1874. The manuscripts gathered by him represent one of the most valuable collections of Judaica in the Russian national library in St.Petersburg.[213] Firkovich's main book, *Avnei Zikkaron* (Vilna, 1872), contains his vision of the history of the Karaite movement, including an absolutely new history of Karaite settlement in the Crimea, epitaphs from the tombstones of the cemeteries of Mangoup, Çufut-Qalé, and Troki, and a discussion of many other controvercial problems in Karaite history. After his death in Çufut-Qalé in 1874, the *Even Reshef*,[214] as he was also called, was buried in the cemetery in the Yehoshafat Valley, whose history he investigated in the last thirty-five years of his life. Debates concerning the veracity and exactness of Firkovich's discoveries, which arose already during his lifetime, are still going on.[215]

---

[213] For details see C.B.Starkova, "Rukopisi kollektsii Firkovicha" [Manuscripts from the Firkovich's collection] in *Pis'mennye pamiatniki Vostoka* (Moscow: Nauka, 1974), 166-192.

[214] Even Reshef (אבן רשף) is Firkovich's acronym, and stands for Avraham **Ben-Rav** Shemu'el Firkovich

[215] For more details concerning Firkovich's biography see Vikhnovich, *Firkovich*. A bibliography of the polemics concerning Firkovich's academic activity is too voluminous to be placed here. For the most important in the favor of his discoveries see: Simon Szyszman, "Centenaire de la mort de Firkowicz," *Supplements to Vetus Testamentum* 28 (1974), 196-216; Simon Szyszman, "Les inscriptions funéraires découvertes par Abraham Firkowicz," *Journal Asiatique* 1975, 231-264; Daniel Chwolson, *Corpus Inscriptionum Hebraicarum Enthaltend Grabschriften aus der Krim* (St.Petersburg, 1882). Against Firkovich: Harkavy A. *Altjüdische Denkmäler aus der Krim* (St.Petersburg, 1876); A.Kunik, "Toktamish i Firkovich"; Abraham Kahana, "Two Letters from Abraham Firkovich," *HUCA* 3 (1926): 359--370; Abraham Geiger, "Abraham Firkowitsch," *Jüdische Zeitschrift für Wissenschaft und Leben* 11 (1874-75): 142-155, 193-195; A. Jellinek, *Abraham Firkowitsch, das religiöse Oberhaupt der Karäer: ein Gedenkblatt* (Vienna 1875); H.L.Strack, "A. Firkowitsch und der Werth seiner Entdeckungen," *Zeitschrift der Deutschen Morgenländischen Geselschaft* 34 (1880), 163-168. Neutral: C.B.Starkova, "Rukopisi kollektsii Firkovicha", 166-192; Zeev Elkin, Menaḥem Ben-Sasson, "Avraham Firkovich WeGenizot Qahir," *Pe'amim* 90 (1002): 51-96; Dan Shapira, "Min "Galuteinu" LiShekhem: Abraham Firkovich Eṣel Shomronim," *Cathedra* 104 (2002): 85-94. The monograph of *Studies in a Karaite Community: The Report of the Epigraphic Expedition of the Ben-Zvi Institute to the Jewish-Karaite Cemetery of Chufut-Qal'eh, the Crimea*, ed. Dan Shapira, Ben-Zvi Foundation, Jerusalem, 2002 (450pp., Hebrew, in print), which is dedicated to the epigraphic monuments from the Karaite cemeteries, would cast light on many problems discussed in the aforementioned publications. Dr. Dan Shapira (Jerusalem) is also carrying out a long-time research project, compiling a full biography of A.Firkovich based mostly on archival sources. Dan Shapira, *Avraham Firkowicz in Istanbul (1830-1832). Paving the Way for Turkic Nationalism* (Ankara: KaraM, 2003).

August von Haxthausen wrote information about Firkovich as early as 1843, at the time of his stay in Feodosia. von Haxthausen's data, paradoxically, reflected the different opinions of the representatives of the various Karaite communities concerning Firkovich's activity. Thus, Feodosian *Hazzan* Koen (a corruption of Kohen), with great veneration, told von Haxthausen about the Evpatorian Karaite "Abram Turkovitch"[216] (a corruption of "Avraham Firkovich") who had brought valuable manuscripts from Armenia with colophons on the history of the Karaites. He also informed von Haxthausen about the warm relations between Firkovich and a governor of the Taurida, count Mikhail Vorontsov.[217] Nevertheless, S.Beim, whom von Haxthausen encountered during his visit to Çufut-Qalé, mentioned, with some annoyance, a certain Evpatorian Karaite rabbi who, with support from the government, had gone to Georgia and found a number of valuable manuscripts there. The data that he had discovered could have been really interesting if not for the rabbi's tendency to make his discoveries look too old. Undoubtedly, Beim meant Firkovich.[218]

Wł.Syrokomla (L.Kondratowicz) dedicated a considerable part of his travel diary to the description of his rendezvous with the *Even Reshef* in Vilno in 1854, where Firkovich, together with his son-in-law Gavri'el Firkovich, was doing some academic work while awaiting the end of the Crimean War.[219] Syrokomla documented Firkovich's activity at a very interesting point, when the scholar, already crowned with world renown and considerable success in his enterprises, was in the process of creating his version of Karaite history, later fully detailed in *Avnei Zikkaron* in 1872.[220] In spite of a very eulogistic evaluation of Firkovich as a historical figure, Syrokomla managed to notice a number of inaccuracies and controvercies in Firkovich's narration. Syrokomla based his

---

[216] The famous twentieth century psychoanalist Erich Fromm made a similar mistake: he called the *Even Reshef* "A.Tirkowitsch" in his doctoral dissertation of 1922. Both German authors made this mistake because of the fact that capital Gothic "T" and "F" look practically identical. See Erich Fromm, *Das juedische Gesetz. Zur Sociologie des Diaspora-Judentums. Dissertation von 1922*, ed. Rainer Funk und Bernd Sahler (Basel: Beltz, 1989), 70.

[217] Haxthausen, *Studien*, 391.

[218] Haxthausen, *Studien*, 402. Haxthausen himself was very ecstatic concerning Firkovich's discoveries: *ibid.* 405-406.

[219] Firkovich left Vilno only in August, 1856, when the war was over: Vikhnovich, *Firkovich*, 120-121.

[220] According to Syrokomla's observation, already at that time Firkovich was preparing this book for publication in Vilno, and planned to print it in two languages: Russian and Hebrew.

information mostly on his personal impressions from his conversations with Firkovich during a stay in Troki, and Karaite documents, which he saw lying on Firkovich's working table. He quoted parts of these documents which had been translated for him by Firkovich.[221]

Syrokomla met Firkovich in "one of the poor, ramshackle houses of *Karaimszczyzna*" (a Karaite district of Troki). He characterized Firkovich as "a venerable old man… well-known in the academic world, an archæologist, member of academic societies, our colleague on the Vilno archæological committee," who "described ancient graves, collected old manuscripts and brought up undoubtful testimonies about the unbelievably old settling of the Israelites, both Rabbanites and Karaites, in the Crimea."[222] Syrokomla dedicated a considerable part of his memoires to the account of Firkovich's vision of the history of the Karaite movement, not only in the Crimea and Poland, but in the whole world. Of great interest, also, are Firkovich's romantic stories and legends concerning the supposed military activity of the Karaites in the Middle Ages and sixteenth-seventeenth centuries.[223] Syrokomla finished his narration about Firkovich with the supposition that the patriarch's unparalleled dedication to archæology "would place his name in the row of the most famous European scholars."[224]

A most apologetic, and simultaneously very observative, description of his encounters with Firkovich was left by Evgeni Markov (in the 1860s). Markov described the *Even Reshef* as a "guardian and patriarch of Çufut-Qalé," "an aged man of considerable height, dignified appearance, dressed in the costume of a real Melchisedek." In Markov's opinion, Firkovich was a peculiar "scholar-monk in the mediæval sense of this word," who strictly kept all religious precepts and was sincerely respected by all members of the Karaite community. Nevertheless, as he relates, the community

---

[221] Among these were various community documents – charters of Polish kings, supposedly belonging to 'Ezra Ben-Nisan – in Latin with some historical notes in Hebrew regarding the historical past of the Karaites in Lithuania. Other documents informed Syrokomla about the life of Troki Karaite community, intrusion of the Russian army in 1665, establishment of the institute of Karaite "woit" (the head of the community), difficult relations between the *woit* family of the Lobanos and the Troki community itself, burst of plague in 1710, anti-Karaite pogrom in 1773, etc. (Syrokomla, *Wycieczki*, 73-85).

[222] Syrokomla, *Wycieczki*, 56-58.

[223] None of them is corroborated by any first-hand written source in Polish, Latin or Hebrew. All available documents tell us about wide and active involvement of the Karaite into trade, arts and commercial activity [see more on Karaite professions in §3.4.1].

[224] Syrokomla, *Wycieczki*, 87-88.

unanimously opposed his wish to imitate Avraham's tradition and marry a 16-year old girl.[225]

Markov was ecstatic about Firkovich's academic achievemenents, and believed in all his discoveries relating to the unbelievable antiquity of the Karaite settlements in the Crimea:

> He read and wrote down all the inscriptions from the innumerable tombstones of the Yehoshefat Valley... He excavated the most ancient tombs... he corrected and filled in lacunæ in the chronology of Karaite history. Rarely can one see a person who knows Holy Scripture with such deep thoroughness... Archæologist is seen in all his views and deeds.

On the other hand, Markov described some prejudices of the patriarch, such as his unwillingness to be photographed[226] or consume his food in the presence of non-Karaites. He also mentioned that even the most educated and emancipated Karaites were afraid of Firkovich's wrath,

---

[225] According to other sources, however, at the age of eighty, Firkovich did marry a young Karaite girl of Luck (Józef Smoliński, "Karaimi i bożnica ich w Łucku," *Ziemia* 3 (1912): 100).

[226] According to A.Zajączkowski, the Çufut-Qalé patriarch allowed himself to be photographed once in his life-time, in Vienna, in 1871. This was the most famous portrait of Firkovich, and all later drawings and depictions of the *Even Reshef* were made from this unique picture ('Ananiasz Zajączkowski, "Firkowicz, Abraham syn Samuela (ok.1786-1874)," in PSB 6: 472-473; see also illustration). I saw one the offprints of this photo in the Karaite museum in Troki. In April, 2002, in the manuscript department of LLAS I found another, hitherto unknown photo of the patriarch, standing together with his wife, daughter and son-in-law Gavri'el Firkovich (F.143-1200; see it published in Elkin, Sasson, "Abraham Firkovich WeGenizot Qahir," 58; Shapira, "Min "Galuteinu" LiShekhem": 87). *Pe'amim* 90 (2002) also published on its frontal page another famous drawing by C.Huhn, depicting Fikovich, his daughter and son-in-law Gavri'el Firkovich against the background of the larger Çufut-Qalé synagogue ("Караимы (Karaimes). Dess. d'après nature par C.Huhn; impr. par J.B.Kuhn a Munich" in T. De Pauly, *Description ethnographique des peuples de la Russie* (St.Petersbourg, 1862), between pages 153 and 154). The fourth character of the painitng, a Europeanly dressed Karaite in his forties, is often wrongly attributed by the Karaite sources, starting from S.Szapszal, as Ephraim Deinard, who, in fact, in 1861, was only a 15-year old boy. In our opinion, this character should be identified as none other as Shelomoh Beim. Many of later East European Karaite authors, who re-published Huhn's masterpiece, erased the figure of "Deinard" from the painting – knowing not that they, in fact, were erasing the only existing portrait of Shelomoh Beim, one of the most important community leaders (cf. publication of the painting in *Pe'amim* 90 (2002) and on the frontal page of *Archeologia. Tresor des Ages* 78 (Janvier 1975), placed there by Simon Szyszman as illustration for his article "Les passionants Manuscrits d'Abraham Firkowicz").

caused by their non-fulfillment of some traditional Karaite prescriptions. Moreover, he remarked that Firkovich opressed those renegades who ventured to eat with non-Karaites, dress in European fashion, and fail to observe religious laws. At the end of his narration, Markov concludes, "Firkovich is far from being a fanatic... but he is a Karaite to the marrow of his bones..."[227]

Markov's description of his conversation with Avraham Firkovich produced, paradoxically, a very strong impression on Dagmar Brandt (the penname of Marta Krüger, née Brandt), who was an active Nazi writer and publicist. In her almost one-thousand-page novel, "Gardariki", she entitled one of the parts of the novel "The Valley of Yehoshafat", and made a "Patriarch Firkowitsch" one of its most important characters (Dagmar Brandt, "Das Tal von Jehoschafat", ninth book of her *Gardariki. Ein Stufenbuch aus Russischem Raum* (Berlin: Wiking Verlag, 1944), 741-837).

As has been mentioned, the most bitter and unfriendly description of Firkovich's activity was left by his secretary Ephraim Deinard, a Rabbanite Jew. However, even Deinard, in spite of the overall contemptuous tone of his memoirs, could not help writing about Firkovich's kindness and general respect from the side of the Karaites and Tatars.[228]

In 1870, when the Polish traveler H.Skirmuntowa (Pojata) visited Çufut-Qalé, Firkovich was away.[229] In spite of this, Pojata was very much impressed to see the manuscript treasures in his collection, which at that time were partially kept in Firkovich's house:

> What a quantity of precious parchments, ancient books and manuscripts looks on you from every bookshelf! Practically everything is filled with them and this is only a small part of the academic treasures that this diligent scholar had found in the course of his forty years long travail, found, excavated, rescued from decay and oblivion, and later placed in a safe place, explained and translated... Firkovich's educated and most polite daughter was our voluntary guide during the

---

[227] Markov, *Ocherki*, 456-461.

[228] See more about Deinard and his work in §1.3.2.

[229] St.Makowski supposed that the penname "Pojata" was used by Helena Skirmuntowa (1827-1874) who spent about two years in 1869-1870 in Balaklava (the Crimea): Stanisław Makowski, *Swiat sonetów krymskich Adama Mickiewicza* (Warszawa, 1969), 18). See more on Pojata and her travels in the Crimea in Mikhail Kizilov, "Krymskie 'peshtchernye goroda' po opisaniyu E.Skirmunt (Pojata)" [Crimean 'cave towns' according to description of E.Skirmunt (Pojata)], *MAIET* 9 (2002): 543-548.

absence of her father.

From Firkovich's daughter, Skirmuntowa received an emotive answer to the question of why Çufut-Qalé looked so abandoned, and almost deserted.[230]

F.Remy who visited Çufut-Qalé in 1871, a short while before the death of the patriarch, also was not lucky enough to see Firkovich himself. Remy highly praised Firkovich's collecting activity, but was quite worried about the authenticity of and possible fasifications in Firkovich's manuscripts. In addition, he was rather sceptical about Firkovich's project to revive the town.[231]

L.Hlebnicki-Józefowicz,[232] who visited the town in 1877 (i.e. three years after Firkovich's death), wrote with deep respect about the late patriarch of Çufut-Qalé:

> Firkovich was known to the whole academic world as a zealous collector of ancient Hebrew and other Oriental manuscripts, an orientalist and an educated person, a rabbi and patriarch of Çufut-Qalé, where he had moved from Vilno... he dedicated all his soul and all his days to the work and study; I was shown his house, working cabinet, and glass balcony (hanging right over the precipice) where he used to sit.

At the time of Hlebnicki-Józefowicz's visit, the only inhabitants of the place were remote relatives of Firkovich from Vilno, who were quite happy to hear the Polish speech of the traveler.[233]

From the monuments of Çufut-Qalé, which are directly connected with the life and activity of A.Firkovich, one should first note his two-story house, which is situated on the southern side of the New Town, right close to the edge of the mountain [see map §4.1]. Until recently, the keepers of the fortress had lived here; however, at present, this duty has been transferred to the hands of the Bakhçeseray (Bakhçeseray) militia, which maintains order within the fortress. In 2002, the ground floor, originally intended for stalls, was re-furnished

---

[230] Pojata [H.Skirmuntowa], "Szkice z Krymu," *Tygodnik Ilustrowany* 8:201 (1871): 221-222.

[231] Remy, *Krim*, 92-95.

[232] L.Hlebnicki-Józefowicz was attributed by St.Makowski as the author of another valuable travel account published in the Polish journal *"Kłosy "* in 1877: Makowski, *Swiat*, 18. The absence of the author's name in most of the Polish reference editions and textbooks testifies that he did not leave any notable trace in Polish literature.

[233] [L.Hlebnicki-Józefowicz], "Wspomnienia Krymu," *Kłosy* 25: 637 (1877): 165.

into a kind of restaurant with Karaite ethnic dishes and a small exhibition related to... You might say Firkovich, but you would be wrong. The exhibition is dedicated to Seraya Szapszal, who, in fact, criticized Firkovich and also accused him of falsifying early tombstone inscriptions.[234]

Of some interest are several markings of graffiti in Hebrew on the walls of the house.[235] One can also visit a small hill situated some 110 meters from the Eastern defensive wall of the fortress, which covers the remains of the mill where, according to the testimony of A.S.Dubinski, Firkovich worked in the first half of the nineteenth century.[236]

---

[234] See one of his early student papers in the manuscript department of LLAS, F.143-891, f.18.

[235] One of them represents two words: "Shalom Firkovich" and might be interpreted either as Firkovich's greeting or the autograph of one of his sons, Shalom Firkovich. The other is more interesting: it represents letters "shin" (abbreviation for "*shaddai*" – "almighty") engraved in stone several times (probably, for training) and "zekher sad" (undoubtedly, abbreviation of "Zekher Saddiqim" – the title of one of the most famous Karaite books, which was written by Firkovich's bitter enemy, Mordekhai Sultanski). One can speculate whether the latter inscription was left by Sultanski, who might have been the owner of the estate before Firkovich, and was also suspected of forging tombstone inscriptions, or by Firkovich and his relatives – Firkovich borrowed much information from "*Zekher Saddiqim*" into his "*Avnei Zikkaron.*"

[236] Akchokrakly, "Novoe," 159. It is known that in his youth Firkovich worked as a miller.

Inside view of the eighteenth century house which once had been in the possession of Avraham Firkovich. (photo by M.Kizilov)

Outside view of the eighteenth century house which once had been in the possession of Avraham Firkovich. (photo by M.Kizilov)

2.4.4. "Simḥah the Deliverer": the Karaite chief Ḥakham Simḥah Ben-Shelomoh Babovich (1790-1855).

"The name of this outstanding man is to be found at every step..."
(Nowosielski, *Stepy*)

Simḥah Ben-Shelomoh Babovich (or Babowicz) was one of the most influential and important figures in the history of the East European Karaites. A wealthy and influential Evpatorian merchant, he became the head of the famous Karaite delegation to St.Petersburg in 1827, which absolved the Karaites of the requirement for army service and provided them with a distinctive legal status, separating them from the main Jewish population. He was also the person who created, in 1837, the Karaite Spiritual Consistory and became its head, the first purely political Karaite *Ḥakham Rashi* (Babovich was not widely educated in religious matters). The chronicle of Yosef Shelomoh Lucki respectfully calls him *"HaSar"* (*i.e.* "prince").[237]

A description of his meeting with "Simeon Baba" (*i.e.* Simḥah Babovich) was left by H.Rzewuski in a letter from June 29th, 1825. Rzewuski characterized Babovich as "le plus riche Caraïte de l'endroit", and described the hospitality of his house, common dinner, and a visit to the Evpatorian Karaite synagogue. Rzewuski was fascinated by the simplistic, Biblical pastoral of Babovich's family life: "des moeurs patriarchales... et sa jeune fille richement habillée, qui nous presentait l'eau, tout cela était un veritable chapitre de La Genèse."[238] Moreover, in his letter Rzewuski mentioned that he introduced his companion on the journey, the famous Polish poet, A.Mickiewicz, to the Karaite leader.

H.Rzewuski mentioned a friendly conversation between him, A.Mickiewicz and a Evpatorian Karaite "Rabbi," who should be identified as Yosef Shelomoh Lucki. Both travelers were greatly impressed by the fact that "le bon Rabbin" knew the Polish literature of the period perfectly, and translated several verses of the Polish poet Trembecki into Hebrew. The travelers and Lucki parted as "amis intimes."[239] Rzewuski's testimony is extremely interesting; however, its authenticity was put under question by Polish scholar St.Makowski.[240]

---

[237] See more about him in Miller, *Separatism*, 20-49; Philip Miller, "Spiritual and Political Leadership among Nineteenth-Century Crimean Karaites" in *Proceedings of the Eleventh World Congress of Jewish Studies*, div.B, vol.III (Jerusalem: World Union of Jewish Studies, 1994): 1-8.

[238] Seraya Szapszal, "Adam Mickiewicz w goscinie u karaimów," *MK* 10 (1934): 3-12.

[239] Szapszal, "Adam Mickiewicz," 6-7. Yosef Shelomoh Ben-Mosheh of Luck, the

On July 3rd – 4th, 1834, the house of "Pabontsch" (a corruption of "Babovich") was visited by another dignified guest, the French marshal Marmont. Marmont characterized Babovich as *le principal Karaite* of the town and found his Oriental house to be perfectly *charmante*. By all means, it was Babovich who headed "une deputation des principaux Juifs Karaïtes" (a delegation of the noblest Karaite Jews), which was sent to meet the marshal on his entering Evpatoria.[241]

Several travel descriptions provide us with information on the quite benevolent attitude of the Russian royal family towards the Crimean Karaite community and its leader, S.Babovich. A wealthy and influential merchant, Babovich played the main role in the rennovation of the Bakhçeseray palace for the visit of Nicholas I (1837) and Grand Duke Konstantin Nikolaevich (1845).[242] Even the horses used by the royal visitors had been purchased by the *Ḥakham*.[243] One of the most famous nineteenth century Russian poets, V.A.Zhukovskiy, happened to be a witness of the solemn welcome given by Babovich to Nicholas I in Bakhçeseray:

---

author of "Iggeret Teshu'at Yisra'el", served as a *Ḥazzan* in the Euvpatorian synagogue until his death in 1844. See more in Miller, *Separatism*, 18-45.

[240] A.Mickiewicz (1798-1855), probably, the most famous Polish poet, the author of the national epic story "Pan Tadeusz"; Henryk Rzewuski (1791-1866), was a member of a noble Polish family, a writer and public figure. St.Makowski considers this letter to be either falsified or incorrectly dated. In his view, it is hardly possible that A.Mickiewicz, who visited the Crimea in August – October, 1825, could be there in June, 1825 (Makowski, *Swiat*, 189). Indeed, there are many strange details concerning Rzewuski's letter. Szapszal published a facsimile of the document without the first and last pages of the letter and "censored" one phrase out of its text. So far I have not been able to find a facsimile or original of the letter in Szapszal's collection in LLAS (Vilnius). There are no doubts about the authenticity of the letter, but there still remains a question whether the "Mickiewicz" mentioned there is indeed Adam Mickiewicz or someone else, whether the letter is correctly dated, and whether its sender was Rzewuski. None of these questions can be convincingly answered without consulting the full original or facsimile of the document, which is nowhere to be found to date.

[241] Marmont. *Voyage du Marechal duc de Raguse*, vol.1 (Paris, 1837), 367-368.

[242] See Safonov, *Opisanie*, 10-11; F.Dombrovskiy, *Dvorets krymskikh khanov v Bakhchisarae* [Palace of the Crimean khans in Bakhçeseray] (Simferopol', 1863), 26. Many later local historians, in fact, rebuked Babovich's restoration for altering the original Oriental style of the Khans' palace.

[243] A detailed description of horses donated by S.Babovich to the royal family is supplied by S.Safonov in his *Opisanie prebyvaniya imperatorskoy familii v Krymu v sentiabre 1837 goda* [Description of the stay of the royal family in the Crimea in September, 1837] (Odessa, 1840), 82. See below the testimony of J.Kohl.

"...the arrival of Vorontsov and Muromtsev. Beautiful view of gathered people. Karaites in white turbans. Sima Babovich, red surtout, green, velvet under dress."[244]

Johann Kohl (1838) portrayed S.Babovich as a "contemporary Crœsus" (der jetzige Krœsus):

'Schima[245] Bobowitch', whose name is far and wide respected among them (*i.e.* the Karaites), is looked upon as a head and patriarchal representative of their tribe. Schima Bobowitch had purchased Turkish horses on which the emperor Nicholas rode during his last visit to the Crimean mountains.[246]

Polish traveler A.Nowosielski (1850) left a very detailed description of his meeting with the Babovich family. Babovich was, in his opinion, the most influential, powerful, and wealthy Crimean Karaite of the period: "The name of this outstanding man is to be found at every step because he is the aristocrat of Kozłow." Nowosielski also described the beautiful house of the *Ḥakham*, whose architecture represented a mixture of European and Oriental traditions.[247] Nowosielski had an opportunity to socialize with Babovich's family ("a brother and three daughters")[248] while traveling

---

[244] See V.A.Zhukovskiy's diary in *Russkaya Starina* (St.Petersburg, 1902), 358. Safonov also depicts a favorable meeting for Babovich with Tsar Nicholas' family (Safonov, *Opisanie*, 24).

[245] "Schima" is, undoubtedly, a misprint of "Simḥah."

[246] Kohl, *Reisen*, vol.2, 260.

[247] The traveler called the house an "architectonic miracle" (Nowosielski, *Stepy*, 25). The 18th century house, with beautiful wooden decorations, where Babovich invited H.Rzewuski and A.Mickiewicz is still in a comparatively good state of preservation on Karaimskaya str.53 (Euvpatoria). Its wooden decorations, however, need to be renovated. At the present moment, it is in the private possession of a Russian family. According to S.Szapszal, on November 1st, 1825, this house was visited by Alexander I; later, Babovich's granddaughter Miryam Shishman donated it to the Karaite spiritual college (Szapszal, "Adam Mickiewicz," 6). One might speculate why this Karaite *Ḥakham*, one of the richest merchants of the Russian Empire of that time, did not want to leave this old house. Perhaps, on the one hand, the dense character of dwelling quarters of old Gözlöw did not allow to him to make a big new house; on the other hand, Babovich did not want to leave the cultural center of Karaite life and build new house outside of the old town. Moreover, constructing a splendid new house might have caused disapproval in conservative Karaite circles.

[248] It seems that Nowosielski encountered here the family of Naḥamu Babovich (1799-1882), the younger brother of Simḥah Babovich. It is possible to suppose that Nowosielski was wrong when he referred to the wife and two daughters of Naḥamu Babovich as "sisters" (the author is greateful to P.Miller and G.Akhiezer for their help in identifying these persons).

together with them on a boat to Sevastopol'. When describing them, he mentioned that in the eyes of his family "sparkled the fire...of a strong feeling, a feeling which could be nourished only in the East, where the members of the family are never divided, but raised, brought up and receive education together over the Bible, whence come all life and all science."[249] In spite of his opinion that Karaite women loose their beauty very early, he was truly impressed by the appearance of the youngest of Babovich's daughters: "She could serve as a vignette for Byron's works. Her beautiful chestnut hair was braided into thousands of plaits falling down on her back..." Nowosielski also mentioned that "the man was dressed in European fashion and spoke Russian in a good way. The women could only speak Tatar..."[250]

Eighteenth century house which was once in the possession of Simḥah Ben-Shelomoh Babovich. Note the beautiful wooden decorations (photo by M.Kizilov)

Of interest also is a short remark of the French officer Beaudoin (1855): "The chief Rabbi of the Karaite Jews (*i.e.* undoubtedly, S.Babovich – M.K.) resides in Evpatoria. He is very rich and [very much disliked] by his co-religionists."[251] When taking into consideration the fact that Beaudoin's informant was, most likely, S.Beim, this remark testifies about unfriendly relations between these

---

[249] Nowosielski, *Stepy*, 48-49.
[250] Nowosielski, *Stepy*, 35-36, 47-49.
[251] Gammer, "Karaites," 77.

two leaders of the Karaite community of that time.

The prominent figure of Simḥah Babovich, which later became ousted by the fame of other charismatic Karaites, such as A.Firkovich, S.Beim, and S.Szapszal, has recently gained the interest of the Crimean audience again. One of Simferopol's local historians, V.Poliakov, has published an article where he raised a question concerning possible connections between the famous finger-ring of the greatest Russian poet A.S.Pushkin, (which he used as a talisman and as a seal for secret love-letters) and Simḥah Babovich.[252] It is well known that A.Pushkin received this ring in Odessa as a present from Elizaveta Ksaverievna Vorontsova, the wife of count M.S.Vorontsov, who had frequent contacts with S.Babovich. In fact this mysterious ring, which originally belonged to a certain "Simḥah Ben-Yosef HaZaqen," whose name is engraved on the ring, could have become the property of Simḥah Babovich. He, indeed could have donated it to Vorontsov, or to his wife, who, in her turn, gave it to Pushkin as a memory of her secret romance with the poet (one may say, perhaps, too many "could" for one little story). Later this ring was a property of such famous Russian men of letters as V.A.Zhukovskii and I.S.Turgenev, until it got stolen from Pushkin's museum at the end of the nineteenth century.[253]

---

[252] V.Poliakov, "Taina pushkinskogo talismana" [The mystery of the Pushkin's talisman] in *Brega Tavridy* 3-4 (1999), 188-193.

[253] Of interest is the *ketubbah* (Kar. "*shettar ketubbah*") of S.Babovich (a widower at that moment) and Nazli Bat-Berakhah Yashish (1851) which was published by V.Poliakov in the same article: "Taina pushkinskogo talismana" [The mystery of Pushkin's talisman] in *Brega Tavridy* 3-4 (1999), 192-193. On Pushkin's talisman and its origin see also Tsiavlovskaia T.G., "Khrani menia, moi talisman" [Keep me, my talisman] *Prometei* 10 (1975): 35-45; Szyszman S. "Le "talisman" de Pouchkine," in *BEK* 1 (1983): 77-84. One Russian journalist, A.Zinuhov, without any grounds, ventured to "suppose" that Pushkin's grandfather was a Karaite (?!) and, consequently, in the veins of Russia's greatest poet flows also Karaite blood: "Abram iz roda Gannibalov" [Abraham from the family of Hannibal] in *Sovershenno sekretno* 6 (2001), 14-16.

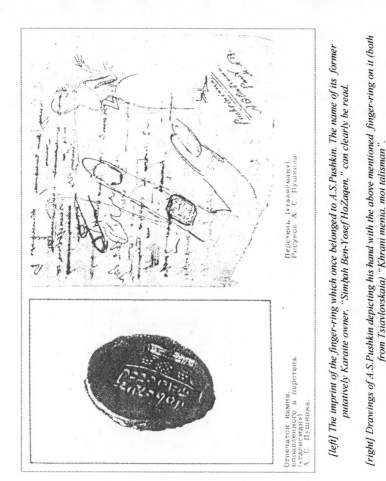

Отпечаток камня, вправленного в перстень («талисман») А. С. Пушкина.

Перстень («талисман»). Рисунок А. С. Пушкина.

[left] The imprint of the finger-ring which once belonged to A.S.Pushkin. The name of its former putatively Karaite owner, "Simḥah Ben-Yosef HaZaqen," can clearly be read.

[right] Drawings of A.S.Pushkin depicting his hand with the above mentioned finger-ring on it (both from Tsiavlovskaia) "Khrani menia, moi talisman".

2.5. Legal status of the Karaites in the Crimean Khanate and Russian Empire.

As all Jews who lived in the territory of the countries of the Ottoman Empire, the Crimean Karaites received the protected minority status of *dhimmis*. According to the pact of 'Umar, which was introduced as a legal and administrative article in the seventh-eighth centuries,[254] *dhimmis*, on the one hand, received many privileges (*e.g.* the right to settle down in Muslim lands and to be protected by Muslim

---

[254] Some scholars consider that this pact was composed during the reign of the caliph 'Umar I (634-644); others suppose that it was introduced by the 'Umayyad caliph 'Umar II (717-720). See Bernard Lewis, *The Jews of Islam* (London, 1984), 24-25.

authorities), on the other, they had to pay *jizya* (a poll-tax) and were subjected to numerous œconomic and ideological restrictions. *Dhimmis* were not allowed, for instance: to build new religious monuments or houses being higher than the houses of Muslims, to manifest their religion publicly, to sell fermented drinks, and to ride horses. They had to show respect towards Muslims, wear special distinctive garments, and give board and lodging to traveling Muslims.[255] Some of these restrictions had exclusively œconomic and administrative significance; others, however, were aimed at emphasizing the inferior and humiliating status of *ahlu 'dh-dhimma*. Moreover, the *jizya* was not only a tax, but also a symbolic expression of subordination.[256]

The life of the Rabbanite and Karaite Jews under Ottoman rule was much less oppressive than that experienced by the Jews under the Mamluks in Egypt or the Safavids in Persia; and Constantinople continued as one of the main seats of the Karaites.[257] The Jews in most provinces of the Ottoman Empire enjoyed prosperity and relative security in the sixteenth century. However, there were still a number of orders reminding *dhimmis* that they were not permitted to ride horses, or own slaves, or sell wine, or ordering them to demolish places of worship.[258]

In general, the status of the Crimean Jews was similar to that of their brethren in all other regions of the Ottoman Empire. However, due to the fact that the Crimea was a remote part of the realm of the Sublime Porte, and had its own semi-independent rulers (the Crimean Khans), there were certain local differences. Some new restrictions were imposed; some traditional ones were softened. Moreover, the Karaites had special privileges, and were exempted from many taxes imposed on other *ahlu 'dh-dhimma*. Once again, travel accounts are the best sources for information on this. They provide a

---

[255] "We shall not build new monasteries... We shall give board and lodging to all Muslims who pass our way... We shall not manifest our religion publicly... We shall show respect towards the Muslims... We shall not mount on saddles, nor shall we gird swords nor bear any kind of arms..." See *Islam from the Prophet Muḥammad to the Capture of Constantinople*, ed. and trans. B.Lewis, pt. 2 (New-York-Oxford, 1897), 217-219.

[256] According to a Muslim source of the eleventh century "The *jizya* shall be taken from them with belittlement and humiliation." See Lewis, *Jews of Islam*, 14-15.

[257] Many talented Sephardic Jews were invited to the realm of the Sublime Porte during the reign of Bayezid II (1481-1512), who issued a number of special *firmans* (orders) ensuring the protection of the newcomers. Normann A. Stillman, *The Jews of Arab Lands* (Philadelphia, 1979), 91.

[258] Lewis, *Jews of Islam*, 137-138.

comprehensive picture of the legal status of Karaim in the Crimean Khanate.

In contradiction to the words ascribed to 'Umar I ("Do not appoint Jews and Christians to public office...") and other responsum of the thirteenth century prescribing that no Jew is allowed to be appointed inspector of coins,[259] there are references to Karaites who were the treasurers of the Khan's mint in Bakhçeseray .[260] Aubry de la Motray, who visited Bakhçeseray {Bakhçeseray] in 1711, mentioned that the head of the Khan's mint was a certain Jew named Abraham.[261] It seems that this "Jew Abraham" was in fact a Karaite, Avraham Ben-Yoshiyah Yerushalmi Çelebi-Sinani, the author of *Emunah Omen*, a philosophical-theological treatise written in 1712, and published in Gözlöw in 1846.[262] Undoubtedly, he was the father of Shemu'el Ben-Avraham Ben-Yoshiyah (1716-1769), a Karaite merchant who received the status of *Ağa* (*i.e.* "noble authority") and fulfilled the duties of the manager of the Khan's mint.[263] Shemu'el left the title of *Ağa* to his scions. One of them, Binyamin Ben-Shemu'el Ağa, was appointed financial advisor to the last Crimean Khan, Shahin Giray, and master of the mint.[264] Thus, it seems that the hereditary status of financial advisor to the Crimean Khan was in the hands of the Karaite clan of Ağa (a branch of Çelebi-Sinani family) for at least a hundred years, from the beginning of the eighteenth century until the Russian annexation of the Crimea in 1783. When taking into consideration the fact that the first Khan's mint was situated in the territory of Qırq-Yer,[265] it is very tempting to suppose that the Karaites fulfilled these duties from much earlier periods.

One of the articles of the pact of 'Umar postulates that non-Muslims should not "seek to resemble the Muslims by imitating any of

---

[259] *ibid.* 29-30.

[260] A highly interesting, but simultaneously quite biased, article of Seraya Szapszal on the role of the Karaites at the court of the Crimean khans is: "Karaimi w sluzbie u chanów krymskich," *MK* 2:2 (1929): 5-22.

[261] Aubrie de la Motray, *Travels through Europe, Asia and into Part of Africa*, vol.2. (London, 1723), 24.

[262] Miller, *Separatism*, 55, ft.34.

[263] His name is also mentioned in the *yarlıq* of Qırım Giray Khan of 1768, which appointed the Karaite merchant Samuel ("kupets Shamuil") to be the head of the aforementioned mint. The *yarlıq* characterizes Samuel as "a man of noble fame, experienced and honest": *Sbornik*, 104-105. According to Dr. P. Miller, Shemu'el Ben-Avraham was a scion of the most influential Karaite clan of Sinan- Çelebis ["Çelebi-Sinani] (Miller, *Separatism*, 10) [see more about Shemu'el Ben-Avraham in §3.3].

[264] Mann, *Texts*, 10.

[265] See more about this mint in Szapszal, "Karaimi," 7-8.

their garments, the turban, the footwear, or parting of the hair."[266] According to testimonies from the travel accounts, however, the Karaites not only adapted the language and many customs of the Crimean Tatars, but also began to dress and wear their hair in Tatar fashion, so that sometimes a traveler could hardly tell a Karaite from a Tatar.[267] Thus, in order to make non-Muslims easily recognized, local Tatar authorities had to introduce some distinguishing signs which would clearly point out non-Muslims. Evliya Çelebi noted that, in order to be distinguished from the Tatars, the Karaites of Qarasubazar (present day Belogorsk in the Crimea) had to wear a piece of yellow fabric sewn to their hats.[268] However, a new problem arised: how to distinguish non-Muslims in public baths where differences in costume do not matter? In Qarasubazar the problem was solved in the following way: local *dhimmis* (*i.e.* non-Muslims subjects, in this case the Rabbanite Jews, Karaites, and Armenians) had to wear shoes with wooden soles and bind small bells to their ankles when visiting the public baths.[269] In other parts of the Ottoman Empire, when attending the public baths, *dhimmis* were supposed to wear distinguishing signs suspended from cords around their necks, so that they might not be mistaken for Muslims when disrobed.[270]

Especially interesting was the status of the Karaites of Çufut-Qalé. On the one hand, they suffered many limitations. First, they were only permitted to live in the territory of Çufut-Qalé. Second, in spite of the fact that the Karaites had a number of shops in Bakhçeseray , the capital of the Crimean Khanate, they were not allowed to stay there overnight. Therefore, the Karaites had to descend from Çufut-Qalé in the morning and return back in the evening (around a 10-12 kilometer journey). Evliya Çelebi reported that a one-way trip from Çufut-Qalé to Bakhçeseray took around an hour for the Karaite merchants.[271] This peculiar detail of the everyday routine of the Karaites of Çufut-Qalé was noted by practically all travelers who visited this place from the seventeenth century onwards.[272]

---

[266] *Islam from the Prophet Muḥammad*, 218.

[267] Henderson, *Researches*, 314; Pallas, *Travels*, 36-37; the same; *Bemerkungen*, 36; D.B., *Otryvok*, 46; Clarke, *Travels*, 189, 194.

[268] Evliya Çelebi, *Kniga Puteshestvij* , 131-132.

[269] *ibid.* 132.

[270] According to Shiite regulations, they were not allowed to use the same baths at all.

[271] Evliya Çelebi, *Kniga*, 94. This journey, in all probability, was not the most secure one: Shemu'el Ben-Avraham Yerushalmi, one of the most distinguished Karaite leaders and master of the Khans' mint, was murdered while travelling from Bakhçeseray to Çufut-Qalé (1769). Mann, *Texts*, 318.

[272] For the earliest data regarding this detail of the status of the Karaites see: Ambrosius

According to the pact of 'Umar, non-Moslems were not allowed to bear arms and ride horses.[273] Thus, in order to ascend Çufut-Qalé and fetch drinking water there, they used mules and asses.[274] Xavier Hommaire de Hell, a later traveler, left quite a curious remark about this. Apparently, the Karaites were actually allowed to ride on horseback, but were bound to alight and proceed on foot when arriving opposite the Khan's palace in Bakhçeseray.[275] It seems that the prohibition to bear arms might well explain Evliya Çelebi's remark that the local Karaites could not use rifles and guns, and had to gather heaps of stones on the slopes of the fortress in order to defend it.[276]

The Karaites were forbidden to erect any buildings in the part of their settlement called Burunçaq [see the map of Çufut-Qalé] due to the fact that the Khans used it as a place for deer hunting on various holidays and festivities.[277]

On the other hand, they enjoyed certain privileges, namely, they were exempted from many public works and additional taxes. Claude de Peyssonel (1753) explained how they obtained these privileges. He states that a certain Karaite physician (Medecin Juif) cured "Ouloukhani,"[278] the sister of "Haci Selim Giray Khan" from a mortal disease. As a consequence, the Karaites of Çufut-Qalé were transferred under the direct patronage of "Ouloukhani," and exempted from the public works aimed at the renovation of the Khan's palace, mosques, and fountains. However, in exchange, they had to provide Ouloukhani with "everything that was necessary for her household, such as timber, coal, coffee and many other provisions of this kind."[279]

Eszer, "Beschreibung," 233-234; Evliya Çelebi, *Kniga*, 94.

[273] "We shall not mount on saddles, nor shall we gird swords, nor bear any kind of arms...": *Islam from the Prophet Muḥammad*, 218.

[274] Some academics have described the types of the mules and asses that were bred by the Karaites: Hablizl (Hablitzl, Habliz, Russ. Gablits), Carl Ludwig, *Fizicheskoe opisanie Tavricheskoy oblasti* [Physical description of the Taurian district] (St.Petersburg, 1785), 169; Demidov, *Voyage*, vol.2, 669.

[275] Hell, *Travels*, 364. In all probability, this softening of a very rigorous Islamic rule would have been introduced very lately, a short while before 1783. The attempt of the Polish Karaite Orientalist A. Dubinski to explain the traveler's remark by a certain Khazar tradition to unmount when passing by Khaqans' graves is more than improbable (Alexander Dubinski, "Osnovy karaimskoi religii," [Basis of the the Karaite religion] in his *Caraimica* (Warsaw, 1994), 58.

[276] Evliya Çelebi, *Kniga*, 94.

[277] See Pallas, *Travels*, 37; the same; *Bemerkungen*, 37; Motray, *Travels*, 64.

[278] "Ouloukhani" is not a name, but a corruption an official term "'Ulu Khanım" ("Great lady"), *i.e.* khan's wife.

[279] Peyssonel, *Traite*, vol.2, 320-321 [see details in §2.2]. Peyssonel's testimony contradicts the remark of the Russian ambassador, Nikiforov, who mentioned that in 1764 (*i.e.* only 10 years after Peyssonel's visit) Qırım Giray forced local Jews (*i.e.*

Ebenezer Henderson mentioned another interesting privilege conceded by the Khans to the Karaites. In conformity with the ordinance of Nehemiah,[280] they were allowed to shut the gates of Çufut-Qalé at sunset on Friday evening and not open them until the evening at the end of the Sabbath.[281]

Many scholars contend that, from the end of the seventeenth through the eighteenth centuries, relations between the *dhimmis* and the Ottomans started to deteriorate.[282] These tendencies were reflected in the Crimea as well. Toward the end of the eighteenth century, the Khans tried to exact enormous payments from the Karaites, in addition to the *jizya* and *kharaj*.[283] Peter Simon Pallas mentioned that the Crimean Khans, when they wanted to get a "present" from the Karaites or to raise a "voluntary" contribution from them, used to threaten them with the extirpation of the sacred trees, which grew in the valley of Yehoshafat adjacent to Çufut-Qalé.[284]

In 1783, the Crimea was annexed to Russia. In accordance with the rules of the new regime, all Muslim institutions were abolished, and the Karaites were allowed to settle throughout the whole Russian Empire. Most of the travel accounts contain some notes about the changes in the legal status of the Karaites under Russian rule. Many travelers also remarked on the respect and reverence with which the Crimean Karaites were treated by the Russian government and the Tsars.[285] However, the data from the travel accounts is not very informative in this respect. Legal documents and memoirs of the Karaite leaders are much more important for the analysis of the status of the Karaites in the administrative framework of the Russian Empire.[286]

---

the Karaites) to take part in the construction works for the palace in Aslama Dere ("the Valley of budding or grafting") without payment. See "Donesenie rossiyskogo rezidenta pri krymskom khane Nikiforova" [Report of Nikiforov, Russian resident at the court of the Crimean khan] in *ZOOID* 1 (1844), 376-377.

[280] Nehemiah, xiii, 19: "... the gates should be shut and... should not be open till after the Sabbath."

[281] Henderson, *Researches*, 322. Once again, this privilege directly contradicts the postulates of the pact of 'Umar: "We shall keep our gates wide open...": *Islam from the Prophet Muḥammad*, 218.

[282] Stillman, *The Jews of Arab Lands* , 91-93.

[283] 'Azaryah Ben-Eliyah, "Sobytiia," 53-55.

[284] Pallas, *Travels*, 35; the same; *Bemerkungen*, 35.

[285] Markov, *Ocherki*, 87.

[286] See *Sbornik*, 109-112; Miller, *Separatism*.

CHAPTER 3
TRADITIONAL CULTURE AND EVERYDAY LIFE
OF THE CRIMEAN KARAITE COMMUNITY

The abundance of cultural and ethnographic details supplied by travelers in their descriptions of the people and places they visited is, probably, the most valuable aspect of the travel accounts as a historical source. No other source provides such an enormous amount of detailed information about the way of life of these Crimean Karaites: their external appearance, customs, manners, and traditions. Moreover, travelers are never as dry and indifferent as, say, chroniclers or authors of legal documents. They are usually inclined to give their own evaluations of what they observe. However, because of their subjectivity, travel accounts should be treated with extreme care, taking into consideration the travelers' political, religious, or national biases. They were often inclined to exaggerate and embellish certain historical aspects, and distort and misrepresent others.

3.1. External appearance of the Karaites.

"The expression of the countenance in the Karaims is, in general, open and prepossessing..."
(Demidov, Travels, 37)

When making observations of the Karaites' external appearance, eighteenth/nineteenth century travelers did not have a unified opinion regarding their ethnic origins. In general, the travelers found the external appearance and dress of the Karaites very similar to that of the Crimean Tatars.[287]

After a further, and more profound acquaintance with the *Benei Miqra'*, travelers usually noticed a close anthropological affinity between the Karaites and other Jews. The account of Russian traveler Anatoli Demidov is very important for the reconstruction of the outer appearance of the Karaites. Demidov not only described the dress of Karaite women, but also placed numerous ethnographic drawings by Raffet, his companion in the travel to the Crimea, in the edition of his work. Moreover, in his anthropological essays, he contended that the Karaites belonged to the Semitic race and shared all its specific features: black eyes, protruding nose, large forehead, oval face and fair

---

[287] Due to this fact, many travelers mistook the Karaites for the Tatars: D.B., *Otryvok*, 46.

complexion.[288] A similar description of Karaites' appearance was left by A.Nowosielski (1850): "pale [face], large black eyes; sharp outline of brows, slightly plump noses, small lips, white teeth, rather oval face".[289] The traveler often emphasized their distinctive, Biblical look, which sharply distinguished them from other European or Turkish inhabitants of the Crimea:

> ...this man with the black beard, black eyes, thick black eyebrows, and large aquiline nose; those women with physiognomies and features of the East... presented the image of Chopin, depicted somewhere in Syria. It would be enough... to give you the image of Rebecca while giving water to the camels of Avraham's servant.[290]

Xavier Hommaire de Hell (around 1843) briefly remarked that the Karaite "rabbi" who had met him in Çufut-Qalé had a typical Jewish appearance.[291] August von Haxthausen was strongly impressed by the appearance of the Feodosian "Rabbi Rebbi Jeschuah Dawidowitch Koen" (i.e. the Ḥazzan Yeshu'ah Ben-Dawid Kohen): "He had one of the most handsome and expressive faces I had seen for a long time".[292] Almost all travelers of the second half of the nineteenth century were greatly impressed by the charismatic, patriarchal appearance of Avraham Firkovich, whom they usually described as similar to the Biblical sages and prophets "the guardian and patriarch of Çufut-Qalé."[293]

A few travelers spoke about the similitude between the Crimean Tatars and Karaites, not only in their everyday life and

---

[288] "...les yeux ordinairement noirs, grands et bien fendus, le nez un peu recourbé a son extremité, le front large, le visage ovale, et le teint pale": Demidov, *Voyage*, vol.2, 742-743, 737.

[289] Nowosielski, *Stepy*, 47.

[290] Nowosielski, *Stepy*, 17-18. H.Rzewuski, who met the family of the future Karaite *Ḥakham* Babovich in 1825, described it in practically the same way (Szapszal, "Adam Mickiewicz," 6). See more in 2.4.4.

[291] Xavier Hommaire de Hell, *Travels in the Steppes of the Caspian Sea, the Crimea, the Caucasus* (London, 1847), 365. Unfortunately, I have not been able to identify precisely this interesting Karaite, the author of "several sacred poems" and "the history of the Karaites from the time of Moses to our days". His description runs as follows: "a little old man with a long white beard... a man of great intellect, vast erudition, and poetic imagination... lives like a patriarch surrounded by ten or a dozen children of all ages..." It is very likely, however, that this "Rabbi" might well have been Firkovich's former teacher and later his bitter enemy, Mordekhai Sultanski.

[292] Haxthausen, *Studien*, 390.

[293] *E.g.* the memoirs of Evgeni Markov: *Ocherki*, 456, 461.

traditional dress, but also in their anthropological type. Johann Kohl – who often emphasized the importance of Muslim influence upon the Karaites, while observing the service in the Odessa Karaite synagogue – mentioned that "Tatar influence left a strong impact on the Karaite appearance".[294] F.Remy, despite his views concerning the Jewish origins of the Karaites, mentioned, "their resemblance to the Turks is more evident than to the Jews".[295]

Another group of travelers was inclined to notice the features of other ethnic groups in the Karaites. Thus, Andrew Neilson wrote, "Karaites in their general style of physiognomy resemble the Armenians a good deal."[296] Laurence Oliphant, who was astonished to see the beauty of the "lovely Karaite Jewesses" of Bakhçeseray , wrote, "there is nothing Israelitish about these Karaite maidens – the Grecian nose and fiery nostril... seem almost to belie their Hebrew origin..."[297] The most extravagant was, perhaps, the testimony of the Polish traveler St.Siestrzencewicz de Bohusz. In his description of Mangoup's population, he mentioned that the town's last inhabitants (the Karaites), preserved many features of the ancient Goths.[298]

In spite of the aforementioned controversial opinions about the ethnic origin of the Karaites, the general opinion was that the Karaites were much tidier, cleaner, and more beautiful than their Rabbanite brethren. Evliya Çelebi wrote that because of the good climate, the Karaite youths of Mangoup were distinguished by "rosy

---

[294] Kohl, *Reisen*, vol.II, 258. This remark of Kohl allowed K.Neumann to state that the descendants of the Khazars are "the Karaites of Southern Russia and former Polish lands, who speak the Turkic language and are similar to the Turks in terms of their body structure and the features of their faces" (Neumann, *Volker*, 125).

[295] Remy, *Krim*, 96-97.

[296] [Neilson A]. *The Crimea: Its Towns, Inhabitants, and Social Customs* (London, 1855), 65. Andrew Neilson was an English traveler, who spent a long time in the Crimea in the 1820s. The name of the author is indicated on the title page as "The Lady resident near the Alma".

[297] Laurence Oliphant, *The Russian Shores of the Black Sea in the Autumn of 1852* (Edinburgh-London, 1854), 277. Laurence Oliphant (1829-1888), English writer, traveler, unexhaustible adventurer, is also known as a Christian mystic, and one of the first active supporters of Zionism. He visited the Crimea in 1852, *i.e.* a short while before the Crimean War.

[298] "La physiognomie des vieillards nichés dans ces décombres me garantit que la main du temps a respecté quelques restes de ces anciens Goths. Quelques familles pauvres, isolées, à peine connues, voilà tout ce qui subsiste ajourd'hui de cette nation...": St.Siestrzencewicz de Bohusz, *Histoire de la Tauride* (the 1800 and 1824 editions), cited by McDonald Stearns, "Crimean Gothic. Analysis and Etymology of the Corpus," *Studia Linguistica et Philologica*, vol.6 (1978): 19-20). Stanislaw Siestrzencewicz de Bohusz (1731-1826) was an archibishop of Mohilev and a Metropolitan of the Roman Catholic churches of Russia.

faces" and the "eyes of a doe and gazelle."[299] Two centuries later, Johann Kohl noticed the beauty of small Karaites: "Karaite boys look as elegant and pretty as the flock of young princes." Paradoxically, the name of the most beautiful of them, the son of the "richest Odessa Karaite", was Mangub.[300] Marshall Marmont mentioned that the Karaites of Çufut-Qalé were "of good figure, calm, with dignity of bearing, and none of the contemptible air that is usually the character of the Jewish nation."[301] Anatoli Demidov held a similar opinion: "The expression of the countenance in the Karaims is, in general, open and prepossessing, and the minute attention with which they perform all acts of external cleanliness distinguish them from... the rabbinical Jews."[302]

Nicholas Kleeman and Maria Guthrie noted the Karaite tradition of shaven heads among males as a specific feature that differentiated them from other Jews.[303] Edward Clarke noticed that the Karaites, as well as the Tatars, "suffer their beards to grow."[304] Johann Kohl described the design of the Karaite's beards, and their manner of shaving in great detail.[305]

---

[299] Evliya Çelebi, *Kniga*, 91.
[300] Kohl, *Reisen*, vol.2, 262. This remark also shows that, by the beginning of the nineteenth century, some members of the former Mangoupian community had emigrated as far as Odessa.
[301] "de belles figures, du calme, de la dignité dans le maintien, et rien de l'air abject qui, en genéral, est le caractère de la nation juive": Marmont, *Voyage*, 297.
[302] Demidov, *Travels*, 37.
[303] Kleeman, *Reisen*, 74; Guthrie, *Tour*, 84. This "haircut" was habitual for many Islamic people including the Ottoman Turks and Tatars as well. Shelomoh Beim mentioned that custom of shaving heads had been introduced among the Karaites in order "to avoid derogatory jokes about their non-shaved heads" (Beim, *Pamiat'*, 72).
[304] Clarke, *Travels*, 194.
[305] Kohl, *Reisen*, vol.2, 262-263.

The drawing by Auguste Raffet (1837) depicting the Karaites of Feodosia. As you may notice, in fact, these are only two individuals portrayed from different perspective. Of interest is also the background depicting the historical setting – nineteenth century Feodosia, its walls, windmills, and a fountain.

Travelers who visited the Crimea were always eager to observe the exotic behavior and mores of the local Oriental women. The style of the Karaite women, which was to a great extent similar to that of Tatar women, attracted much of the travelers' interest. The travelers usually noted that the Karaite women were very shy, and afraid of strangers. Nevertheless, some of them managed to overcome the obstacle of Oriental habits and describe the Karaite women more closely (this might be especially said with the regard to the second half of the nineteenth century, when the Karaites started to adopt European manners).

According to A.I.Mikhailovskiy-Danilevskiy (18.05.1818), even the Russian emperor Alexander I, in order to satisfy his inquisitiveness, visited the "harem" (*i.e.* the female part of the house) of a certain "rich inhabitant" (undoubtedly, Benjamin Ağa). The Tsar, when seeing the astonishment of the women witnessing the ruler of the country in their own house, quoted in French: "Dites a ces dames, que je suis enchante d'avoir fait leur connaissance," and departed.[306]

A.Afanasyev-Chuzhbinskiy (1863) confessed that he "had a strong wish to be present in female Karaite society." Soon, when the traveler had been invited to a certain Karaite house, his desire was satisfied. The traveler devoted much space to the necessity of emancipating the Karaite women from the yoke of the Oriental habits of their men.[307]

Robert Lyall stole into the house of Yiṣḥaq Ben-Shelomoh when he was away. The absence of the latticed windows, which half-veiled Yiṣḥaq's wife and his four daughters during traveler's previous visit, destroyed his illusions which "fancied them beautiful as houris... they were clumsy, pock-marked, and even ugly. They were excessively shy..." [308] However, most other travelers praised the exquisite, unusual appearance and manner of the Karaite women's dress.

Johann Kohl, when describing the beauty of the Karaite women, mentioned that they looked "somewhat manly... like young Amazons."[309] A.Nowosielski (1850) – in spite of the fact that, in his opinion, Karaite women loose their beauty very early – was truly impressed by the appearance of the youngest of S.Babovich's daughters: "She could serve as a vignette for Byron's works. Her beautiful chestnut hair was braided into thousands of plaits falling down on her back..."[310] The Marquise de Castelnau was deeply impressed by the beauty of the pretty young Karaites of Çufut-Qalé, and mentioned that "the most beautiful woman born in the Crimea is the daughter of a [Karaite] Jew, who accorded me a short, but very hearty welcome". A Russian aristocrat, who wanted to check the verity of this opinion, confirmed to de Castelnau that she "had never seen anything so beautiful and simultaneously so awkward".[311] A.Koshliakov was also mesmerized by the appearance of the "young pretty Karaite maidens" of Çufut-Qalé: "In general, local women are unusually beautiful; the reasons are, perhaps, mountain air, simplistic life, and first of all, pristine type, which was kept untouched by the

---

[306] See travel notes of A.I.Mikhailovskiy-Danilevskiy, published in *Istoricheskiy vestnik* (May, 1892): 371, and quoted by S.Szapszal (MS LLAS, F.143-918).

[307] A.Afanasyev-Chuzhbinskiy, *Poezdka v Yuzhnuyu Rossiyu* (St.Petersburg, 1863), 322-323.

[308] Lyall, *Travels*, 273-274.

[309] Kohl, *Reisen*, vol.2, 263.

[310] Nowosielski, *Stepy*, 35-36, 47-49.

[311] Castelnau, *Essai*, 179.

separation of the fair sex from the strangers."[312] Laurence Oliphant was sure that the "lovely Jewesses" – Karaite women of Bakhçeseray – would overshadow the beauty of their "waddling" Tatar companions.[313]

To sum up, it is possible to distinguish the following three approaches of the travelers concerning the Karaites' ethnic origins on the basis of the external appearance of the Karaites. Most of the travelers considered the Karaites representatives of the Jewish nation who were similar to the Turkic and Oriental nations in their behavior and manner of dressing. A few travelers, however, focused on their Turkic and Tatar features. Others noticed features in the Karaites of other non-Muslim and non-Jewish ethnic groups inhabiting the Crimea. Practically all of them paid great attention to what was, in their view, the exotic and "Oriental" appearance of the Karaite women.

3.2. Manners and customs.

> *"Their way of life and character, represents a mixture of Tatar and*
> *Jewish..."*
> (Kohl, Reisen, vol.2, 260)

When analyzing information from the travel accounts regarding the manners and customs of the Crimean Karaites, it is possible to conclude (once again) that practically all the travelers noticed the close cultural affinity between the lives of the Karaites and the Crimean Tatars.[314] The travelers documented many cultural borrowings of the Karaites from their Tatar surrounding. For example there is what they viewed as the patriarchal Oriental attitude of the Karaites towards their wives, who were isolated from the external world, and bound to spend their lives within the close walls of their dwellings.[315] They interpreted the way in which the Karaites spent their leisure time as very Islamic, and Oriental. A.Nowosielski described in detail the atmosphere of the Tatar coffee-houses in Gözlöw, where "the Tatars, Karaites, and Greeks sit, drink coffee, smoke pipes and keep silence or talk slowly."[316]

---

[312] [A.Koshliakov], *Desiatidnevnaya poezdka*, 38-39.

[313] Oliphant, *Russian Shores*, 277.

[314] The first traveler who noticed this fact was Evliya Çelebi (seventeenth century). In his opinion the Karaites of that time did not speak any Hebrew, and knew only the Tatar language: *Kniga*, 90.

[315] E.Chojecki mentioned that "the Karaite women are not used to being shown to strangers:" Chojecki, *Wspomnienia*, 218.

[316] Nowosielski, *Stepy*, 29. describes a similar picture of mutual friendship and consent

Equally Oriental and strange was the architecture of the Karaite's dwellings.[317] When speaking about the linguistic peculiarities of the Crimean Karaites, the travelers mentioned that they used the language of their neighbours, the Tatars, for the everyday matters and retained Hebrew as the sacred language used during prayers. In addition, in the nineteenth century, many from the younger generation (especially men) already spoke the Slavic vernaculars of their neighbours, the Russians and Poles.[318] However, the travelers also noted and described many other features of Karaite culture.

3.2.1. Religious views, traditions and practices.

As has been mentioned, the main difference between the religious doctrine of the Karaite and Rabbanite Jews is found in the Karaite's negation of the binding authority of the Talmud, and their recognition of the *TaNaKh* as the only true source of religious law. In addition, the Karaites did not recognize the use of Rabbanite paraphernalia such as the *mezuzah*, *tefillin*, and the strictures of a *miqweh*[319]. There were also a number of other differences, first of all, in the sphere of the calendar, dietary and marriage laws, [320] rights of inheritance, ceremony of circumcision, &c.[321]

Many of the religious practices of the East European Karaites bore a seemingly Oriental character, examples inlcude: ablution before entering the synagogue (called by the present-day East European Karaites *"kenasa/kenese"* [sing; pl.*"kenasalar/keneseler"*], derived from the Hebrew *Beit Keneset*, "house of assembly", *i.e.* synagogue);

---

between various Crimean ethnic groups (Jews, Karaites, Tatars, Greeks, Armenians) sitting in coffee-houses was depicted by A.Demidov (1837): *Voyage*, vol.1, 499.

[317] The German traveler F.Remy (1871) noticed the Oriental "egoism" of the Karaite and Tatar isolated "house-existence" for women (Remy, *Krim*, 8) [see §3.4.3].

[318] Nowosielski, *Stepy*, 195-196, 47, 40; Kaczkowski, *Dziennik*, 103 (Karol Kaczkowski (1797-1867), an author of many scientific works, and famous Polish physician); [L.Hlebnicki-Józefowicz], "Wspomnienia," 165. A.Nowosielski called the Turkic dialect of the Karaites "idiomat czagaltajski" (*i.e.* a Çağatay dialect) (Nowosielski, *Stepy*, 195). H.Rzewuski mentioned that "le Turc est leur langue maternelle, l'hebreux n'est pour eux qu'une langue savante et theologique, exclusif apanage de leur clergé" (Szapszal, "Adam Mickiewicz," 6).

[319] Ritual cleansing is used by Karaites. It is only the Rabbanite requirements for the ritual and structure of ritual cleansing, requiring a specific structure (*i.e.* the *miqweh* itself) that Karaites object to. [*ed.* For an example, consider the ritual washing troughs at the entrance of Karaite synagogues.]

[320] Shelomoh Beim left a highly interesting and detailed description of the traditional Karaite wedding: "O svad'be u Karaimov, kak ona sovershalas' za sto let tomu nazad" [On the Karaite wedding, the way it was performed a hundred years ago], in Beim, *Pamiat'*, 63-81.

[321] See more details in Leon Nemoy, "Karaites," *EJ* 10 (1971), 777-781.

116

the directing of the Torah closet to the South;[322] and, entering the synagogue sanctuary bare-footed (there are no benches inside a Karaite sanctuary, and it is covered by carpeted floors). Some scholars explain these observances by tracing them to Islamic influence, others say they are drawn or interpreted from an understanding of Biblical laws. The Karaites contend that these practices stem from the observance of Biblical purity laws, which were extended from the temple, at a ceremonial level, to the synagogue.

Practically all travelers, starting from the times of Evliya Çelebi (mid-seventeenth century), noticed that the Karaites were proponents of the "pure" law of Mosheh, who rejected later Rabbanite additions, such as the Talmud and Qabbalah. The most detailed account of such matters was, perhaps, the writings of the French officer Beaudoin (1855). Beaudoin described not only the religious views of the Karaites, but also such ceremonies as funerals, circumcision, engagement, drawing up a marriage contract, wedding, *et alia*.[323] He quite correctly recorded the general structure of the administration of the Karaite community of that time: the *Ḥakham* (*"Khakam"* or *"Khrakam"* according to the traveler's spelling) was the head of the community, followed by the *cantors-Ḥazzanim* (*"Khazan"*), whose helpers were *shammashim* (*"Shamash"*), and, finally, the administrators-*gabbayim* (*"Gabay"*).[324]

Most travelers mentioned that the Karaites professed a special type of Judaism peculiar to their sect, and described Karaite religious practices as the features which differentiated the Karaites from their Muslim, Christian, and Talmudic neighbours. One of the very distinctive Karaite practices, which distinguished them from both the Talmudists and Tatars, was their rigorous, and strict observance of the Sabbath.

The Marquise de Castelnau noted that Çufut-Qalé looks very impressive and interesting only on Saturdays, whereas during the weekdays the town is ruled by an "atmosphere of abandonment". Only on Saturday, in his opinion, did the town look completely different, because "on the Sabbath the Jew ("le Juif", *i.e.* a Karaite) is very open and happy to greet a stranger," offering him various dishes and even

---

[322] Gustav Peringer (the end of the seventeenth century) explained the southern orientation of the Karaite synagogues by a Karaite tradition according to which King Salmanassar had carried the Karaites away from Palestine Northward, consequently, all prayers should be directed in the direction of Jerusalem, *i.e.* to the South. See Peringer's letters in Szyszman, "Gustaf Peringers Mission," 228. Some explain it by a literal understanding of *Daniel* 6:10 (*i.e.* prayer in the direction of Jerusalem).

[323] Gammer, "Karaites," 66-78.

[324] Gammer, "Karaites," 72-73.

allowing [him] to have a look upon his wife and daughters.[325] K.Kaczkowski, who happened to be there on Saturday, possessed a similar impression from his visit to Gözlöw: "All the streets were filled with the Karaites, because it was *szabas*."[326]

According to Ebenezer Henderson, the gates of Çufut-Qalé were shut from Friday evening until sunset at the end of the Sabbath,[327] because the Karaites "sanctify the Sabbath by rigid abstinence, and a close application of the mind to the duties of religion."[328] Some travelers noted that the Crimean Karaites managed to preserve the centuries-old precept prohibiting the burning of any fire or candle on the Sabbath day.[329] Edward Clarke noticed that the Karaites abstained even from snuff and smoking during the Sabbath.[330] Henderson wrote that "In the houses of Karaim... you will neither see a candle nor fire, from sunset on Friday evening till the same time the evening following. They eat nothing but cold meat during the whole of this period" (meaning cold foods, not just flesh). In contrast to E.Clarke, he mentioned that the Karaites allowed themselves to smoke their pipes on the condition that they were leaning out of a window; a Rabbanite, however, supplied this information, to him.[331]

Similar information concerning the rigid preservation of Sabbath was left by Beaudoin: "On Friday all the food for the following day has to be ready by one hour before sunset... They do not warm it up... they do not light the lights to see. They do not touch the food prepared on Saturday by a stranger."[332] It is worth mentioning (in spite of the very ambiguous character of this source) that the claim regarding Karaite fasting during the Sabbath is very similar to that of certain *minim* (heretics) described by Rabbi Petaḥyah as early as the end of the twelfth century.[333] Evgeni Markov also added that, during the Sabbath, the Karaites "do not dare to wear a watch or take a book"[334] Because of the Sabbath, a "Jewish rabbi" of Çufut-Qalé (undoubtedly, Yiṣḥaq Ben-Shelomoh) could not, himself, read the

---

[325] Castelnau, *Essai*, 179.

[326] Kaczkowski, *Dziennik*, 38-40.

[327] In accordance with Nehemiyah 13:19.

[328] Henderson, *Researches*, 321-322.

[329] Preserving this tradition had to be quite a hard task, taking into consideration cold Crimean winters. The Karaites of Lithuania preserved this rule at least until the end of the fifteenth century: Mann, *Texts*, 558.

[330] Clarke, *Travels*, 193.

[331] Henderson, *Researches*, 321.

[332] Gammer, "Karaites," 75.

[333] Petaḥyah of Ratisbon, *Travels of Rabbi Petachia*, 6-9.

[334] Markov, *Ocherki*, 461.

letter of recommendation that was brought by Robert Lyall; as a consequence he (*i.e.* Lyall) gave it to his secretary.[335]

Of great interest is a brief remark by James Webster (1828) concerning Karaite ablution before entering the synagogue. During his visit to Çufut-Qalé, the local rabbi informed Webster that "washing (*i.e.* the rite of *miqweh*) did not form part of the ceremonies of their faith; but that those who chose to undergo an ablution before entering the synagogue, did so." The traveler ventured to suppose, "The custom of ablution... is probably local, resulting from their (*i.e.* the Karaites') intercourse with the Tatars..."[336] This, however, does not take into account the fact that Karaites in all other countries where they lived practiced the same ritual.

---

[335] Lyall, *Travels*, 266.

[336] [See more details in §4.1.2]. James Webster, *Travels through the Crimea, Turkey, and Egypt*, vol.1 (London 1830), 81-82. James Webster (1802-1828) was a young British traveler, who died soon after the end of his travels. Of interest is also the fact that the traveler found the local Karaite "rabbi" to be "exceedingly ignorant" concerning religious matters. Paradoxically, the difference between the Karaite and Rabbanite creed was explained to him not by a local Karaite, but by a certain "German (*i.e.* Ashkenazic) Jew" who resided in the town at that time.

Nineteenth century fountain for ablution at the entrance to Evpatorian Beit HaKeneset.

Robert Lyall left a detailed description of the service in the large synagogue of Çufut-Qalé in the "commemoration of God's giving the commandments to Mosheh" (*i.e.* probably, on the Pentecost [*Hagh HaShavu'ot*, also known as *Mattan Torah* – or the giving of the Torah]): "The Rabbi, robed in white, and with his face toward the altar, sometimes remained mute, and sometimes spoke with considerable gesticulation [...] All who could make use of it held the Hebrew Psalter in their hands; and, at times, accompanied each other in reading. As a mark of distinction, they had a white linen scarf thrown over their shoulders, and small silk bags descending from their left arms. Those who could not read had neither books, nor these ornaments; and, among them, were remarked some youths, but very few adults. [...] the congregation stood up, or knelt...".[337]

---

[337] Lyall, *Travels*, 275. [*ed.* Lyall obviously mistook the Karaite *Siddur* for the Psalter,

A.Nowosielski was present at the prayer in the Gözlöw synagogue: "During the prayer the Karaites take [their] places before the partition, whereas women are placed on the balconies, which reach the middle of the temple. While preparing themselves for the prayer, the Karaites put on their heads a big cap made of white sheepskin instead of the usual black *krymka*..."[338]

Johann Kohl left a detailed description of the celebration of *Yom HaKippurim*, which he saw in the Karaite synagogue in Odessa on September 20th, 1838. Unlike other travelers, who compared Karaite *batei keneset* with the synagogues of the Talmudic Jews, Kohl found a lot of similarities between the former and Muslim mosques. Kohl distinguished several parts of the synagogues: a small part with benches, situated near the entrance, a gallery for women – the central part of the temple, covered with carpets – and the "shrine" (*i.e.* *heikhal*) which held the liturgical scrolls. Kohl noticed that the Karaites entered the synagogue "almost like Muslims, bare-footed, they kneel, sit or lie..." During the prayer men had to wear a "*qalpaq*" on their heads and, while sitting on a carpet, they read passages in turns from the prayer books (most of the Karaite service is antiphonal). Even during prayer, the Karaites were divided into several groups: children, elders, adults, well-to-do Karaites, and so on. Kohl, who was visiting on the Sabbath when lamps were prohibited, noted that, after sunset, in order to read more distinctively, believers moved closer to windows and leaned the books over the heads of those who were in front of them in order to catch the last rays of the setting sun.[339]

These testimonies of Lyall, Nowosielski and Kohl are supplemented by a very detailed description of the Karaite service in Luck left by E.Henderson (1821), and by the remarks of Wł.Syrokomla concerning the liturgy in the Karaite synagogue of Troki.[340]

As has been mentioned, the belief in the coming of the Messiah constitutes a part of Karaite religious doctrine.[341] Some

---

because much of Karaite prayer is derived from the book of Psalms. The scarves were obviously the *tallit*.]

[338] Nowosielski, *Stepy*, 39. Some other Polish travelers supplied important information concerning the inner furnishings and external view of the Karaite synagogues in Gözlöw and Çufut-Qalé: Kaczkowski, *Dziennik*, 39, 100-101; [L.Hlebnicki-Józefowicz], "Wspomnienia," 165; Chojecki, *Wspomnienia*, 219; Nowosielski, *Stepy*, 36-40.

[339] Kohl, *Reisen*, vol.2, 263-266.

[340] Henderson, *Researches*, 324-330; Syrokomla, *Wycieczki*, 89-90.

[341] Even such a "dark" figure of the Karaite history as Seraya Szapszal mentioned it in one of his interviews: Warren Green, "The Karaite Community in Interwar Poland," *Nationalities Papers* 14: 1-2 (1986): 101-109.

travelers noted the messianic expectations of the Karaites. Thus, Russian poet S.Bobrov (1804) poeticized the messianic expectations of the Karaites in one of his verses.[342] V.Izmailov (1799) wrote with disapproval, after his visit to Çufut-Qalé: "Rabbis spend their life-time in misery and expect the Messiah".[343] E.Henderson mentioned that the Karaites have a much more considerate and rational attitude concerning the coming of the Messiah than the Rabbanites.[344]

Of interest, also, is a discussion concerning the coming of the Messiah, which was written down by J.Kohl in Odessa. The dialogue took place between a Rabbanite market-woman and a Karaite near whose house she usually sold her goods. The Karaite told Kohl that the Karaites "are always waiting for Him to come, both during the day and night. Perhaps, he is already amongst us, but we do not know this yet." When hearing this, the woman replied: "Tomorrow is the *Schabbes,* and if the Messiah comes tomorrow, yuhh! I would give him all my food". Then they started a discussion about whether the food and other things would be still of importance after the coming of the Messiah. In order to say a final word in the discussion and to show what he considered its groundlessness, Kohl asked both interlocutors: Will He [the Messiah] give peace and friendship to abide between you, Dschuffut and Karaites?" – To this question of mine none of them, irreconcilable [rivals], gave me an answer!"[345] Beaudoin (1855) also asked the Karaites several questions concerning the expected coming of the Messiah. One of his informants (S.Beim?) with a smile replied: "the messiah should arrive 6,000 years after the creation of Adam and then the world will be destroyed. [...] the messiah will arrive to reunite in Jerusalem the dispersed Hebrews... he will rebuild the temple."[346]

French travelers who visited the peninsula during the Crimean War, left a description of Karaite funerals, performed by "the Sacred Society" (*i.e.* "hevra qadisha"), consisting of three persons only:

> The *Gabay* is forewarned of the death and is asked to authorize the interment, which in any case take place only 18-

[342] О Караибы! – вы кого
При храминах отвесных ждете? -
Того ль что в молниях багряных
И в громе от страны восточной
На ваш камнистый снидет холм...

[343] Izmailov, Vladimir. *Puteshestvie v poludennuiu Rossiiu* [Travel to the Southern Russia]. Part 2. (Moscow, 1805), 142.

[344] Henderson, *Researches*, 330.

[345] Kohl, *Reisen*, vol.2, 266.

[346] Gammer, "Karaites," 66-67.

20 hours after the deceased had departed this world... the men of the Sacred Society wash the corpse in order to purify it and dress it in white... Only men take part in the funeral, women are not to be seen. The procession advances sometimes in silence, sometimes chanting prayers... the coffin is separated, the body is lowered into the grave and placed in it the head pointing north and the feet – south.[347] Several pieces of earth imported from Jerusalem... are placed on his shut eyelids. Then the grave is covered. The assistants disperse immediately to their homes [...] If the deceased is a man remarkable for his virtues and talent, he is carried, before turning to the cemetery, to the synagogue and the *Khakam* gives a eulogy pleading to Heaven. The ceremonies of interment for women are similar, only the corps is being purified by women.[348]

E.Henderson mentioned that, in spite of the sternness of the Karaite religious laws, some of their sages – from time to time, especially in difficult cases – consulted the Talmud; he even mentioned that some of them were acquainted with the texts of the New Testament.[349]

Even more paradoxical is a Karaite tradition to use ostrich eggs as means for concentration during prayer. This tradition was mentioned by S.Beim, A.Koshliakov, E.Deinard and much later, by S.Szapszal [see details in §4.1.2, the synagogues of Çufut-Qalé].

3.2.2. Beliefs and superstitions.

The travelers usually wrote that the Karaites were free from various superstitions, such as belief in the power of talismans and

---

[347] A very important detail – southern orientation of the Karaite graves, as well as the altar part of the Karaite synagogue [see above].

[348] Gammer, "Karaites, 75-76. Cf. another French report as retold in William Harris Rule, *History*, 186: "when the time for burial arrives the corpse is laid on a bier, and so carried to the cemetery, men only following. The procession moves on slowly, in profound silence, except when silence is broken by the chanting or intoning a psalm of prayer. On reaching the cemetery they lay the corpse in the grave on its back, with the head towards the north, and feet to the south. A little dust, brought from the Holy Land by some pilgrim, is laid on the closed eyelids. The grave is filled with earth, and the followers disperse." Rule makes a mistake when he says that the funeral takes place 18-20 *days* after the death (should be 18-20 *hours*; see *ibid.*). It seems that French reporters based their data on information received from Shelomoh Beim (cf. Beim, *Pamiat'*, 61-62).

[349] Henderson, *Researches*, 320, 330. The last observation might be explained, perhaps, by Henderson's missionary zeal and tendency to overestimate the Karaites' readiness to come closer to the Christian religion.

transmigration of souls, which were typical for the Rabbanite Jews.[350] Nevertheless, some of them noticed certain peculiar beliefs and superstitions of the Crimean Karaites.

Practically every nation inhabiting the world has its own traditions, beliefs, and legends related to burial grounds. The Jews, for example, in spite of their venerable attitude towards cemeteries as sacred places where their ancestors and forefathers had been buried, believed evil ghosts and dæmons haunted them.[351] Of great interest are the unusual beliefs of the Karaites related to their necropoli in Çufut-Qalé and Mangoup. D.Chwolson, while carrying out an epigraphic and archæological exploration in the territory of the cemetery in Çufut-Qalé, mentioned that the Karaites often informed him that a non-Jewish population of enormous height had been buried on the part of the cemetery with the largest tombstones (probably, a section with the supposed graves of the Sangari family).[352] Firkovich's daughter informed the Polish traveler Pojata (1870) that the Sangari family was distinguished by their gigantic height.[353] V.Ch.Kondaraki left an amusing remark that the cemetery in the Tabana-dere in Mangoup looked quite eerie, even during the daytime, and that the brother of his Tatar informant had seen "a woman of extraordinary corpulence, surrounded by a countless crowd of hunchbacked people" there.[354]

Travelers often remarked that the beautiful, mighty oaks and other trees growing in the Yehoshafat Valley necropolis (Çufut-Qalé), when compared against its sorrowful background of innumerable, marble-white tombstones, engrossed them in pious contemplations regarding the vanity of earthly life. P.S.Pallas (1793-1794) left a very important remark concerning the reverent attitude of the Karaites towards this valley and the trees growing there. According to his information, the Karaites held this "kleine Thal Josaphats" (Germ. "small valley of Yehoshafat", so called to distinguish it from the Valley of Yehoshafat in Jerusalem for which it is named) so dear that in order to get "voluntary gifts" from them ("ein freywilliges Geschenk", i.e. some extra-payments) it was enough for the Crimean Khans just to threaten the Karaites with the extirpation of the trees growing in this valley.[355] In the twentieth century the Karaites started to

---

[350] Henderson, *Researches*, 322.
[351] "Cemetery" *EJ* 5 (1971), 272.
[352] Chwolson, *Corpus*, 34-35, 37.
[353] Pojata [H.Skirmuntowa], "Szkice z Krymu," *Tygodnik Ilustrowany* 8:201 (1871): 222.
[354] V.Ch.Kondaraki, *Universalnoe opisanie Kryma* [Universal description of the Crimea], pt.1 (Nikolaev, 1873), 95.
[355] Pallas, *Bemerkungen*, 35; the same, *Travels*, 35. The scholar does not mention what

call the cemetery "*Balta tiymez*" (Karaite-Tatar "axe does not touch"), and connect this toponym with the reverent attitude towards the oaks in the Yehoshafat Valley.[356]

The remark above of P.S.Pallas is too brief to derive any serious conclusions. In the Rabbanite tradition, an oak (Hebrew "*allon*" – "strong") symbolizes pride and loftiness; in the book of the prophet Isaiah, the Jewish people are compared to an old oak (*Isaiah 6:13*); though, it is difficult to see how scripturalist Karaites would compare themselves to the oak in this passage.[357] There were numerous sacred trees mentioned in the Torah; one of them, the so-called "oak of Avraham", was mentioned in one of the travel diaries of A.Firkovich.[358] Again, however, it is difficult to see how the Karaites would adopt what was clearly viewed as a pagan practice[359].

The Karaites' reverent attitude towards the oaks and other trees in the Yehoshafat Valley might be explained by the generally reverent attitude towards the trees in cemeteries typical in both Jewish and non-Jewish lore. Taking all these into consideration, it is no wonder that the Karaites were terrified to hear the Khans threaten the trees growing in the Yehoshafat Valley. Moreover, cutting down the trees, with the aim of obtaining timber, would undoubtedly constitute a sacrilegious action towards their ancient burial ground. In addition, some sources testify there was a Karaite tradition that prescribed the preservation of the trees and weeds in the territory of the cemetery, so that it would gradually return to its original natural state.[360]

Quizzically, the motif of sacred oaks has received unbelievable attention in twentieth century Karaite scholarship. On the

---

sort of trees were growing there at that time – oaks or some other trees as well. Scholars of the dendochronological laboratoty of the Institute of Archæology at the Ukrainian Academy of Sciences (September, 1998), on the basis of dendochronological analysis, came to the conclusion that the earliest oak explored by them started to grow in 1780-1785.

[356] It is highly probable, that *Balta tiymez*, the Turkic name for the "*'Emeq Yehoshafat*" (Hebr. "Yehoshafat Valley"), so popular among the present-day Crimean Karaites was, in fact, invented by S.Szapszal (cf. his early work of 1896, where calls this Valley exclusively "*Iosafatova dolina*" (Russ. "Yehoshafat Valley"), and fragments from his later (1950s) unpublished work "Istoriia tiurkov-karaimov v Krymu, Litve i Polshe" [The history of the Turks-Karaites in the Crimea, Lithuania, and Poland] where he calls it *Balta tiymez*: Szapszal, *Karaimy*, 10, 26-27, 33).

[357] Jehuda Feliks, "Oak", *EJ* 12 (1971): 1293-1294.

[358] A.S.Firkovich, "Palomnichestvo." Transl. B.Y.Kokenai. Ed. M.Eizeri. *Leningradskii evreiskii almanakh* II (1986), 39.

[359] cf. Isaiah 1:29, Hosea 4:13

[360] Pelczynski, *Najmniejsza mniejszosc*, 42; Trevisan Semi, "Brief Survey," 102.

basis of this brief remark of Pallas, later Karaite leaders propounded a rather awkward contention that, in addition to Judaism, the East European Karaites also professed a kind of shamanistic belief, with the cult of sacred oaks as its central part.[361] However, as noted above, there is not a single source that testifies in favor of this hypothesis.

Of interest is an odd tradition prohibiting Karaites from eating together with strangers.[362] Evgeni Markov and Mary Holderness wrote that the Karaites, according to their traditional custom, were forbidden to eat anything in the presence of strangers.[363] Anatoli Demidov was not aware of this tradition, but noticed that the Karaite "Rabbi," to whose house he and his companions were invited, did not eat with them.[364] From the remark of E.Markov, it is possible to conclude that, by the second half of the nineteenth century, this custom was perceived as an anachronism.[365]

The travelers also remarked on other, various odd behaviors or superstitious beliefs of the Crimean Karaites. Evliya Çelebi, for example, mentioned that the Karaites did not have any guns or rifles to defend Çufut-Qalé, because of the fact that they (as well as the Tatars) could not stand the sound of their roar.[366] Markov mentioned that he had understood Avraham Firkovich's unwillingness to be

---

[361] One of the earliest important and significant references to this non-existing pagan cult was made, perhaps, by Seraya Szapszal in his review of Alexander Baschmakoff, *Cinquante siècles l'evolution ethnique autour de la Mer Noire* (Paris, 1937) published in *MK* 12 (1938): 14-20. See also fragments from his later (1950s) unpublished work in his *Karaimy*, 33. In our opinion, in order to invent this shamanistic tradition, the *Ḥakham* used the story from the Vita of St.Constantine (Cyrill) concerning the cult of oaks among the Khazars. For the culmination of praising this pagan tradition in Karaite scholarship see *Karai (Krymskie karaimy)*, 22-27.

[362] [ed. The prohibition Karaites observe which keeps them from eating with non-Jews stems from their observance of the ritual purity laws (*tahorah* and *tum'ah*). Karaites observe the dietary laws, in keeping with the Torah, as an extension of the purity laws. Consequently, women in their period are not allowed in the kitchen, and eat at separate tables; as well, non-Jews, who must be presumed unclean, are not permitted with food.]

[363] Markov, *Ocherki*, 461; Mary Holderness, *Journey from Riga to the Crimea* (London, 1827), 179.

[364] Demidov, *Travels*, 34; the same; *Voyage*, vol.1, 369.

[365] Markov, *Ocherki*, 461.

[366] Evliya Çelebi, *Kniga*, 94. The traveler also mentioned that, in order to defend the fortress, the Karaites used stones. This data may be corroborated by a very late Karaite legend "*Tas yağqan yol*" ("the road raining stones"), which tells about the defeat of the Kumans, beleaguering the town by a "rain of stones" thrown by the Karaite defenders of Çufut-Qalé (narrated to A.Szyszman by T.S.Levi-Babovich on 04.03.1937: LLAS F143-1531: 5-6).

photographed as "absurd Tartar superstitions".[367]

The southern tower of the Middle Wall of Çufut-Qalé. The cavern on the left from the Tower is Sakyz-Koba ("Mastic/Putty Cave"); close to it is Khamam Koba ("Bath Cave"). According to a late Karaite tradition, Karaite women used to take baths in the latter cave and then went to the former to have a chat and to smear themselves with fragrant mastic.

---

[367] The patriarch of Çufut-Qalé explained that he considered it to be sinful: Markov, *Ocherki*, 461 [see more in §2.4.3].

3.3. Legends and traditions.[368]

The travel memoirs of A.Nowosielski (1850) contain a real treasure house of Karaite folklore collected in Simferopol' by Fr.Dombrovski.[369] They represent a precious anthology of the Karaite folklore of the first half of the nineteenth century, where historical persons and events are intertwined with fantasy and imagination.[370]

Nowosielski starts his narration with a set of stories related to the Çelebi-Sinani family and their settling in the Crimea. The founder of this dynasty, *Moszesinan* [Mosheh Sinan] (1300s), a favorite counselor of the Persian shah, was sent to the Crimea through the efforts of his rivals.[371] His son *Izaak* (*i.e.* Yiṣḥaq), who inherited father's honorable title *Czelebi* [Çelebi],[372] became an advisor to the Tatar Khan Mengli Giray after showing Giray his acumen in solving a very intricate legal case. While in such an important office, Yiṣḥaq turned his attention to his people, who were belittled and oppressed by the Muslim authorities to the extent of forcible conversion to Islam. He received permission from Giray to settle the Karaites in Çufut-Qalé. There, he built a synagogue, school, and printing house.[373]

---

[368] Members of The al-Qirqisani Center for the Promotion of Karaite Studies (including M.Kizilov, H.Aaronson, A.Qanaï, A.Eidlisz, and Y.Yaron, with consultation from P.Miller), are preparing an anthology of Karaite foklore from the mediæval period up to the present.

[369] Franz Dombrovski (Dabrowski) – nineteenth century Crimean historian. He was interested in the history of the Karaites and was preparing a large work, "Opisanie byta krymskikh Karaimov" [Description of the everyday life of the Crimean Karaites], which, unfortunately, has not been published. He was also engaged in correspondence with S.Beim. See the letter of Fr.Dombrovski to S.Beim (1860): RGADA F.188.Opis' 1. Delo 365: 97r-98r. The destiny of the manuscript of "*Opisanie byta krymskikh Karaimov*" and its present-day location are not known.

[370] In all probability, A.Nowosielski derived his folk-stories from some rare newspaper publication of Fr.Dombrovski whose precise location I have not been able to identify so far, or from his personal contact with the latter. Thus, A.Nowosielski's travel diary seems to be the only accessible source of these legends.

[371] According to a local tradition recorded by A.Firkovich, a Persian Karaite Sinan Ben-Yosef (Sinan Çelebi), the founder of the clan Sinan-Çelebis, arrived in the Crimea much later, in 1501 (Miller, *Separatism*, 9-10).

[372] In the Crimea and Ottoman Turkey the term *çelebi* was initially used for the designation of the Muslim spiritual authorities and young men from noble families; later it was used as the title of civil servants and intelligentsia. This *Izaak Czelebi* is undoubtedly, Yiṣḥaq Ben-Mosheh Çelebi Sinani (ca.1696-1756), under whose auspices the first Karaite printing press was established in Çufut-Qalé in 1734.

[373] Not counting the attempt to organise a printing house in Constantinople, the typography in Çufut-Qalé (later transferred to Euvpatoria) was the first typography in the Crimean Khanate, and the only independent Karaite typography in world history. See more in P. Miller, "Prayer Book Politics," *Studies in Bibliography and Booklore* 18 (1993), 15-26.

128

After Yiṣḥaq's death, his dynasty looses its importance and a new family, *Aǧa*, comes to the fore. The first Karaite leader who got the noble title *Aǧa* and gave it to his posterity was *Mardochaj-Ben-Berach* (other variants *Ben-Beach, Ben-Berech*) (*i.e.* Mordekhai Ben-Berakhah), who was the master of the Khan's mint during the reign of *Kajlan Girej*.[374] Among other important deeds, Mordekhai Ben-Berakhah invited a famous Karaite scholar *Mardochaj-Ben-Nisan* (*i.e.* Mordekhai Ben-Nisan of Kokizov [Krasny Ostrów]) to publish his book in the Crimea. Alas, on his way there, Mordekhai Ben-Nisan was killed by the Talmudists of *Halicz*, who bitterly hated him. However, his book was later published in Çufut-Qalé under the title "Ma'amar-Mordekhai."[375] Mordekhai Ben-Berakhah died on the island of Samos on his way to Jerusalem; as a consequence every Karaite going to the Holy city had to visit his tomb.[376]

During the time of his successor, Shemu'el Aǧa, the morality of the Karaites started to deteriorate. In order to improve the situation, Shemu'el Aǧa, who also was a master of the Khan's mint, brought in many Karaite scholars from abroad (among them *Symche Izaak* of Luck[377]). In spite of a general respect and veneration in his community, Shemu'el Aǧa very soon earned the envy of two rivals, *Szomolak Aǧa* and *Dawid Aǧa*. These two organized his assassination and, in about 1768, Shemu'el Aǧa was shot dead on the way to Çufut-Qalé.

---

[374] In the Crimea and Ottoman Turkey, the title *Aǧa* (Turk."elder brother") was used as a designation for important military and civil servants; in the Crimea, it was also the title of the khans' vizirs, *Qalga* and *Nüreddin*. In the opinion of P.Miller, the Karaite leaders who had the title *Aǧa* were the scions of the Çelebi-Sinani family (Miller, *Separatism*, 10). *Kajlan Girej* is the Crimean khan Qaplan Giray I, well remembered by the Karaites because of the fact that the printing press was established in Çufut-Qalé during his third rule (1730-1736).

[375] Mordekhai Ben-Nisan of Kokizow is one of the most authoritative Karaite scholars of the seventeenth/eighteenth centuries, the author of the books "Dod Mordekhai," "Ma'amar Mordekhai" and many other works and treatises. Mordekhai's works were never published in Çufut-Qalé. It is very interesting that Mordekhai, together with his son, was indeed killed on his way from Halicz to the Crimea after 1709; the exact place and time of his murder, as well as the place of his grave, remain unknown. See below and Mann, *Texts*, 588-589, 1265-1266, 1274.

[376] The very interesting and influential Karaite figure, Mordekhai Ben- Berakhah, who invited Simḥah Yiṣḥaq of Luck to the Crimea, and supplied him with students and a *beit-midrash*, indeed died on Sakız Adası (island of Chios), not Samos, on his return trip from the Holy Land in 1757. The Crimean khan who was there at that time ordered that Mordekhai's funeral be very dignified. See more on Mordekhai Ben-Berakhah in Mann, *Texts*, 335, 750.

[377] Simḥah Yiṣḥaq Ben-Mosheh Lucki (d.1766) was one of the most famous Karaite scholars, who moved to the Crimea at the request of Mordekhai Ben- Berakhah (not of Shemu'el Aǧa as the legend has it!) in 1751 (Mann, *Texts*, 335, 750).

However, his murderer, Dawid Ağa, did not enjoy his victim's office for a long time, and was soon displaced by *Binyamin Ağa*.[378]

Wł.Syrokomla (L.Kondratowicz) also documented a number of romantic stories and legends about the Karaites and their outstanding persons, which were narrated to him by A.Firkovich in Vilna, in 1854. Firkovich told tales about Karaite knights who – every morning, after prayer in the synagogue – proudly rode to the Troki castle to serve as armed guards of Grand Duke Vitold. In spite of his blind belief in everything that was said by Firkovich, Syrokomla was rather skeptical about this story, and considered it a legend.[379] Of interest also is the story about the seventeenth century Karaite knight Natan. Having been sent with an embassy to the Crimean Khanate, on the way back Natan met a gang of robbers. In the fight he cut off an ear of their leader, acquired his respect, and was even awarded for his military courage.[380] In addition, Firkovich mentioned some other half-legendary Karaite figures such as the standard-bearer squire (*chorąży*) Nisan Jozefowicz, and the physician at the Radziwill court, Jezza Nizanowicz (1595-1666).[381]

---

[378] The story about the assasination of Shemu'el Ağa, which was told by his wife *Giulus* (*i.e.* Gülüş), is especially lenghty and detailed. Gülüsh-tota, as the wise leader of the Karaite community who saved Çufut-Qalé from its enemies, is mentioned in another Karaite legend. See "Gulush-tota" in A. Szyszman, *Legendy i predaniya karaimov* (1932-1944), MS LLAS, f.143 (S.Szapszal's collection): 1531, 6v-8v. Shemu'el Ağa or Shemu'el Ben-Avraham Ben-Yoshiyah Yerushalmi (1716-1769) was the financial advisor to the khan; in 1768 he was appointed master of the mint [see *Sbornik*, 104-105] and in 1769 was killed in the ravine close to Çufut-Qalé (later called *Qanlı Dere* ["Valley of Blood"] in commemoration of the event; according to S.Beim, "inhabitants of Çufut-Qalé could not enter the town through this place without fear". (Beim, *Pamiat'*, 46). Binyamin Ben- Shemu'el Ağa (d.1824) was his son, who served as financial advisor and mint-master to the last Crimean Khan, Shahin Giray. *Symche Izaak* is Simḥah Yiṣḥaq Ben-Mosheh Lucki (d.1766), a famous Karaite scholar, who moved to Çufut-Qalé from Luck in 1751.

[379] Syrokomla, *Wycieczki*, 73.

[380] Syrokomla, *Wycieczki*, 82. A very similar folk-tale in the Karaite language tells about the Karaite soldier Alankasar who served Vatat-biy (Vitold): *Karaimsko-russko-pol'skii slovar'* [Karaite-Russian-Polish dictionary] (Moscow, 1974), 685-687. There are, however, many reasons to suppose that the editor of this dictionary, Seraya Szapszal, made up this folk-tale, taking Firkovich's story and its later Szyszman-version as the basis. See A. Szyszman, "Gonec velikogo kniazia," in his *Legendy i predaniia karaimov*, 1932-1944, MS department of LLAS, f.143 (S.Szapszal's collection), s.1531, 31-37 (v).

[381] The figure of *Jezza Nizanowicz* (a corruption of 'Ezra Ben-Nisan) seems to be especially important for Firkovich. Firkovich showed to Syrokomla 'Ezra Ben-Nisan's medical books and private diary in Hebrew (Syrokomla, *Wycieczki*, 84). In the opinion of M.Balaban, the tombstone inscription upon 'Ezra Ben-Nisan's grave, published by Firkovich in *Avnei Zikkaron* (p.251) looks very suspicious (Balaban, "Karaici," 86, ft.2). The text of the inscription on the grave of 'Ezra Ben-Nisan,

To conclude with, we should mention that, in the twentieth century, with the transformation of Karaite ethnic self-identification, instead of preserving their genuine ancient legends and folklore, Karaite authors preferred to "invent" a folk-past that would prove their alleged links to the Turkic people, or praise their non-existing military valor.[382] Thus, the legends and oral traditions documented by travelers are one of the few, quite rare sources which have preserved genuine samples of pre-ideological Karaite folklore.

3.4. Everyday life.

Travel accounts often contain much valuable information concerning the details of everyday life. Travelers frequently mentioned that in manners, customs, language, cuisine, and traditional dress the Karaites resembled their Muslim neighbours, the Crimean Tatars.[383] This seeming affinity with Muslims rarely deceived the voyagers: practically all of them considered the Karaites a part of Jewish people, who differed from the more numerous Rabbanite Jews only in religious and everyday matters.

3.4.1. Professions.

According to the travelers' data, most of the professions of the Crimean Karaites were traditionally Jewish. They were tanners, merchants, jewelers, and other petty craftsmen. Legal documents, however, are full of references regarding the involvement of the Karaites in such branches of agriculture as bee keeping, farming, horticulture, and viticulture.[384]

Tanning hides was especially developed in the territory of Mangoup. According to Evliya Çelebi, there were eighty shops of tanners in the territory of Mangoup. The Karaites of this town were renowned for producing "thick Mangoubian leather."[385] The French traveler de Peyssonel, mentioned that Mangoup was famous for its

---

however, which was seen by me in the Troki cemetery in December, 2000, exactly corresponds with the text supplied by A.Firkovich [see more on 'Ezra b.Nisan in §2.2].

[382] *E.g.* A. Szyszman, *Legendy i predaniia karaimov*, 1932-1944, MS department of LLAS, f.143-153; *Legendy i predaniia karaev*; Lebedeva, *Ocherki*, 12-16; Fuki, *Karaimy*, 12-18.

[383] See *e.g.* J.Kohl: "[the] life of the Karaites, in constant contact with the Mohammedans... left an imprint on their present day development, and gave them not only their language, appearance and spiritual state, but also dress, kitchen, and way of life... in everything, both in their mores and way of life, there is a mixture of Tatar and Jewish..." (Kohl, *Reisen*, vol.2, 258, 260).

[384] Gertsen, Mogarichev, *Krepost'*, 98.

[385] Evliya Çelebi, *Kniga*, 90.

woollen and leather manufacture.[386] The weaving of wool and tanning of hides were traditional industries of the Byzantine Karaites as well.[387] At the time of Pallas' travel (1793-1794), Mangoup was already abandoned. He mentioned that "the Jewish curriers of Dshufut-Kale" still visited the forsaken settlement during the summer in order to dress their hides with tan extracted from the local plants.[388] Numerous stone baths used for this purpose can still be seen in Tabana-Dere.[389]

A.Nowosielski noted that in maritime towns (Odessa, Evpatoria), the Karaites, together with the Greeks, worked as wagoners and ferrymen. He also mentioned that some of them were involved in farming, viticulture, and sheep-breeding.[390]

However, practically all travel accounts agree that the most widespread branch of Karaite professional activity was involvement in trade and arts. Many travelers of the nineteenth century remarked on the prosperity and wealth enjoyed by the Karaites because of their diligent work in trade and manufacture. The Karaites of Gözlöw (Evpatoria) were especially influential and rich. Anatoli Demidov mentioned that they "form the elite of the population of Koslof."[391] Mary Holderness wrote that the Karaites of Gözlöw were called *Million Tcheks* (a corruption of a Russian *Millionschick*, i.e. "a millionaire").[392] Simḥah Babovich's family was often referred to in the travel accounts as the richest, and most influential family in Gözlöw.[393] Most of the travelers mentioned that the Karaites were well known as

---

[386] Peyssonel, *Traite*, vol.1, 25, 118.

[387] Ankori, *Karaites*, 174-178.

[388] These plants were *Rhus Coriaria* [Tanners' Sumac] and *Rhus Cotinus* [Venice Sumac or False Fringe Tree]; moreover, in the traveler's opinion, even the water afforded by Mangoup was good for leather-processing: Pallas, *Travels*, 122; the same; *Bemerkungen*, 122.

[389] Crimean historian V.Ch.Kondaraki counted about ten baths for tanning, situated in the upper part of the Tabana dere (V.Ch.Kondaraki, 'Mangup-Kale," *ZOOID* 8 (1872): 421). [ed. In Russian scholarship starting from the mid-nineteenth century the toponym Tabana Dere is usually translated as "Kozhevennyj ovrag" ("Valley of Hides" or "Valley of Tanners"). The problem with this is that while "Taban" means "sole of a foot" or "foundation of a wall", "Tabana" means "directly opposite". It is a variant (due to Ottoman influence) of Tabanga, which is the dative case of Taban [literally "to the sole"], which is short for "taban tabana" [diametrically opposed, literally "sole to sole" or "foundation to foundation"]. If "Valley of sole leather" were meant it would be "Tabannıng deresi" or even in an abbreviated form "Taban deresi" or "Taban dere", not "Tabana dere".]

[390] Nowosielski, *Stepy*, 44-45.

[391] Demidov, *Travels*, 156; the same, *Voyage*, vol.1, 477.

[392] Mary Holderness, *Journey from Riga to the Crimea* (London, 1827), 178.

[393] Nowosielski, *Stepy*, 35-36; the letter of Rzewuski in Szapszal, "Adam Mickiewicz," 5-8.

wealthy, influential merchants: "the trade of the whole Crimea is concentrated in the hands of the Karaites. Their excellent knowledge of the region, their capital and diligence are the reasons for this; nobody is able to trade here without their help."[394] N.Berg also highly esteemed the trading activity of the Karaites, considering them "real merchants": "they are much more enterprising than their teachers (*i.e.* Tatars) and far much smarter them in the trade. The best shops in Bakhçeseray belong to the Karaites..." [395]

Especially peculiar was the position of the Karaite merchants of Çufut-Qalé: because of the fact that they had a number of shops in Bakhçeseray , the capital of the Crimean Khanate, the merchants had to descend from Çufut-Qalé in the morning and return back in the evening (around a 1-1.2 mile journey). K.Kaczkowski, for example, wrote: "During the daytime only women and a few men remain in the town; in the beginning of the day everybody descends to *Bakczyseraj* where they (*i.e.* the Karaites) have their shops." He also added that in Bakhçeseray "the Karaites held the biggest trade in their hand".[396] From other travel accounts, we know that the Karaites were also known as leather workers, goldsmiths and jewelers.[397]

It seems in earlier periods, especially in the sixteenth – seventeenth centuries, that the Karaites actively participated in the slave trade, sometimes buying them for their own use, sometimes acting as mediators between the Tatars and representatives of the countries who wanted to redeem their countrymen from Tatar captivity.

The Turkish defter (register) of the Kaffa Eyalet [Kaffa Eyalet' in Vergi Defteri] (1542) mentions six females who were slaves (*esirler*) belonging to the members of the Karaite community of Kaffa: Esir-i-Şalom Aslan, marya rus; Esir-i-İşḥaq nam, marya; Esir-i-Ğan-Gıray, marya rus; Esir-i-Muşi Kızı, marya; Esir-i-Muşi, marya; Esir-i-İşḥaq, marya, rus Ulyana.[398] A seventeenth century archival document

---

[394] Nowosielski, *Stepy*, 43. Such a statement was not an exaggeration: according to some estimates, before World War I, about 40% of the tobacco trade in Russia was concentrated in the hands of Karaite merchants (Lebedeva, *Ocherki*, 28).

[395] Berg, Nicholas. *Bakhchisaray*. N.p., 1856, 7.

[396] Kaczkowski, *Dziennik*, 92, 130.

[397] Demidov, *Voyage*, vol.1, 475; Pallas, *Bemerkungen*, 122; the same, *Travels*, 122.

[398] Oleksander Halenko, "Iudeiski gromady Osmanskoi Kefy seredyny XVI st" [Jewish Communities of the Ottoman Kaffa in the mid-Sixteenth century], *Skhodoznavstvo* 3-4 (1998), 59. According to their names and other details, these female slaves were of Slavic origin, probably from Poland and Russia. Evliya Çelebi mentioned that in the Crimean Khanate female-slaves were usually called "difka" (a corruption of Polish "dziewica" or Russian "devka") and "maria" (probably because "Maria" was one of the most widespread names of these captives: Evliya Czelebi, *Ksiega*, 355,

mentioned that one of the Polish servants captured in the battle of Czudnow (1661) was kept in Çufut-Qalé. According to B.Baranowski he was "na Kale zaprzedany" ("sold to Qalé");[399] however, while quoting the text he slightly "emended" the document, which in fact says "u Żyda na Kale zaprzedany" ("sold to the Jew in Kale").[400] The text of the document suggests that this Jew (most likely, a Karaite) was keeping the Pole for domestic purposes. Russian ambassadors to the Crimea, Stepan Tarbeev and Ivan Basov (1628) were informed that Canı Beğü Giray had to gather Turkish captives ("turskikh liudey") from the Tatar nobility and the Jews (perhaps, the Karaites) in order to return them to Turkey.[401] Other sources mention that the Jewish population of the Crimean Khanate (without specifying whether it was Karaite or Rabbanite) bought slaves and prisoners. [402]

3.4.2. Traditional dress.

An ancient Near Eastern proverb, appearing also in post-Biblical Aramaic and Hebrew, says "Waste on your back and save on your belly," which means "spend on your food and drink less than you are able to do, but on your clothing and outer wear spend as much as you can."[403] In mediæval and early modern times, the symbolic significance of a costume was much more important than it is today. Representatives of certain professions would recognize each other by their dress. Some ethnic or marginal groups also wore (or were

ft.454; Evliya Çelebi, *Kniga*, 172-173, ft.441).

[399] Bohdan Baranowski, "Dzieje jasyru na Gródku karaimskim," *MK* s.n. 2 (1947): 49. It worth mentioning that the author did not indicate the title and page of the document (on purpose?); as a consequence, it was rather hard to find the place quoted by him.

[400] AGAD AKW Dz.Tatarskie, k.60, t.117, nr122. List W.Szmelinga, posla na Krym, do Jana Kazimierza króla Polskiego, s.7. In our opinion, this "emendation" of the text could have been done either by Baranowski himself or by one of the Karaite editors of *MK*, most likely by S.Szapszal.

[401] "Is istorii snosheniy Moskvy s Krymom pri tsare Mikhaile Feodoroviche" [From the history of the diplomatic relations between Moscow and the Crimea at the time of the Tsar Mikhail Feodorovich] in *ITUAK* 39 (1906): 72.

[402] One of the Dominican friars, Giovanni da Lucca (around 1630), mentioned that, in the Tatar towns of the Crimea, "there are always slaves to be sold. The Turks, Arabs, Jews, Armenians, and Greeks often buy them..." (Lucca, "Fatta da me," 55; Lucca, "Opisanie," 482). Pierre Chevalier in his "Histoire de la Guerre des Cosaques contre la Pologne" (1663) wrote that the Tatars used to sell their captives to Christian and Jewish merchants of Kaffa. As payment for the captives, the Tatars usually received Turkish horses, weapons, clothes and some other goods (Pierre Chevalier, *Istoriia viini kozakiv proty Polshchi* [The history of the war of the Cossacks against Poland], transl. Yu.I.Nazarenko (Kiev 1993), 60-61).

[403] See mediæval Karaite and Jewish documents in S.D.Goitein, *A Mediterranean Society*. Vol. 4: *Daily Life* (Berkeley-London), 150-200.

sometimes forced to wear) specific garments or signs. For the Jews, costume was not a fashion, but, rather, a reflection of their moral and religious principles.[404]

Travelers left so many detailed references to this important aspect of everyday Karaite life that it would be enough to compare the data from travel accounts with nineteenth century drawings and materials from ethnographic collections to reconstruct traditional Karaite dress.[405] The most common remark made by the travelers was that the costume of the Crimean Tatars and the Karaites was quite similar. However, having mentioned this fact, travelers often described what was specific to traditional Karaite costume.

What the travelers usually singled out was the Karaite head-dress, which was a traditional Turkic-style hat. Evliya Çelebi, when describing the Karaite community of Mangoup, wrote that the local Karaites, unlike all other Jews, did not wear hats, but dark, lilac colored Tatar caps made from a thick, woolen fabric. In his opinion, a similar kind of cap called a *shapartma* was worn by all *kafirs* (*i.e.* non-Muslim subjects including the Karaites) of Qarasubazar. However, the Karaites, in order to be distinguished from other nations inhabiting the town, sewed a badge in the form of a piece of yellow fabric of the size of *kuruş* (a Turkish coin of a small denomination) to these head-gears.[406]

The same kind of Karaite cap was probably described by Edward Clarke: "a lofty thick felt cap, faced with wool: this is heavy, and keeps the head very hot.".[407] A slightly different type of headgear was worn by the patriarch of Çufut-Qalé, Avraham Firkovich: "something between the turban of Shamil and a mitre of the Biblical high priests."[408]

According to the observation of A.Nowosielski, the Karaites "dress themselves in the Tatar fashion and live like the Tatars; their dress usually consists of a long robe made of a light silky cloth, which

---

[404] See in general Abrahams, *Jewish Life*, 273-290.

[405] Cf. also Seraya Szapszal's detailed description of the Karaite dress in his "Nauchnyi obzor predmetov material'noy kultury khraniashtchikhsia v karaismkom otdele Istoriko-Etnograficheskogo Muzeya AN Litovskoy SSR" [Scientific review of the objects of material culture housed in the Karaite department of the Museum of History and Ethnography, Academy of Sciences of the Lithuanian SSR], kept in MS LLAS, F.143-859: 20-22.

[406] Evliya Çelebi, *Kniga*, 90-91, 131-132. On the origin and symbolic significance of the Jewish badge see Abrahams, *Jewish Life*, 291-306.

[407] Clarke, *Travels*, 194. One can compare travelers' descriptions with the drawings by Raffet.

[408] My translation from Evgeni Markov, *Ocherki*, 456. cf. the drawing depicting this scholar in illustrations.

is girded with a belt, and a wide cloth garment with wide sleeves, which is worn above... *Krymka* made of sheepskin is worn on the head. Old people wear beards, whereas young ones are shaved."[409] K.Kaczkowski left a similar description of Karaite dress:

> The dress of the Karaites is quite decent and to a great extent similar to the Turkish one: a wide striped gown with short sleeves constitutes the upper dress, under which is worn a striped gown with long sleeves; *kolpack* [qalpaq], which is worn on the head, is usually made of black sheepskin, and is peculiar only to the Karaites.[410]

Nevertheless, A.Nowosielski noted that the younger generation of Karaites, especially those in large cities, preferred wearing European dress.[411] J.Kohl also noticed that, in Odessa, the Karaites started to exchange their "Tatar Kalpak" [qalpaq] for European headgear.[412]

Andrew Neilson described the Karaite costume in the following way: "Their dress consists of a kaftan, or long, loose surtout, confined round the waist by a colored silk sash and a fur cap, which is exchanged when in the house for one made of silk, fitting close to the head."[413] According to A.Demidov, the Karaites of Qarasubazar paid great attention to their outer appearance. Specifically, he noted how they kept their beards, and wore massive, precious finger-rings.[414]

A comparative analysis of the travelers' descriptions distinguishes several main parts of the traditional Karaite dress of the end of the eighteenth/first half of the nineteenth centuries:

1. Long, Oriental gowns with extended sleeves [gömläk/kölmek, entarı, or qaftan], usually of dark color (sometimes striped), girded by a sash [quşaq, belbağı, or inçkir]; over this long-sleeved gown, another gown, with short sleeves [yelek; the

---

[409] Nowosielski, *Stepy*, 195. E.Clarke (1801) noticed that the Karaites, as well as the Tatars, "suffer their beards to grow" (Clarke, *Travels*, 194). J.Kohl (1838) mentioned that the Karaites had very peculiar beards, which were almost entirely shaved at whiskers and allowed to grow at the full length on a chin: Kohl, *Reisen*, vol.2, 262-263.

[410] Kaczkowski, *Dziennik*, 40.

[411] However, even such Europeanized Karaites wore *krymka* which would differentiate them from other people: Nowosielski, *Stepy*, 195.

[412] Kohl, *Reisen*, vol.2, 261.

[413] Neilson, *Crimea*, 65.

[414] Demidov, *Voyage*, vol.1, 499. Undoubtedly, these finger-rings were of the same type as the famous, misterious finger-ring of A.S.Pushkin, which was supposedly of Karaite origin [see more details in §2.4.4].

136

wide long-sleeved robe was called cübbe (jübbe)] (the travelers, usually unfamiliar with Oriental terminology, called them "sarafan", "kaftan", or "surtout").

2. Hats of two types: "kalpak" [qalpaq] and "krymka" (a Russian word) (both made of sheepskin). These hats served as distinguishing signs for the Karaites, and continued to be worn in practically all Karaite families (even in the most Europeanized) of the nineteenth century.

3. Footwear, which consisted of Oriental slippers [papuçlar], shoes [ayaqqabılar], and boots [etikler, çedikler, mestler, or çizmeler].[415]

4. Massive finger-rings [yüzükler] (perhaps, to show off their wealth and status).

As has been mentioned, the travelers paid special attention to the description of Karaite women; this is why we have several detailed descriptions of women's traditional dress.[416]

The most detailed description of the female dress was left by J.Kohl (1838). Kohl noticed that, on the streets, the Karaite women were usually covered by European shawls, which were taken off only at the entrance to the synagogue "to show the radiance of the pair of beautiful eyes, as well as the shining of gold and pearls". On their heads, the Karaite women wore "*fez* [*Fetz*; small hats still worn in Turkey] embroidered with gold and decorated with pearls, with ancient Hebrew letters on the sides... which were phrases from the Bible". Married women plaited their hair in one plait and hid it under the *Fetz*, whereas unmarried Karaites used to braid their hair into numerous plaits: Kohl counted from forty to fifty plaits. He was particularly struck by a Karaite woman who had four daughters (which was quite common at that time), and had to plait about 200 plaits.[417]

---

[415] This is according to J.Kohl who had seen the Karaite footwear, which was left at the entrance to the Odessa Karaite synagogue (Kohl, *Reisen*, vol.2, 265).

[416] Demidov, *Voyage*, vol.1, 369-370; the same, *Travels*, 34-36. The travel account of Anatoli Demidov provides an opportunity to reconstruct the costume of the Karaite women: the traveler not only scrupulously described their garments, but also placed a drawing in his book portraying the Karaite women. See also Lyall, *Travels*, 274; Nowosielski, *Stepy*, 47-48; Haxthausen, *Studien*, 390-391.

[417] According to twentieth century Karaite authors, the Karaites believed that a pious Karaite maiden, in case of dangerous situation, would be saved by angels, who would lift her by her plaits in the air and take her out of trouble (N.M Sultan Girej, "Kartki z kroniki eupatoryjskiej rodziny," *Awazymyz* 1 (4) (2000): 15). Plaits indeed were worn only by unmarried Karaite maidens, and were unplaited on the wedding day (Tadeusz Kowalski, "Pieśni obrzędowe w narzeczu Karaimów z Trok," *Rocznik Orientalistyczny* III (1925): 227, 243). According to Solomon Beim, the most

Kohl continues with a description of married women's dress:

> All matrons are usually dressed in gorgeous garments. The underskirt... consists of a purple-red material, embroidered with gold, over which is worn wide and long dress that reaches the floor... usually of lilac color. This dress is without buttons, and allows [one]... to see the radiance and shining of the underclothing.

Kohl remarked that in this lower dress was concentrated "all the wealth and radiance of the beautiful Karaite ladies." He also mentioned that the Karaite women used to wear several rows of necklaces. These necklaces usually consisted of golden and silver coins. Small Turkish coins were found at the bottom, then larger ducats from Holland, and finally massive Spanish doubloons so that "their breast was so densely and thoroughly covered by this golden decoration, it was as if it was a real armor". To complete the picture, a necklace of pearls was usually worn on the top.[418]

Another interesting description has been left by Edmund Spenser (1836), who concentrated his attention mostly on the Karaite jewelry:

> ...her head-dress, composed of a sort of turban embroidered with gold, from which a chain of pearls was suspended across her forehead... A purple velvet jacket, over a white silk dress, embroidered with gold... a massive gold chain, of the most exquisite workmanship, several times encircled her neck; while bracelets of the same material, enriched with precious stones, superb earrings, and a multitude of rings on her fingers, completed her costume...[419]

---

specific sign that differentiated a married Crimean Karaite woman from unmarried were special earlocks, called in Crimean Tatar "*zuluf*" (Beim, *Pamiat'*, 70-71).

[418] Kohl, *Reisen*, vol.2, 263-264. In the private collection of the Çoref [= Hebrew Şoref, "gold smith"] family (Bakhçesaray) I saw several examples of the coins that were worn as decorations by Karaite women; of interest is the fact that Çufut-Qalé Karaites themselves sometimes struck imitations of Turkish coins to be worn on such necklaces (the author is greatful to the Karaite Çoref family, especially to M.M.Çoref, the son of the late M.Y.Çoref, the well-known Crimean historian and collector, for showing him these imitations, and explaining their usage). Acording to Solomon Beim, precious golden coins, worn by the Karaite women as decorations, often saved the family in the time of famine or other difficult circumstances (Beim, *Pamiat'*, 67-68).

[419] Edmund Spenser, *Travels in Circassia, Krim-Tartary*, pt.1 (London, 1839), 220. As well as A.Nowosielski, the traveler met a pretty Karaite woman whose dress he is

A comparative analysis of the travelers' descriptions distinguishes several main parts of the traditional dress of the Crimean Karaite women of the end of the eighteenth/first half of the nineteenth centuries:

1. A long dress, often ornamented. The travelers disagreed concerning its form. Demidov considered it perfectly fit, whereas Lyall found it loose and baggy.[420]
2. Long silk mantles that almost entirely covered a short petticoat worn over cloth trousers. In rich families the women wore small satin coats embroidered with gold.
3. For a head covering, young maidens wore small hats, somewhat similar to a *fez*. Married and adult women wore silky shawls, tied like turbans. Outside of the house, women usually wore veils, which served a function similar to those of the veils [*yaşmaqlar*] of the Crimean Tatar, Arab, and Turkish women.[421]
4. A wide leather belt with a large ornamented buckle of bronze or silver, which was worn a bit lower than waist level.
5. Necklaces with golden objects, coins, and pearls.[422]

---

describing on the steam-boat going from Odessa to the Crimea.

[420] Demidov, *Voyage*, vol.1, 369-370; the same, *Travels*, 34-36; Lyall, *Travels*, 274;

[421] A most detailed description of Karaite women's head gear was left in A.Afanasyev-Chuzhbinskiy, *Poezdka v Yuzhnuyu Rossiyu* [Travel to Southern Russia] (St.Petersburg, 1863), 322.

[422] The only thing that is absent from this list is their footwear. Unfortunately, none of the travelers supplied information on this. However, one can see slippers/papuche worn by the women in the drawings of Raffet [see illustration].

*The drawing by Auguste Raffet (1837) depicting a Karaite woman
with two children and a servant (?).*

Johann Kohl was, probably, the only traveler, who devoted
some of his time to socializing with Karaite children. He noticed a lack
of difference in the dress of Karaite boys and girls, and described the
garments of "der kleine Mangub" [German "small Mangub"], a son of
one of the richest Karaite merchants of Odessa, whom he met at the
entrance to the local synagogue:

> The Karaite dress, as shown to me by a small Mangubi was
> the following: a silky mantle, which represented something
> similar to our shirt, and was called 'Kuelmek'
> [kölmek/gömlek], trousers, also regularly made of silk, called
> 'Kontschak' [qonçaq] or 'Schalwar' [şalvar]. A long folded
> drapery, buttoned only above the breast, with a number of
> small, silver buttonhooks, was pulled over *shalvar* and
> *kuelmek*, and above it 'Ton', which was girdled in the middle
> of a body by a 'Kuschak' [quşaq] (a belt). Another dress, a

140

short furry waistcoat called 'Dschubae' was usually worn above this upper dress".[423] Kohl also mentioned children's slippers/papuçlar ("Babuschen").[424]

3.4.3. Houses.

"Karaite dwellings [resemble] eagles' nests, on the top of the high, inaccessible mountain."
(Muraviev-Apostol, Puteshestvie, 127)

According to an ancient Hebrew saying, three things set a man at ease: a beautiful home, a comely wife, and fine clothing. Notably, the home comes first, because a man should build a house before taking a wife.[425] This proverb illustrates the importance of homes in Jewish life. An important part of understanding the Karaim, then, is understanding their domestic architecture.

According to A.G.Gertsen, Karaite domestic architecture is very similar to the architecture of the so-called "Tatar houses," which was common in the Crimea from the late Middle Ages.[426] Almost all travelers mentioned that Karaite houses were generally built in *"manière Tartare."* Some of them described the inner appearance of Karaite dwellings, which was Oriental and also very similar to the Tatar abodes.

A very early description of Karaite homes was left by Evliya Çelebi. When visiting the Karaite community of Mangoup, which was in decline at that time, Çelebi saw numerous "misfortunate, dirty, and neglected" Karaite houses. Evliya found the houses of the Çufut-Qalé Karaites, however, "beautiful and splendid... with roof-tiles, in a good state".[427] I.M.Muraviev-Apostol poetically wrote, in the nineteenth century, that Çufut-Qalé looks like "airy town" with "Karaite dwellings resembling eagles' nests, on the top of the high, inaccessible mountain."[428]

Edward Clarke described the house of a *"principal Jew"* of Çufut-Qalé (*i.e.* probably, of Binyamin Ben-Shemu'el Ağa). It was divided into two parts: the women's quarters, and those of the master of the family. The master of the house also had his private room, which

---

[423] The photo of one of such "Dschubae" was published in Zajaczkowski, *Karaims*, 57.
[424] Kohl, *Reisen*, vol.2, 262.
[425] Goitein, *Mediterranean Society*, 47.
[426] Gertsen, Mogarichev, *Krepost'*, 88.
[427] Evliya Çelebi, *Kniga*, 90, 93.
[428] Muraviev-Apostol, *Puteshestvie*, 127.

was intended for smoking, reading, sleeping, and receiving guests.[429] A similar description of the house of Binyamin Ben-Shemu'el Ağa was left by Ebenezer Henderson, who was impressed by Ağa's oriental carpets, which covered a "guest chamber or upper-room" (*i.e.* the chambers of the master of the family).[430] Anatoli Demidov, who probably visited the same house, was honored with the exclusive and rare opportunity to visit the women's quarters.[431] Pojata who, in 1871, took a walk on the streets of the practically abandoned Çufut-Qalé, mentioned that the houses of the town were mostly one or two stories, with bars and decorated windows.[432] D.B. mentioned that there was no glass in the windows of the Karaite houses, but wooden bars.[433] N.Zhukov – deceived by the seeming primitiveness of the houses of Çufut-Qalé, hanging "on the slopes like birds' nests" – was equally astonished to find their gorgeous oriental interiors.[434] O.Shishkina praised the beauty of the house of S.Beim, which was arranged "in the Tatar style, with gilded stars placed on the ceiling".[435]

J.Kohl wrote that the houses of the Çufut-Qalé Karaites are "small, low, without windows, with flat roofs, all of them, without exception, made of large blocks of stone". When visiting the estate of the wealthy and loquacious Karaite "Tschausch Awram",[436] Kohl mentioned its considerable size, and beautiful wooden balcony. The traveler also wrote about the contrast between the houses of wealthy Karaites and those of poor ones, which usually looked like "heaps of piled stones".[437]

A.Nowosielski described the magnificent view of the beautiful house of "Kozlov [Gözlöw] aristocrat", Simḥah Babovich, which he termed an "architectonic miracle"; this dwelling represented a mixture of European and Oriental traditions.[438] August von Haxthausen noticed, in 1843, the introduction of European elements in the rich Karaite houses of Feodosia: "We were conducted into papered

---

[429] Clarke, *Travels*, 191.
[430] Henderson, *Researches*, 309-310.
[431] Demidov, *Voyage*, vol.1, 369-370; the same, *Travels*, 34-36.
[432] Pojata [H.Skirmuntowa], "Szkice z Krymu," *Tygodnik Ilustrowany* 8: 201 (1871): 220.
[433] D.B., "Otryvok," 51.
[434] N.Zhukov, "Zametki v puti na yuzhnyi bereg Kryma" , 284.
[435] Shishkina, *Zametki*, 110.
[436] It is possible to identify this "Tschausch Awram", whom Haxthausen met on the streets of Çufut-Qalé in 1843, with Çavuş Avraham Ben-No'aḥ HaKohen, who lived in Çufut-Qalé and subscribed to A.Firkovich's "Massa' UMerivah" in 1838 (a word of thanks goes to Golda Akhiezer for her help with this).
[437] Kohl, *Reisen*, vol.1, 236, 238.
[438] Nowosielski, *Stepy*, 25.

rooms, furnished with a sofa, mirrors, a writing-table, and modern tables and chairs."[439]

Some travelers rebuked the oriental "egoism" and isolated character of the Karaite houses. Their grim walls without any windows reminded K.Kaczkowski of "mad-houses."[440] N.Berg left a description of the hearths-*tandurlar*, which were obligatory in every Karaite house: "Instead of fireplaces... they often have tandurs, a kind of underground hearth, which are stoked and closed as well as those of ours." According to S.Beim, these *tandurs* had been used not only for heating, but also for baking bread.[441] In general, Berg retained a rather unpleasant impression from visiting the Karaite houses of Bakhçeseray : "They [the Karaites] live very dirty, not much cleaner that the Tatars. If one says 'Asia', so Asia it must be."[442]

These travelers' descriptions can be supplemented by the comments of S.Szapszal who, at the end of the nineteenth century, described the houses of Çufut-Qalé: "... with two small balconies and windows directed to the inner yard, predominantly consisting of two stories; a master usually lived on the first floor, whereas the ground floor was used as stables... The houses were heated by means of primitive hearths/tandurs, which usually stood in the soil in the middle of the rooms..." [443]

The results of archæological excavations in the territories of Mangoup and Çufut-Qalé have shown that caves, which are very numerous there, were used as the basements for houses. Evliya Çelebi, however, remarked that the poorest layers of the Karaite population of Çufut-Qalé lived in the caves situated near the southern gate of the settlement [see map §4.1]. A.Berthier-Delagarde, in the beginning of the twentieth century, had a conversation with an old Karaite who showed him a cave where he, together with his family, had lived some forty years ago.[444]

Thus, the travelers' descriptions suggest the following: Karaite houses, which were usually divided into two main parts, looked quite different depending on the wealth and status of their

---

[439] Haxthausen, *Studien*, 390-391.
[440] Kaczkowski, *Dziennik*, 38-40.
[441] Beim, *Pamiat'*, 46.
[442] Berg, *Bakhchisaray*, 19
[443] Szapszal, *Karaimy*, 21.
[444] A.Berthier-Delagarde, "Issledovanie nekotorykh nedoumennykh voprosov srednevekovia v Tavrike" [Investigation of some complicated questions of the Middle Ages of Taurica]. *ITUAK* 57 (1920): 120. In general, the usage of caves (as dwellings, burial and sacred places) was a common practice among the Jews dating from Biblical and early mediæval times: "Caves in Palestine," *EJ*, vol.3, 633-634.

owners. The poorest classes might have used caves as their living places. Rather modest from the outside, the houses of the Karaite aristocracy often much impressed the visitors by their exquisite and costly oriental interior. An especially beautiful and impressive aspect of these Karaite houses was the wooden decorations and ornaments made out of small pieces of wood (this type of marquetry is called *Khatam*).[445] The nineteenth century marked the introduction of European elements into the once ascetic design of Karaite dwellings. With the acculturation of the Karaites into the lay world of European culture, the late nineteenth/early twentieth century Karaite dwellings of Evpatoria and Feodosia were some of the most splendid and gorgeous buildings in these cities. Today, they are important administrative buildings, museums, and sanatoriums.

3.4.4. Traditional kitchen.

> *"Breakfast at the place of a Karaite. A pie and jam."*
> (V.A.Zhukovskiy, *Ballady. Nal' i Dayamanta* [Ballads. Nal' and
> Dayamanta] (Moscow, 1987), 252)

In academic literature, the Karaites are usually portrayed as much more rigorous in their dietary and purity laws than the Rabbanites.[446] They differed in regulations of ritual slaughter, regarding as prohibited the meat of animals slaughtered according to Rabbanite regulations. The Karaites only permit the consumption of the meat of those animals enumerated in the Torah. They do not recognize the criteria for permitted mammals and birds in the Talmud.[447] In contrast with the Rabbanites, however, Karaites permit the consumption of meat and milk.[448]

---

[445] A visitor to the Crimea still can see (if he is lucky enough to get inside) examples of such exquisite wooden decorations in the house of A.Firkovich (Çufut-Qalé) and Simḥah Babovich (Eupatoriia).

[446] [ed. In practice, the differences between Rabbanite and Karaite Jews stem from legal interpretation rather than a strictness or laxity on either party (*cf. note 448 below*).]

[447] See the writings of 'Anan Ben-Dawid and Dani'el al-Qumisi in Nemoy, *Karaite Anthology*, 16-17, 31-34.

[448] [ed. Generally, Karaite commentators conclude that there is no prohibition in the Torah against mixing meat and milk (outside of cooking a kid in its own mother's milk). Al-Qirqisani notes the origin of this prohibition as resulting from a pagan practice he observed in his days. So, the prohibition has more to do with *'avodah zarah* (idol worship and its practices), than purity laws and their dietary extensions. There is a small, relatively unknown opinion that one should not mix any mammal with its own mother's milk (its specific mother) – c.f. Aharon Ben-Eliyahu's *Keter*

As has been mentioned in §3.2.2., most of the Karaites would not eat in the company of a stranger. However, with genuinely oriental hospitality, many travelers were offered various kinds of confectionery, cold snacks, alcohol, and coffee. Edward Clarke was served with conserved rose petals, eggs, cheese, cold pies, and brandy; Ebenezer Henderson found on a guest table: bread, butter, dates, pears, mulberries, brandy, and wine. Anatoli Demidov tasted a profusion of light viands, cakes, preserves, coffee, and different sorts of wine.[449] S.Beim offered his visitors, A.Koshliakov and his companions, fruits, jams, and champagne.[450] The family of Russian emperor Nicholas I, who visited the house of a wealthy Çufut-Qalé Karaite Mangubi in 1837, "was offered a breakfast which, in accordance with oriental customs, consisted mostly of jam, sweets, and an Asiatic dish called "*gelvah* (halvah)", made of sugar, eggs, flour, and parts of honey."[451] Inserting in his welcoming speech "a hundred thanks and a thousand compliments" the wealthy and loquacious Tschausch Awram supplied J.Kohl and his colleagues with "*Confect Alwa*" (*i.e.* halvah), *Ragat al kum [rahat-luqum]*, and various liquors.[452] Avraham Firkovich served his guest, Evgeni Markov, coffee, and *galvah* (*i.e.* halvah).[453]

However, in many Europeanized Karaite families of the nineteenth century, the tradition of not eating together with strangers was abandoned. Thus, future Karaite *Ḥakham* Simḥah Babovich, in 1825, welcomed his Polish visitors, writer and journalist H.Rzewuski and poet A.Mickiewicz, with a lavish oriental dinner, which his guests found to be "delicious", either because of the "original beauty of his wife and daughters", or because of their "terrible hunger".[454] A.von Haxthausen, while having dinner at the house of Mordekhai Ben-

---

Torah. This interepretation, however, was based on a misunderstanding of the word *gedi* (which means a kid of a goat or sheep, which is differentiated from cattle in Hebrew). There is a custom, not law, that some people observe, which is late and likely comes from the Rabbanites, of avoiding the milk of any animal with the meat of the same type of animal unless you are 100% sure that the milk is not from mother of the animal being eaten.

[449] Clarke, *Travels*, 190; Henderson, *Researches*, 310; Demidov, *Voyage*, vol.1, 369; the same, *Travels*, 34.

[450] [A.Koshliakov], *Desiatidnevnaya poezdka*, 37-38. It seems that Beim strongly liked this European drink, which was popular among the Russian aristocrates of that time. See also Haxthausen, *Studien*, 401.

[451] Safonov, *Opisanie*, 21. See exact recipe for preparing of various kinds of *halvah* in E.I.Lebedeva, *Retsepty karaimskoy kukhni* [Recipes from Karaite Cuisine] (Simferopol', 1992), 223-225.

[452] Kohl, *Reisen*, vol.1, 238.

[453] Markov, *Ocherki*, 461.

[454] Szapszal, "Adam Mickiewicz", 9-10.

Mosheh – together with its owner, a rich Karaite merchant of Feodosia – was especially impressed by the "thick white honey" and a "jam made of rose petals".[455]

Edward Clarke was surprized to see vine-leaves sold on the streets of Çufut-Qalé. Soon, he found an explanation for this fact. He was informed that they were widely used in the Crimea for producing a special dish: "Minced meat is rolled up in vine-leaves, and is sent to the table in the form of sausages".[456] This local speciality was also tasted by Robert Lyall: "... balls of minced mutton rolled up in vine leaves".[457]

Varied and rich traditions of Karaite oriental cuisine are still preserved in many Karaite families in Eastern Europe. Many Karaite and non-Karaite authors, however, complain that the traditional kitchen is, unfortunately, perhaps, the only ancient tradition that has been preserved by East European Karaites in its entirety.[458]

---

[455] Haxthausen, *Studien*, 391.

[456] Clarke, *Travels*, 194.

[457] Lyall, *Travels*, 271. See exact recipe for this dish, called by the Karaite author, E.I.Lebedeva, "*yuzium yaprak sarmasy*," [üzüm yapraq sarması] in her *Retsepty*, 76-77. For those familiar with Russian kitchen this dish is called "golubtsy v vinogradnykh listyakh" ("*golubtsy* in vine-leaves). [ed. This dish is a common Mediterranian and Central Asian food: *yaprak dolması* or *sarması* (the Turkish name), *maḥshi waraq 'inab* (the Arabic name), *dolmeh-e-mo* (the Farsi name), *dolmadhes* (the Greek name).]

[458] A *Ḥazzan* of the Karaite community in Ashdod, Avraham Kefeli, stated that many of the Crimean Karaite emigrants to Israel only had knowledge of the Karaite traditional kitchen, and no idea about religious Karaite traditions (Kefeli, *Karaimy*, 2).

CHAPTER 4
KARAITE SETTLEMENTS AND QUARTERS ACCORDING TO TRAVELERS' DESCRIPTIONS

Travel accounts supply data that is very important for the analysis of the urban structure of the Crimea in general, and for the history of each settlement as well. Moreover, important conclusions about the history of these settlements can be made when comparing the travelers' data with information from other sources (archæological, epigraphic, legal documents, literary works, etc.). Travelers' accounts also contain precious information on the history and topography of the settlements that were once inhabited by Karaite communities.

An attempt herein has been made to reconstruct the life and history of the main Karaite communities of the Crimean peninsula until the end of the nineteenth century on the basis of the accessible travelers' reports – and data from other sources, including personal observations acquired over many years of acquaintance with these unique monuments, the mute and simultaneously very loquacious eye-witnesses of Karaite history. It is hoped that the right key has been found to make the silent ruins of these monuments speak up, and reveal some of their secrets.

The magnificent ruins of Mangoup and Çufut-Qalé – two settlements that, since the late mediæval period, were inhabited by large Karaite communities – always attracted the eyes of warlike invaders, merchants, diplomats, scholars, and tourists, not only by their beauty and advantageous position, but also by the unusual ethnic groups that inhabited them. The Goths, Alans, Byzantines, Khazars, Turks, and Crimean Tatars strove together in the fight for dominance over these settlements until the seventeenth/eighteenth centuries, when both settlements were *de facto* left in the ownership of the Karaites, their last inhabitants. In spite of the fact that the mediæval history and archæology of Mangoup and Çufut-Qalé looks rather well-investigated,[459] the last chapters of their history, related to the life and

---

[459] See Gertsen, Mogarichev, *Krepost'*; Alexander Vasiliev, *The Goths in the Crimea* (Cambridge, 1936), 182-266; A.G.Gertsen, "Krepostnoi ansambl' Mangupa" [The defensive ensemble of Mangoup], *MAIET* 1 (1990): 87-166; A.G.Gertsen, "K probleme tipologii srednevekovykh gorodishtch yugo-zapadnoy Tavriki" [On the problem of the typology of mediéval settlements of the south-western Taurica], in *Vizantiya i srednevekovyi Krym* (Simferopol', 1995): 85-90; A.L. Yakobson, *Srednevekovyi Krym* [The Mediæval Crimea] (Moscow 1973), 128-135; J.Bayer, *Istoriya krymskikh gotov kak interpretaciya Skazaniya Matfeya o gorode Feodoro* [The history of the Crimean Goths as intrepreted in Matthew's poem about the town of Theodoro] (Ekaterinburg, 2001), 285-309.

activity of the Karaite communities, are still to be written.

Çufut-Qalé, the main settlement of the Crimean Karaites in the fifteenth – eighteenth centuries, was described more comprehensively than any other Karaite settlement. Especially detailed and interesting accounts regarding the history of this town were left by the travelers of the nineteenth century, who were fascinated by its eerie atmosphere and the ancient, Judaic beliefs preserved by its enigmatic inhabitants.

The Karaite community of Mangoup, a similar town in the mountainous region of the south-western Crimea, was not described in such detail. This can be explained by the much earlier date of its abandonment (the 1790s), and its more inaccessible location, far away from Bakhçeseray, the capital of the Crimean Khanate.

In addition to the Karaite districts in the settlements of Mangoup and Çufut-Qalé, there also were Karaite quarters in larger Crimean towns, such as: Eski-Qırım (Staryi Krym), Kaffa (Feodosia), Qarasubazar (Belogorsk), and Gözlöw (Evpatoria). Many nineteenth century travelers left detailed and interesting descriptions of the Karaite communities of Gözlöw, which became the new Karaite capital in the nineteenth century, after the decline of Çufut-Qalé. At the end of the eighteenth/beginning of the nineteenth centuries, Karaite communities appeared in Bakhçeseray, Or (Ferakh-Kerman, Perekop), Armianskiy Bazar (Armiansk), Sevastopol', Simferopol', and Kerch. In spite of the fact that these small Karaite communities seemed much less interesting for voyagers, travel accounts still contain some important remarks about their history. As a separate problem, the controversial data concerning the presence of a Karaite population in the Crimean settlements of Yaşlov, Taş-Cargan, and Tepe-Kermen will be discussed.

Although there is an abundance of interesting architectural and historical monuments in the territory of the towns where the Karaites lived, to keep on topic, only those which have a direct relationship to the Karaite community will be examined.

4.1. Jerusalem of the Crimean Karaites: Çufut-Qalé (Qırq-Yer)
4.1.1. Outline of its history.

"Oh, nature! thy creations are unimitatable! Could all Princes of this universe, even when joined together, establish fortifications resembling those of yours, could thousands of Crœsus' riches erect another Dchu-foot-Kale?"

(Pavel Sumarokov, *Puteshestvie po vsemu Krymu i Bessarabii v 1799 godu* [Travel through the whole Crimea and Bessarabia in 1799], (Moscow, 1800), 141)

A general description, and problems of early history.

The remains of one of the most interesting monuments of the Crimea's Middle Ages – the town of Çufut-Qalé (Qırq-Yer), an important Crimean fortress that once housed a large and influential Karaite community – are situated on an isolated rock on the inner chain of the Crimean mountains. Çufut-Qalé is located in an advantageous place in terms of its natural fortification. It is surrounded on three sides by cliffs reaching, in some places, fifty meters in height. It reaches 200 meters above the level of its adjacent valleys.[460] Evliya Çelebi wrote that the fortress did not need any additional fortifications, apart from its two walls, because of the fact that "it is surrounded by rocks of a thousand *arshins* in height... Underneath there are precipices of immeasurable depth resembling the jaws of Hell."[461]

---

[460] Gertsen, Mogarichev, *Krepost'*, 6.
[461] Evliya Çelebi, *Kniga*, 93.

OLD TOWN

NEW TOWN

JEHOSAPHATH VALLEY

1. *Burunchack wall*
2. *Southern gate*
3. *Synagogues*
4. *Middle wall*
5. *Well*
6. *The house of A. Firkovitch*
7. *The house of S. Beim*
8. *Eastern wall*
9. *Bath*
10. *Supposed prisons*
11. *The house of Simon-Chelebis*
12. *Eastern gate*
13. *The house of Chadluri*
14. *Typography*
15. *Well with Hebrew graphiti*

Fig. 5. Topographic plan of Chufut-Kale (from the plans by E. Chikalin (1980) and O. Akchokrakly (1927)).

Yehoshafat Valley Map.

There are several valleys adjacent to Çufut-Qalé. One is *Maryam-Dere* ("Valley of St. Mary") with the remains of a Greek settlement, called Mariampolis, and a cemetery dating back to the sixth-ninth centuries. There is also the Muslim cemetery *Gazi-Mansur* ("Mansur the pilgrim") situated a bit farther to the north, and the Karaite cemetery in the *Yehoshafat Valley*. There is a settlement belonging to the Qızıl-Qoba culture, and an uninvestigated early

150

mediæval cemetery in the valley of *Aşlama-Dere*, which is situated to the north east of the plateau.

The town may be entered using the footpath leading to *Kiçik-Qapı* ("Small" or Southern Gate) or by the road coming through Maryam-Dere and the Yehoshafat Valley to *Büyük-Qapı* ("Big" or Eastern Gate; *see the map of Çufut-Qalé*).[462] Because of the fact that the town has been deserted only in the nineteenth century, its defensive complex has been preserved to such a degree that it is still barely possible to enter Çufut-Qalé when these mediæval gates are closed. The territory of the town is clearly divided into three parts: the empty western part called Burunçaq ("Little Cape") or "Kiiklyk" with an area of about thirty-six hectares,[463] the so called *Old Town*, with an area of about seven hectares (between Burunçaq and the Middle defensive wall), and the *New Town*, with an area of about three hectares, situated between the middle and eastern defensive walls.[464]

In contrast to Mangup, with its numerous natural springs, from at least the second half of the seventeenth century, Çufut-Qalé started to suffer from a lack of water on its territory.[465] Most of the travel reports of the seventeenth – nineteenth centuries mentioned that water was carried up to Çufut-Qalé from the valleys situated underneath the fortress. S.Szapszal described the process of carrying water up to the fortress in the following way:

> Barrels are filled with water, tightly covered with lids and then hanged on *koromysla* [Russ. "shoulder-yokes"], which one should be aware of when put across the backbone of an animal

---

[462] Solomon Beim mentioned three different road used by the Karaites: *At-yol ["horse road"]*, *Aylanma-yol ["loafing/idling road"]*, and *Aşlama-yol ["buddıng/cool" road]* (Beim, *Pamiat'*, 44).

[463] According to the testimonies of the travelers of the eighteenth/nineteenth centuries, Burunçaq, a section of Çufut-Qalé that is empty of buildilngs, was used by the Tatar khans as a place for having special festivities, hunting, and merry-making (Pallas, *Travels*, 37; the same; *Bemerkungen*, 36; Castelnau, *Essai*, 187; Motray, *Travels*, 64).

[464] Gertsen, Mogarichev, *Krepost'*, 8-9.

[465] The problem of the water supply system of mediæval Qırq-Yer (Çufut-Qalé) was explored by E.V.Veimarn, and later, A.G.Gertsen. Because of the lack of information from written sources, neither scholar came to a decisive solution of the problem (Gertsen, Mogarichev, *Krepost'*, 31-33). In all probability, the key data for this problem can be extracted from the excavations of the underground water supply complex recently discovered near the Southern gates of the fortress. Unfortunately, the speliologists who carried out excavations of this highly interesting monument did not provide the academic world with precise information regarding the archæological materials found there [see more details in §4.1.2, subchapter "other monuments"].

[usually a horse or donkey], tightly fit to its sides; at the bottom, the barrels are joined together with a wide belt, which tightly embraces the stomach of an animal.[466]

Pojata (1871) once saw one of these water carrying donkeys in the estate of A.Firkovich.[467] Delivering of water up to Çufut-Qalé was one of the occupations for the poorest classes of the Karaite population.[468] According to L.Oliphant (1852), near the spring from which the water was usually taken, there was a special official who filled vessels with water.[469] Shelomoh Beim mentioned that Çufut-Qalé's most important spring, situated at the footing of Beşik-Dağ ("cradle mountain"), was called "Yusuf Çoqraq " ("spring of Yusuf"). In his opinion, the "fountain" was built by a certain Karaite named Yosef.[470]

The way to carry the water up to Çufut-Qalé.

The history of Çufut-Qalé is interesting and complicated, with a number of mysteries that still surround it. While the first traces of the human presence on its territory go back to the Neolithic period, the foundation of the first defensive complex of Çufut-Qalé, as well as the

---

[466] Szapszal, *Karaimy*, 17, ft.2. One may compare Szapszal's description with one of the early twentieth century pictures in *MS LLAS*. F.143-1249, 5.

[467] Pojata [H.Skirmuntowa], "Szkice z Krymu," *Tygodnik Ilustrowany* 8: 201 (1871): 221.

[468] Pavel Sumarokov, *Puteshestvie po vsemu Krymu i Bessarabii v 1799 godu* [Travel through the whole Crimea and Bessarabia in 1799] (Moscow, 1800), 145.

[469] Oliphant, *Russian Shores*, 277-278.

[470] Beim, *Pamiat'*, 41. Was it Yosef Ağa, the scion of the Sinan-Çelebi clan? Yusuf however is the Muslim form of the name Yosef.

construction of the fortifications of Theodoro (Mangoup), might be attributed to the period of the Byzantine Emperor Justinian I (527-565). During Byzantine times, the main population of this territory was mixed, with the Christians/Alans as its predominant inhabitants. With the exception of several earlier sources that mentioned the town of Phoullæ,[471] we do not have at our disposal any written testimonies concerning the settlement until the thirteenth/fourteenth centuries.[472]

During the Middle Ages, Çufut-Qalé was known in its Turkic form as "Qırq-Yer/Er." Practically all variants of the Turkic etymology of the toponym were analyzed by V.D.Smirnov.[473] Still, scholars do not agree on the meaning, origins and etymology of this term. It might be well explained by a process of the homonymic changing of the town's supposed early Greek name. This suggests that the Tatars, who used the toponym "Qırq-Yer"/"Qırq-Or", in the fourteenth-sixteenth centuries, simply adapted the former Alanian name, transforming it into a form more understandable for them. However, this tells us nothing about the original name of the town.[474]

---

[471] Some scholars are inclined to contend that, in the Early Middle Ages, the town was called Phoullæ (Berthier-Delagarde, "Issledovanie," 89).

[472] Abulfeda, the Arab geographer of the fourteenth century, wrote about the castle of *Kerker* or *Kerkri* situated in the country of the Alans (*The Arabic Text of Abulfeda*, ed. M. Reinaud, and M. de Slane (Paris 1840)). Bishop Theodore (thirteenth century) reported about a certain settlement of the Alans (most likely, Qırq-Yer) whose inhabitants (the Alans) were "neither wanted nor voluntary [settlers]" and served for Kherson (Chersonese, present-day Sevastopol') as "a sort of wall and fortified enclosure". See "Episkopa Feodora alanskoe poslanie" (Bishop Theodore Alanian epistle), trans. Julian Kulakovskiy, *ZOOID* 21 (1898): 17. Of great importance also is the remark of William de Rubruquis (1253), who wrote about "quadraginta castella," (most likely, the Latin translation of Turkic "Qırq-Or") located somewhere between Kherson and Sudak (Willielmus de Rubruquis, "Itinerarium fratris Willielmi de Rubruquis de ordine fratrum Minorum, Galli, Anno gratie 1253 ad Partes Orientales," in *The Texts and Versions of John de Plano Carpini and William de Rubruquis*, ed. Ch.R.Beazley (London, 1903; repr., Nendeln, 1967), 145-147). See more details concerning the early history of Qırq-Yer in Gertsen, Mogarichev, *Krepost'*, 4-58.

[473] The scholar suggested the following interpretations: "qırq-er" – "forty men"; qırq-yer – "forty places"; qırq-il" – "forty tribes"; "qırq-yel" – "forty winds" (V.D.Smirnov, *Krymskoe khanstvo pod verkhovenstvom Ottomanskoy Porty* [The Crimean Khanate under the jurisdiction of the Ottoman Turkey] (St. Petersburg, 1888, 109-110).

[474] A.Harkavy, who denied the presence of Turkic elements in this toponym, suggested that its Indo-European origin was from the root "kar", which is present in Latin in the form "carcer" and in German as "kerker" (Smirnov, *Krymskoe khanstvo*, 108-109). Both words mean "prison" or "underground". Harkavy's etymology is very tempting, taking into consideration the presence of a mediæval prison and a number of underground cave monuments in the territory of Çufut-Qalé. P.Koeppen tried to explain the toponym as deriving from the Greek "κιρκος (kirkos)" or

153

Numerous variations used in transcribing the town's name, common in the fourteenth/fifteenth centuries, allow one to suppose that there was no unified interpretation of the meaning of the toponym at that time. The most widespread of these variations, perhaps, was the form "Qırq-Yer" ("forty places") or "Qırq-Er" ("forty men").[475] This interpretation received a further development in nineteenth century Karaite folklore. According to one such legend, the Tatar Khan Batu brought forty Karaite families with him to the Crimea.[476] There are also other, late legends that talk about the establishment of Qırq-Or by forty Karaite brothers, or about forty Karaite families who fought together with Tokhtamış and Mengli Giray.[477] According to another widespread transcription of the toponym, however, it should be understood as "Qırqk-Or", *i.e.* "forty castles".[478]

The population of mediæval Qırq-Yer was not homogeneous. In addition to the Alanian population, mediæval travelers also indicated the presence of the Goths. In the opinion of Josaphath Barbaro, the regions of the Crimean Alania and Gothia were situated very close to each other and inhabited by a mixed ethnic group, called the "Gothalani," who appeared as a consequence of mixing between the Alans and the Goths.[479]

In the thirteenth century, not only the eastern, but also the western part of the Crimea suffered from the invasions of the Tatars. Qırq-Yer was injured from at least one other invasion, that of the *emir* Noğai in 1299.[480] In the fourteenth century, Tatar expansion to the

"κρικος (krikos)" ("ring") in the sense of "surrounded" and defended by the wall space (Koeppen, *Sbornik*, 312). V.D.Smirnov suggested that the toponym was derived from the Greek "καλλιακρια (kalliakria) ("beautiful hilltop") (Smirnov, *Krymskoe khanstvo*, 111-115). If one takes into consideration the suggestion of the toponym's Germanic origins (at some point Qırq-Yer, undoubtedly, was a part of the Crimean Gothia and Alania where Christians-Goths lived), it is also quite possible that "Qırq-Yer" was a distortion of a Germanic root that is present in English as "church" and in German as "kirche".

[475] If one takes into consideration the fact that, in the Turkic languages, the numeral "qırq" (40) has a connotation "numerous", one may well translate the toponym as "full of people" or "densely populated".

[476] Kohl, *Reisen*, vol.2, 259-260.

[477] Markov, *Ocherki*, 454; Beim, *Pamiat'*, 37.

[478] If one takes into account the aforementioned additional meaning of the word 'forty' in the Turkic languages, one may translate "Qırq-Or" as "[a town] with numerous fortifications" or "well-defended [town]".

[479] *Barbaro i Contarini o Rossii* [Barbaro and Contarini on Russia] (Leningrad, 1971), 132.

[480] See the chronicle of Rukn-ad-din Beybars in *Sbornik materialov otnosiashtchikhsia k istorii Zolotoy Ordy* [The collection of the materials related to the history of the Golden Horde], ed. V. Tizengauzen, vol.1 (St. Petersburg, 1884), 112.

Western Crimea considerably grew and, as a consequence, Qırq-Yer was seized by the Tatars. This event happened, most likely, during the reign of Canıbeğ, the Khan of the Golden Horde in 1342-1357.[481] It seems that Yaşlov beys, one of the most important clans of the Tatar nobility took a very active role in the seizure of the fortress.[482]

The history of the Karaite community of the town (fourteenth-eighteenth centuries).

With the accession of the Tatars to power in Qırq-Yer, the ethnic situation there considerably changed. The Christian population (*i.e.* the Greeks, Goths, and Alans) was probably moved to the adjacent valley of Maryam-Dere. There are no written sources that confirm this, but the establishment of the monastery of the Assumption in this valley at the close of the fifteenth/beginning of the sixteenth century testifies in the favor of this hypothesis. However, the Tatar invaders, who led a half-nomadic life, still needed the assistance of other nations (more sedentary than their own) to support them. Therefore, the vacuum which appeared after the removal of the Goths and Alans, was soon filled up with the newcomers, the Karaites and Armenians.[483] Thus, already in the second half of the fifteenth century, Qırq-Yer was inhabited by the representatives of the Muslim (Crimean Tatar), Jewish (most likely, Karaite), and Christian (Armenian[484]) communities. These

---

[481] Gertsen, Mogarichev, *Krepost'*, 56. [*ed.* Canıbeğ reigned only from 1342 to 1357 and was succeded by Berdibeğ 1357-1359, Qulpa 1359-1360, Nawruz Beğ 1360-1361, Khıdr 1361-1362, Tımur Khoca 1362-1382, Keldibeğ 1362-1362, and Murid 1362-1364.]

[482] See the legend of Sa'id Muḥammad Riza about the seizure of Qırq-Yer and legal documents of the seventeenth/eighteenth centuries, which mentioned the beys of Yashlov as the owners of the town (Smirnov, *Krymskoe khanstvo*, 104-106, 120-121).

[483] According to the chronicle of Sa'id Muḥammad Riza (eighteenth century), "the Jewish tribe of the Karaites" was settled down in Qırq-Yer not by its own will, but obeying the force of the Tatars (Smirnov, *Krymskoe khanstvo*, 104-106).

[484] In spite of the absence of the references to the Armenian population of the town in all other written sources, the Armenians are mentioned as the inhabitants of Çufut-Qalé in legal documents as late as the eighteenth century (Smirnov, *Krymskoe khanstvo*, 107). There is also archæological evidence to the presence of Armenians in Çufut-Qalé. A small weight, with the name "Manurk, a son of Markos", was found during the excavations of the Qopqa-Quyu (Tat. "bucket-well") (Gertsen, Mogarichev, *Krepost'*, 95, 97). In August, 2000, Dr. D.Shapira and M.Kizilov found an Armenian graffito on the gate of the synagogue compound of Çufut-Qalé; the compound was built in the late eighteenth century, after the Armenians left the Crimea – including Çufut-Qalé – to Russia. D.Shapira suggests reading the graphito as *ro k·aluiik* , "*ro* (?) from/of Qal'eh." According to him, this inscription was made by a local Armenian, testifying thus again to the existence of an Armenian community in the town before the end of the eighteenth century (full publication of

three communities are mentioned as the inhabitants of Qırq-Yer in the earliest *yarlıqlar* [edicts] of the Crimean Khans of 1459 and 1468. The leader of the Jewish community at that time was "teacher Yahuda."[485] It seems, however, that the Karaites may have settled in Qırq-Yer earlier, but not later than the fourteenth century.[486] We lack written sources in this regard (apart from late nineteenth century Karaite legends), but it is very likely that the early Karaite settlers could have come there two ways: 1) together with the Tatar invaders in the mid-14th century, or 2) from Byzantine Karaite colonies.

In addition to the Karaite community, it is highly probable that there also was a very small Rabbanite (Qrımçaq) community in Çufut-Qalé, which most likely left the town in the eighteenth century.[487] Unfortunately, to date there is no written source that can supply us with more details about the role of the Rabbanite community in the history of the town. In general, when speaking about the Jewish history of the Crimea in the fifteenth-eighteenth centuries, a very difficult terminological problem arises because most non-Jewish sources of this period did not differentiate between the Rabbanite and Karaite Jews. Thus, when a Gentile source mentions a certain Jewish person active in the Crimea in this time, we may only guess whether this Jew was of Karaite or Rabbanite denomination.[488] Undoubtedly,

---

the graffito soon to appear).

[485] V.D.Smirnov, "Tataro-Khanskie yarlyki iz kollektsii TUAK" [The yarlıqlar of the Tatar Khans from the collection of TUAK], *ITUAK* 54 (1918): 9-10.

[486] See more details in the forthcoming *Studies in a Karaite Community: The Report of the Epigraphic Expedition of the Ben-Zvi Institute to the Jewish-Karaite Cemetery of Çufut-Qal'eh, the Crimea,* ed. Dan Shapira, Ben-Zvi Foundation, Jerusalem, 2002 (450pp., Hebrew, in print).

[487] See epitaphs from several Rabbanite tombstones from the cemetery in the Yehoshafat Valley published by A.Firkovich in his *Avenei Zikkaron,* 79, nr310 *et alia.* In spite of the fact that the inscriptions from the Rabbanite tombs situated in the Yehoshafat Valley were published by Firkovich, perhaps the most authoritative Karaite leader, the twentieth century Karaites vigorously oppose even the slightiest hint to the presence of the Rabbanites in Çufut-Qalé (*e.g.* Leonid Lavrin, in his letter to the president of the Ukraine L.D.Kuchma says that "the only Jew who had ever lived in Çufut-Qalé was Ephraim Deinard, the flunky of the archæologist Abraham Firkovich": *KV* 6 (49) (1999)). The official position of S.Szapszal was similar with the regard to this problem (*e.g.* Seraja Szapszal, "Karaimi w służbie u chanów krymskich," *MK* 2:2 (1929): 5-22.). Nevertheless, among the books in his private possession, I found a copy of *Avenei Zikkaron,* where Szapszal himself underlined one of the Ashkenazic tombs and wrote on a margin "*ravvin*" (here, undoubtedly, a "Rabbanite"). This proves that Szapszal was aware of the presence of the Rabbanite tombs in the Yehoshafat Valley [see MS LLAS F.143-1182, 79].

[488] Travelers of the fifteenth-seventeenth centuries did not differentiate between the Karaite and Rabbanite Jews, and referred to them in the same manner: *Giudei, Juifs, Juden* or *Judaei.* Official Tatar documents, however, referred to the Karaite and

only a comprehensive and unbiased exploration of the tombstone inscriptions of the cemetery in the Yehoshafat Valley will provide a more exact date for establishing the foundations of the Karaite and Rabbanite communities in Qırq-Yer.

In all probability, the Muslims lived within the boundaries of the so called *Old Town*, while the Karaites and Armenians lived beyond its limits, in the territory of the adjacent suburb, which was surrounded by a wall in the beginning of the sixteenth century (in modern scholarly literature it is called the *New Town* [see the map of Çufut-Qalé].

Qırq-Yer was such a significant acquisition for the Tatars that, in the middle of the fifteenth century, the founder of the dynasty of the Crimean Khans, Haci-Giray, transferred the capital of the Crimean Tatars there.[489] Moreover, the first Khan's mint, where the first Giray dynasty coins were minted, was also situated in Qırq-Yer.[490] The first peace treaties between the Crimean Khanate and the Polish-Lithuanian Commonwealth were also signed there, in Qırq-Yer.[491]

However, in the beginning of the sixteenth century, the capital of the Crimean Khanate was transferred to a more appropriate place, the town of Bakhçeseray.[492] It is possible to suppose that, from this moment on, Qırq-Yer was transferred into the jurisdiction of the Yaşlov beys, whose ancient rights to possess the town find their roots in the active role of the beys in the seizure of the fortress in the fourteenth century. The *yarlıq* (charter/edict) of Bahadur Giray of 1047 (1637 a.h.), where the beys are named as the "ancient owners of the town of Qırqı," is the oldest known document which confirms these

---

Rabbanite subjects using the word *yahudi* (*Sbornik*, 62-93).

[489] Gertsen, Mogarichev, *Krepost'*, 64.

[490] G.Karaulov mentioned that among the Tatars there was an opinion that "the Karaites re-coined the khans' good silver coins into bad-quality copper ones" (G. Karaulov, "Chufut-Kale i Evrei-Karaimy" [Çufut-Qalé and the Jews-Karaites], *ZOOID* 13 (1893): 99); these rumours caused a reply of S.Szapszal, who vigorously opposed this point of view (Seraya Szapszal, "Karaimi w służbie u chanów krymskich ," *MK* 2:2 (1929), 5-22). However, the author saw, in a private collection, fake seventeenth century Russian coins forged – according to Mr. M.M.Çoref (Bakhçesaray), the owner of the collection – in the Çufut-Qalé mint [see also §2.5].

[491] The first treaty was signed in "Kirkiery" in 1480 (AGAD, Metryka Litewska, ks.191a, f.344-345. List przymierzy Mengli Gereja z 1479 lub 1480 roku: "Pisan w Kirkiery w let: 885 (=1480)"). The next was signed on 27.11.1514 "In Cherchere in doucat saraj" (AGAD AKW Dz.Tatarskie, k.65, t.1, nr575-576, "Traktat Mengli Gereja I chana krymskiego z Zygmuntem I królem polskim").

[492] V.D.Smirnov mentioned that the Tatars, "inhabitants of the steppe, who spent half of their life on a horse, in fact, had no need of the steep and waterless rock of Qirqor" (Smirnov, *Krymskoe khanstvo*, 106).

rights.[493]

Because of the removal of the Tatar administration to Bakhçeseray, in the course of the sixteenth, and especially in the first half of the seventeenth century, Qırq-Yer lost its former administrative significance. The yarlıq of Selamet Giray of 1608 still mentions the presence of the Tatar administration (a military garrison, *qadi* (judge), and *bek* (governor) Ahmed Pasha). However, Evliya Çelebi, who visited the fortress in 1666, already wrote that "There are no Muslims there at all, and even its commandant, garrison, guards, and door-keepers are all Jews." This situation seemed to Çelebi quite an extraordinary one. He remarked that he had not seen "such an independent Jewish fortress" in any other country of the world.[494] However, when taking into consideration new data regarding the prison that functioned in Çufut-Qalé in the fifteenth-eighteenth centuries [see below], it seems that there could have been a small Tatar garrison for taking care of prisoners. Moreover, one very late charter, the yarlıq of Devlet Giray of 1773, mentions the appointment of Yaşlov bey Qutluş to the office of the governor of the fortress.[495]

On the basis of the travelers' reports, it is possible to characterize the main reasons why the Tatars decided to leave the town. First, in the sixteenth/seventeenth centuries, the town lost its military significance due to a lack of water. Many travelers thought the Tatars left Çufut-Qalé in the possession of the Karaites because of its problems with water supply.[496] Second, the Tatars still needed the Karaites as skillful merchants and artisans. In the opinion of M.Guthrie and some other travelers, the Karaites were allowed to settle down in Çufut-Qalé mostly because of their diligence in crafts and trade.[497] As a consequence, in the seventeenth/eighteenth centuries, the town started to play a role as the center of trade and arts.

By the beginning of the seventeenth century, the Karaites had become the main population of the town. This change in the ethnic structure of the town is distinctively reflected by the replacement of the old mediæval name of the town, Qırq-Yer/Er/Or, by the new one, Çufut-Qalé (*the Jews' Castle/Town*). On the basis a comparative

---

[493] Smirnov, *Krymskoe khanstvo*, 107. Gertsen and Mogarichev erroneously attribute this document to 1612 (Gertsen, Mogarichev, *Krepost'*, 95).

[494] Evliya Çelebi, *Ksiega*, 266-267; Evliya Çelebi, *Kniga*, 93-94.

[495] Gertsen, Mogarichev, *Krepost'*, 95-96.

[496] Kleeman, *Reisen*, 74; Guthrie, *Tour*, 85. P.Savelov wrote that during his stay in the town the price of a bucket of water was as high as two *altyns* [altınlar] ["gold (pieces)"] ("Posylki v Krym v XVII veke" [Embassies to the Crimea in the seventeenth century], *ZOOID* 24 (1902): 75).

[497] Guthrie, *Tour*, 85.

analysis of travelers' data and legal documents from the seventeenth/eighteenth centuries, it is possible conclude that the process of supplanting the old name of the town was as follows. In the first half of the seventeenth century, with the removal of the Khan's administration, the town started loosing its military and administrative significance. In the later half of the 1600s, when the representatives of the Jewish community (Karaites, and, possibly, a few Rabbanites) became practically the only inhabitants of the place, the adjective "Jewish" ("Çufut") became a fixed part of the town's name. In the eighteenth century "Çufut-Qalé" was the established name of the town.[498]

East European Karaites, however, up to the present day, avoid using the first part of this placename, *Çufut*, because of its derogatory meaning. As it is evident from their correspondence and other documents, the Karaites called their main Crimean settlement *Qalé* ("castle/town"), Qırq-Or/Yer ("forty castles/men," former Tatar name) or Sela' HaYehudim ("Jews' Rock"). [499]

This situation was precisely reflected by J.Kohl (1838), who wrote down an extremely interesting version (based on the local oral tradition) of the origins and circumstances of the supplanting of the toponym "Qırq-Yer" with "Çufut-Qalé". According to this tradition, Batu Khan brought with him about forty Karaite families to the Crimea. The settlement that was established by these forty families was called "Kürkiwli" [Qırq Evli], which means "forty Wirtschaften"

---

[498] A.N.Samoilovich indicated that "Çufut-Qalé" (derogatory "Jewish Castle") appeared in the spoken Crimean-Tatar as the unofficial variant of "*Qalé-i yahudian*" ("Jewish Castle") used in legal docments of the khan's administration. Paradoxically, it was this derogatory spoken variant that became the main term used for the town in the eighteenth/nineteenth centuries. Samoilovich mentioned that – in order to restore the historical truth, derogatory both for the Karaites and Rabbanite Qrımçaqlar, "Çufut-Qalé" should be changed to "Qalé" or "Qaray-Qalé" (A.N.Samoilovich, "O materialakh Radlova po narodnoi slovesnosti krymskikh tatar i karaimov" [On the Radloff's materials related to the folklore of the Crimean Tatars and Karaites], in A.N.Samoilovich, *Izbrannye trudy o Kryme* (Simferopol', 2000), 121.

[499] See Mann, *Texts*, 285-550. In the opinion of D.Shapira, the toponym "*Sela' HaYehudim*" was invented by A.Firkovich or one of his contemporaries (private communication). On the marble monument commemorating the visit of the emperor Alexander III to Çufut-Qalé on 4.05. 1886 (until Autumn 2001 it was kept in one of the caves, and later in the smaller synagogue of the town) the town is called "*Sela' HaQara'im*" ("Karaites' Rock"), undoubtedly a later version of "*Sela' HaYehudim*". Twentieth century scholarship of the East European Karaites popularized the attempt to explain the meaning of the toponym as "Double Castle" (from the Turk. "çift/cift/cüft" – "double" (from the Farsi *jift*]; *e.g.* Fuki, *Karaimy*, 16); however, none of the seventeenth-nineteenth century documents interpreted the town's name in this way.

159

(*i.e.* "forty estates/houses"). Later, when this settlement became a capital of the Tatar ruler, the name was lost, and "the Tatars called this town 'Çufut-Qalé', which means 'Jews' town'... whereas the Karaites, who only call the Talmudists 'Çufut', instead of this say simply 'Qalé' (fortress/castle)."[500] In addition to this interesting legend about the establishment of the town, we should also notice that, according to this tradition, the town was originally called "Kürkiwli" (*i.e.* "forty estates/houses") [Qırq Evli].

August von Haxthausen, similarly, also called the town "Kürkiwli" or "Kyrkor", but translated the former placename as "forty Stämme" ("forty tribes/clans").[501]

In the yarlıq of Canıbeğ Giray of 1610, the town is called *Qalé*, while the yarlıq of 1637 notes that the town "Qırki" was called *Jewish Town* within the Armenian and Jewish (*i.e.* Karaite) communities.[502] Russian ambassadors of the seventeenth century also called the settlement *Жидовский Городок* (*Zhidovskiy Gorodok* – "*Jews' Town,"* undoubtedly, a Russian translation of "Çufut-Qalé;" cf. also German "*Judenfestung*" or French "*Chateau des Juifs*").[503]

Almost all sources named the settlement and interpreted the meaning of its name in the same way: *Çufut-Qalé* – the "Jews' Castle." The only point of disagreement was in the spelling of this placename; it is possible to come across such variants as *Chufudkalesi, Dschufut-Kale, Tchifout Kalchsi, Dschoufout Kale, Juffut-Kale, Juft-Kale, Joofud-Kalah, Tschonfort Kale*, etc.[504]

---

[500] Kohl, *Reisen*, vol.2, 259-260.

[501] Haxthausen, *Studien*, 401.

[502] *Sbornik*, 69; Smirnov, *Krymskoe Khanstvo*, 120.

[503] "Stateinyi spisok stol'nika Vasiliya Tiapkina and diaka Nikity Zotova, posol'stva v Krym v 1680 godu" [Account of the stol'nik Vasiliy Tiapkin and deacon Nikita Zotov, an embassy to the Crimea in 1680], *ZOOID* 2 (1848): 587-588, 604, 615, 616; "Posylki," 75; "Skazanie sviashtchennika Iakova" [The narration of the priest Jacob], *ZOOID* 2:2 (1848): 686.

[504] Similar toponyms containing the root "chufut" (derogatory "Jewish") can be found in other districts of the former Ottoman Empire. *e.g.* *Tchifut-Burgaz* in Constantinople and *Chufut-Katta* in the Caucasus (Danon, " Karaites," 301; David, *Istoriya*, vol.1, 86). Some travelers, quite rarely, referred to the town in the Karaite manner *Kale, Kalo, Ghala.* Vasiliy Zuev (1782) even named the town *Карайкале* (*Qaray-Qalé*), *i.e.* "the Karaites' castle" (Vasiliy Zuev, "Vypiska iz putevykh zapisok Vasiliya Zueva" [A note from the travel memoires of Vasiliy Zuev], in *Ottisk iz mesiatseslova na 1783 god*, 289). Polish traveler from Danzig quoted by N.Witsen, called the fortress *Siaput Cabasse*, which also seems to be a corruption of Chufut-Kalesi. [*ed.* It is also possible that "Cabasse" is a corruption of "Kobasy", *i.e.* "big cave" (Witsen, *Noord en Oost Tartarye*, 577). Çufut Qalési in Tatar literally means "Jews' fortress/castle".]

Nevertheless, some travelers used other toponyms: De Peyssonel (1753) used the naming *Chateau des Juifs*, a French translation of *Çufut-Qalé*.[505] P.S.Pallas, similarly, often called the town *Judenfestung* or *Judenstadt*, using names well understood by the readers of his travel notes.[506] Evliya Çelebi(1665-1666) supplied two other placenames: *Butmai* and *Gevherkerman*. The origins of the first toponym are unclear, whereas "Gevherkerman", translated from the Turkish, means the *"Fortress of Jewels."* Çelebi recorded a legend according to which the town was called this because of precious stones once placed in its walls.[507] However, it is more likely that the first part of the toponym, *"gevher"* is a corruption of "Qırq-Yer," the former name of the town.

During the sixteenth-eighteenth centuries, the architectural ensemble of the town underwent a number of considerable changes. Especially important was the construction of the Eastern defensive wall surrounding the *New Town* [see map §4.1]. A very interesting remark about the *"civitas Kirkel"* was left, in 1517, by Polish scholar Matthias de Miechov (Maciej Miechowski or Miechowita). De Miechov wrote that the fortifications of the town of Qırq-Yer were built of wood and clay.[508] Portelli D'Ascoli (1630s) called Qırq-Yer *"Topracala"* – which means, translated from Turkish *Topraq Qalé* [*Toprak Kale* in modern Turkish], the "Earthen Castle."[509] These two testimonies allowed A.Gertsen to suggest that travelers, who entered the town from the eastern side, could see an earthen mound covering the outer portion of the eastern wall. This view might give them the false impression that the entire town was built of earth or clay.[510] The remark of de Miechov suggests that the time of the construction of this

---

[505] Peyssonel, *Traite*, vol.1, 259.

[506] Pallas, *Bemerkungen*, 34-35, 82, 374.

[507] Evliya Çelebi, *Kniga*, 92-93. His usage of the latter toponym allowed A.G.Gertsen and Y.M.Mogarichev to entitle their book about Çufut-Qalé poetically *Krepost' Dragotsennostey*, *i.e.* "Fortress of Jewels". However, no other source used this toponym, provided by the Ottoman traveler.

[508] He also supplied the legend about the dragon who plundered the town and the surrounding area: "Alia civitas minor est Kirkel, et supra eam in rupe alta est castrum ex lignis, et argilla factum. In hac rupe (ut fertur) draco commorabatur, et trucidabat homines..." (Matthias a Michovia, "De Sarmatia Asiana et Europeana," in *Polonicae Historiae Corpus* (Basel, 1582), 139). A similar fortification of clay and wood was recorded by French traveler, Guillebert de Lannoy (c.1421) in Troki: *Oeuvres de Ghillebert de Lannoy,* ed.Ch.Potvin (Louvain, 1878), 40.

[509] According to the traveler's information, this "Topracala" (*i.e.* Çufut-Qalé) was inhabited by the Jewish merchants who used to descend every day to their shops in Bakhçeseray and return back to the castle in the evening (Eszer, *"Beschreibung,"* 233-234).

[510] Gertsen, Mogarichev, *Krepost'*, 84-85.

161

alleged fortification was not later than the first quarter of the sixteenth century.

One of the rare still standing houses of Çufut-Qalé, once a possession of a Karaite named Çalbörü. (photo by M.Kizilov)

As noted, in the fifteenth-sixteenth centuries, Karaites and Armenians lived in the territory of Çufut-Qalé's *New Town*, while the *Old Town* was reserved mostly for Muslim inhabitants. However, from the seventeenth century on, practically the whole territory of the settlement was occupied by the Karaites. Evliya Çelebi (1665-1666) was the first to leave some data concerning the dwelling quarters of the town. According to Çelebi, the Karaites lived not only in dwelling houses made of stone, but also in caves. He notes that there were 200 houses in the territory of the *New Town*.[511]

As has been mentioned, in the seventeenth – eighteenth century, Qırq-Yer lost its military and administrative significance. However, according to the travelers' reports, in the seventeenth century, at the time of frequent internal conflicts in the Crimean

---

[511] Evliya Çelebi, *Kniga*, 93. However, later Evliya writes about "1530 Jewish houses" in the fortress, a number which should be understood as one of the frequent traveler's mistakes or a scribe's error (*ibid.*). The "530 houses", allegedly mentioned by Çelebi, supplied by A.Gertsen and Y.Mogarichev and their attempts to estimate town's Karaite population as 3500 souls (Gertsen, Mogarichev, *Krepost'*, 87), are undoubtedly erroneous: the only numerals which Çelebi mentioned are the aforementioned "200" or "1530" houses.

Khanate and the devastating raids of the Cossacks, Çufut-Qalé was still often used as a fort. Petr Savelov (1628) mentioned, in his account to Tsar Mikhail Romanov, that, because of the "war" in the Crimea, he and other members of the embassy were forced to spend about nine weeks in the beleaguered *Жидовский Городок* (Russ. "Jews' Town"), almost dying from starvation, purchasing victuals from the local Jewish inhabitants (undoubtedly, the Karaites).[512]

In addition to its weakening importance as a military and trading center of the region, Çufut-Qalé fulfilled some other, quite unusual functions. From the end of the fifteenth century, almost until the Russian annexation of the Crimea in 1783, Tatar officials used Çufut-Qalé as a place for housing important prisoners.[513] Evliya Çelebi (1666) wrote that, "There is no way to get out of this prison in Chufudkalesi, unless your remains are taken from there in a coffin. To this extent, this prison resembles the *inferno*."[514] In his opinion, from the mid-seventeenth century on, the task of guarding and keeping prisoners was carried out by the Jewish (Karaite) population of the town.[515]

In spite of Evliya's information, we may suppose that there still was a small Tatar garrison in the fortress, which had to take care of important prisoners. In our opinion, some of the prisoners were too significant to the Crimean Khans to be guarded by the non-Muslims, who did not have the right to bear arms.[516]

A Karaite document of rather suspicious origin, allegedly found by Seraya Szapszal in the Karaite library "Karay Bitikliği", tells about the attempt to house Timophei, the son of the infamous Cossack hetman Bogdan Khmelnitski (responsible for the seventeenth-century Khmelnitski massacres), in Çufut-Qalé. According to this document (or, rather, to its Russian translation published by Szapszal), the Karaite community refused to house Timophey because of their hatred

---

[512] "Posylki," 75. The ambassadors' "war" refers to the lengthy conflict between the ruling Khan Muḥammad Giray and his rivals, Canıbeğ Giray and Devlet Giray, who invited Noğays and Cossacks to support them. See Xačatur's Kafaĵeci chronicle in E.Schutz, "Eine Armenische Chronik von Kaffa aus der ersten halfte des 17. Jahrhunderts," *AOASH* 29 (1975): 142-145.

[513] The prison functioned for at least three hundred years. Its earliest known prisoner was the Lithuanian ambassador Lez (1493) (Smirnov, *Khanstvo*, 103), whereas Selim-Shah-Murza was imprisoned there as late as 1777, *i.e.* only a few years before the Russian annexation of the Crimea ('Azaryah Ben-Eliyah, "Sobytiya," 74-75).

[514] Evliya Çelebi, *Kniga*, 94. Similar "penitentiary" functions had been fullfilled by Mangoup, another cave-town with the Karaite population [see more in §4.2.2].

[515] Evliya Çelebi, *Księga*, 266-267; Evliya Çelebi, *Kniga*, 93-94.

[516] Cf. Evliya's remark that Çufut-Qalé Jews (Karaites) did not have any weapons in the town (Evliya Çelebi, *Kniga*, 94).

towards the Zaporozhian Cossacks who killed colonel Eljasz Karaimowicz (according to Szapszal, this colonel belonged to the non-existent Karaite clan of the Uzuns).[517] A close glance at this document, the absence of its original, and its suspicious style, not to mention the striking improbability of the story, strongly suggest to the reader that it is a Szapszal forgery. My suspicions were justified in April, 2002, when – browsing one of Szapszal's notebooks, which he started in Constantinople in 1927, among quotations from other sources related to Eljasz Karaimowicz – I found a document in Hebrew characters written in Szapszal's hand. This document, composed in Crimean Tatar, represents two *different* versions of the "draft" of this "seventeenth century" Karaite document, evidently composed by Szapszal, most likely in the 1930s.[518]

During this period, in addition to prisoners of war, Çufut-Qalé often housed "unofficial" prisoners, *i.e.* members of disagreeable foreign embassies. Their position was often worse than that of important captives: they were not allowed to leave Çufut-Qalé, did not receive any money or food, and were often threatened and humiliated.[519] Very often it was Karaite merchants who facilitated their position by lending them money and food. Andrey Nepeitsyn (1634) remarked that he had left his goods to be kept in "Zhidovskiy Gorodok" at the place of the Jew 'Ezra of Yaşlov (Russ. «у жидовина у Изрыну Яшловскова»).[520]

More details concerning the drastic circumstances of Nepeitsyn and Dvorianinov's stay at the embassy in the Crimea (1634) are provided by Russian sources, which were analyzed by the twentieth century Russian scholar A.Novoselski (not to be confused with nineteenth century Polish traveler A.Nowosielski!). According to them, the ambassadors left their valuables at the homes of some Jewish moneylenders (undoubtedly, the Karaite merchants of Çufut-Qalé and Yaşlov). However, under torture they confessed this fact. The

---

[517] S.M. Szapszal, "O prebyvanii Bogdana Khmelnitskogo i ego syna Timofeya v Krymu" [On the stay of Bogdan Khmelnitski and his son Timophey in the Crimea], *Voprosy Istorii* 8 (1955): 145. I plan to dedicate a separate article to Eljasz Karaimowicz (often confused with Wadowski or Barabash), as an historical fugure, a colonel of Cossacks, and legendary figure of twentieth century Karaite scholarship.

[518] Both version are heavily corrected with Szapszal's own hand, some names are written in a completely different manner, some new characters are introduced into the story – an impossible thing when someone is dealing with the original of a document (MS LLAS, F.143-918, 2r).

[519] Leszek Podhorodecki, *Chanat Krymski i jego stosunki z Polską, w XV-XVIII* (Warsaw, 1987), 75.

[520] "Skazanie sviashtchennika Iakova [The legend of the priest Jacob]," *ZOOID* 2:2 (1848): 686.

moneylenders, when taken to Bakhçeseray, "uboyas' i vidia pytku" («убоясь и видя пытку» – Russ. "being terrified of the tortures"), informed the officials of the exact location of the hidden valuables.[521]

In addition to its unusual "penitentiary" functions, in the seventeenth/eighteenth centuries, Çufut-Qalé was used as a sort of ghetto. Behind its walls, the Karaites could feel comparatively safe, and secure. Marshall Marmont noted the Karaites' wish to "secure themselves" as one of the most important reasons for their settling down in Çufut-Qalé.[522] A.Nowosielski, similarly, described Çufut-Qalé as a mediæval settlement where "the Karaite Jews had to be aware of the attacks of the Tatars, a people who hated the Jews".[523]

However, even behind the mighty walls of the Çufut-Qalé, the Karaites could not entirely secure themselves from the oppressive requests of the Tatar government. In 1764, for example, the Khan Qırım Giray extorted from the local Jews (most likely the Karaites) large sums of money, and forced them to participate in the construction of his palace in Aşlama-Dere.[524] The Karaite author 'Azaryah Ben-Eliyah described the tensions between the Karaites and Crimean Tatars, and the oppressions that the Karaites suffered during the last years before the Russian annexation of the Crimea.[525]

---

[521] Novoselski, *Bor'ba*, 243.
[522] Marmont, *Voyage*, 296.
[523] Nowosielski, *Stepy*, 190.
[524] "Donesenie rossiyskogo rezidenta pri krymskom khane Nikiforova", 376-377.
[525] See 'Azaryah Ben-Eliyah, "Sobytija," 52-79.

General view of Çufut-Qalé. Two buildings in the middle are Batei Keneset; the house of A.Firkovich is on the right (photo by M.Kizilov)

The Karaite last of the Mohicans: the Karaite community of Çufut-Qalé from the end of the eighteenth through the nineteenth century.

In the 1790s, the Karaite community of Çufut-Qalé grew considerably, because of the migration to Çufut-Qalé of the Mangoup community [see §4.2.1]. In general, in the nineteenth century, when the mediæval town became too old-fashioned, even for its rather conservative inhabitants, the Karaites gradually abandoned Çufut-Qalé. The center of Crimean Karaism shifted to the west, to a new important port of the Russian Empire, Evpatoria (Gözlöw) [see §4.3.2]. In this period, the town became a very attractive destination for international tourism.

The travelers, who visited the fortress at that period, provided data regarding the density of Çufut-Qalé's dwelling quarters and the number of houses in the town. N.Kleeman supplies the unusually small number of only 120 houses (1769), while G.Romm (1786) and P.S.Pallas (1793-1794) speak about 200 houses.[526] The Russian traveler D.B. and German voyager von Haxthausen recorded 300 houses.[527]

---

[526] Kleeman, *Reisen*, 74; Charles Gilbert Romme , *Puteshestvie v Krym v 1785 godu* [The travel to the Crimea in 1785] (Leningrad, 1941), 70; Pallas, *Travels*, 36; the same, *Bemerkungen*, 36.

[527] D.B., "Otryvok," 49; Haxthausen, *Empire*, 111.

However, two other travelers provided the most accurate data: P.Sumarokov (1799), who recorded 227 houses – and Dubois de Montpereux (1838), who recorded 212 houses.[528] These two figures are very close to the government statistics of 1783, according to which there were 217 houses in Çufut-Qalé.[529]

In 1818 and in 1824 Çufut-Qalé was visited by Russian emperor Alexander I. and A.I.Mikhailovskiy-Danilevskiy. Those who witnessed the first visit of the Tsar (on May 18th, 1818), mentioned that Alexander enjoyed the hospitality of the house of a certain "rich inhabitant" (undoubtedly, Benjamin Ağa), and, moreover, even paid a visit to his "harem" (*i.e.* to the female part of the house).[530]

According to Gustav Olizar, who stayed in the Crimea from 1823-1825, the second visit of Tsar Alexander I to Çufut-Qalé played an interesting role in Russia's history.[531] Olizar maintains that the real reason for Alexander's mortal disease was the cold caused by his visit to "bardzo chłodną górę, dla zwiedzenia Karaitskiego miasta Kale" ("a very cold mountain while visiting the Karaite town of Kale"), which he undertook in a very light uniform, in spite of the warning of his Tatar guide, general *Kaja Bej* [Qaya Bey].[532] With the death of Alexander I, and the later, unsuccessful uprising of the so-called "Dekabritsy" [Decembrists"] (December, 1825), Russia's mild, democratic government was easily overcome by the oppressive, authoritarian rule of Nicholas I.

Among other famous nineteenth century visitors to the fortress, one should mention the Polish poet A.Mickiewicz, who visited the Crimea in August – October, 1825. Mickiewicz entitled one of his Crimean sonnets "Droga nad przepaścią w Czufut-Kale" ("The

---

[528] Sumarokov, *Puteshestvie*, 144; Montpereux, *Voyage*, 339.

[529] "Statisticheskie svedeniya o Kryme" [Statistical data on the Crimea], *ZOOID* 14 (1866): 103.

[530] See travel notes of A.I.Mikhailovskiy-Danilevskiy, published in *Istoricheskiy vestnik* (May, 1892): 371, and quoted by S.Szapszal (MS LLAS, F.143-918).

[531] Exact list of royal visitors of the fortress was compiled by S.Beim: *Pamiat'*, 50-51 and later by S.Szapszal: *Karaimy*, 25-26.

[532] Gustav Olizar, *Pamiętniki Gustava Olizara* (Lwow, 1892), 181. Gustav Olizar (1798-1865), a Polish poet, writer, and public figure. Here, Olizar supplies a hitherto unknown version of the emperor's death. "Kaja Bej" is a historical person, the wealthy Tatar landowner Kaya Bey Balatuqov, the owner of part of the lands of the former Mangoup qadılıq, who was in charge of organizing a visit of Alexander I to Çufut-Qalé and Bakhçeseray in 1824. During the next visits of the members of the ruling dynasty to Bakhçeseray , in 1837 and 1845, similar hospitable functions were carried out by Simḥah Babovich (Dombrovskiy, *Dvorets krymskich khanov*, 26). According to Szapszal, and Beim, however, the emperor visited Çufut-Qalé only in 1824, *i.e.* a year earlier than his sudden death (Beim, *Pamiat'*, 50; Szapszal, *Karaimy*, 25).

Road over the Precipice in Çufut-Qalé"), and dedicated several lines of his commentary on the sonnets to his brief description of this town.[533] It seems, though, that Mickiewicz originally entitled this sonnet "Kikineis" (a mountainous village on the Crimea's southern coast) and only later renamed it to "The Road over the Precipice in Çufut-Qalé". This would explain why the reader of the sonnet would not find in Çufut-Qalé the "terrible precipice" poeticized by Mickiewicz. In fact, this precipice was seen by the poet in Kikineis. Moreover, while reading Mickiewicz's commentaries on the sonnet, one can notice that some of his information on Çufut-Qalé is almost a direct translation of data from the travel diary of I.M.Muraviev-Apostol (1820).[534]

In the nineteenth century, when Çufut-Qalé became one the most interesting tourist sights of the Crimea, many of well-known Russian men of letters dedicated their time and attention to this place. One of the most famous Russian writers and poets of the nineteenth century, Alexey Konstantinovich Tolstoy (1817-1875) poeticized Çufut-Qalé, and its last inhabitants, in two beautiful sonnets, dedicated to his visit of the town in 1856.[535] Beautiful verses dedicated to Çufut-Qalé and the Yehoshafat Valley were left by S.Bobrov (1804), P.A.Viazemskiy (1867), and G.P.Danilevskiy. V.A.Zhukovski (1837), and A.S.Griboedov (1825), two other famous Russian men of letters – poets, writers, translators, and public figures (less known in the West) – left interesting notes in their diaries relating to their visit to Çufut-Qalé.[536] The Russian painter N.I.Kramskoi, who visited the Crimea in 1867, composed one of his most important paintings, "Christ in a desert", under the influence of his visit to Bakhçesaray, and Çufut-Qalé and its vicinities. One of the most famous Israeli poets of Crimean origin, Sha'ul Tchernichowsky – while following the steps of A.Mickiewicz in the Crimea, in the turbulent 1920s, when the peninsula became an arena of contest between the White and Red Armies, composed three eloquent verses dedicated to Çufut-Qalé and its *Beit Keneset*, which seem to ignore all the terrible events of the Civil War and Revolution in Russia.[537]

Using data from the travel accounts, it is possible to reasonably speculate on the size of Çufut-Qalé's population from the

---

[533] Adam Mickiewicz, *Sonety* (Moscow 1826), 47-48.
[534] Muraviev-Apostol, *Puteshestvie*, 127-128.
[535] Tolstoy, *Sobranie sochineniy*, vol.1, 102, 109.
[536] Griboedov, *Sochineniya*, 439-441; Zhukovskiy, *Ballady*, 252.
[537] "Chufut-Qal'e – Sela' HaYehudim" (in two parts) and "Beit HaKeneset BeChufut-Qal'e (1920)."

end of the eighteenth through the nineteenth centuries. P.S.Pallas (1793-1794) estimated the Karaite population of the town at 1200. Taking into consideration the fact that he also notes the number of their houses (two hundred), it is possible to assume that each household (family) consisted roughly of six people.[538] D.B. [D.N. Bantysh-Kamenskiy?] (1816), noted that the population of Çufut-Qalé was around 1500, while E.Henderson (1821) speaks about 250 families (which is roughly equal to 1500 people).[539]

Exact data concerning the population of the town was supplied by R.Lyall (1822), with reference to the work of another English traveler. He calculates 1120 inhabitants (645 men and 575 women).[540] Dubois de Montpereux (1838), with reference to the work of Peter Koeppen, was equally scrupulous: 1109 inhabitants (492 males and 617 females).[541] Unfortunately, neither traveler indicated whether their numbers were inclusive of Çufut-Qalé and Bakhçeseray, or whether the population they tallied referred only to the Karaites of Çufut-Qalé.

K.Kaczkowski, who visited Çufut-Qalé in 1825, described the town as the seat of the main Karaite rabbi, full of people, with hundreds of houses built right on the rocky surface of the mountain.[542] N.Murzakevich, who visited Çufut-Qalé in 1836, mentioned the recent trend of Karaite emigration from the town, and estimated its population at 800 people.[543] A similar picture of the gradual abandonment of the town was depicted by O.Shishkina (1845).[544] E.Chojecki (1843) was lucky to see Çufut-Qalé still inhabited by a considerable amount of people, and estimated its population at 500 Karaites.[545] The French travelers Xavier Hommaire de Hell and his wife visited Çufut-Qalé in the 1840s. They note that the population was reduced to only twelve families, living there exclusively for religious reasons. They described the town by its "sepulchral silence and the desolation of its dilapidated streets."[546]

---

[538] Pallas, *Travels*, 36; the same; *Bemerkungen*, 36.
[539] D.B. "Otryvok," 49; Henderson, *Researches*, 311.
[540] Lyall, *Travels*, 264-265. We should add, however, that 645 and 575 give us a sum of 1220, not 1120 as the traveler has it.
[541] Montpereux, *Voyage*, 339.
[542] Kaczkowski, *Dziennik*, 100.
[543] N.Murzakevich, "Poezdka v Krym in 1836 godu" [Trip to the Crimea in 1836], *ZhMNP* 3 (1837): 642.
[544] O.Shishkina mentioned that the town looked like "a fairy-tale, a hazy dream" (Shishkina, *Zametki*, 116).
[545] Chojecki, *Wspomnienia*, 217.
[546] Hell, *Travels*, 365.

According to S.Szapszal, the emigration of the Karaites *en masse* started in 1846, when only thirty families remained in Çufut-Qalé.[547] The main destinations of the migrants were Bakhçeseray, Evpatoria [Gözlöw], Feodosia [Kaffa], Cherson [Kherson], Odessa, Nikolaev and other trading cities situated nearby.[548] A report sent to the attention of the governor of Taurida (24.06.1852) mentioned that the population of Çufut-Qalé was reduced to ninety-four inhabitants.[549]

Temporarily reversing this trend, the population of Çufut-Qalé considerably grew during the Crimean War (1853-1856). The town's Karaite community was enlarged by a number of Gözlöw Karaites who decided to leave Evpatoria, because of its location in dangerous proximity to the arena of military actions. A.Markevich estimated that, before the seizure of Evpatoria in 1854, about 500 families of well-to-do local Karaites left the town; in all probability, part of them moved to Çufut-Qalé.[550] However, after the end of the war not only the newcomers, but also most of old residents of the town decided to leave. The German traveler S.Steinhard (1855) mentioned that, during the war, practically the whole Crimean Karaite community had gathered in Çufut-Qalé, and then left it after the end of military actions.[551] N.Berg, who lived in Bakhçeseray during the Crimean War (1856), described Çufut-Qalé as a "hardly breathing", half-mythical town inhabited by several Karaite families, who were retained there only by the efforts of the "Rabbi" Shelomoh Beim.[552]

Shemu'el Pigit, who witnessed these events as a small boy, left a very picturesque description of Çufut-Qalé at the time of the Crimean War. According to Pigit, the Karaites from Evpatoria [Gözlöw] and Sevastopol', who migrated to Çufut-Qalé, were mostly from poor and middle-class families, whereas well-to-do Karaites migrated to remoter and safer cities of the Russian Empire (such as Moscow, St.Petersburg, Elisavetgrad, Ekaterinoslav, Kremenchug,

---

[547] Szapszal, *Karaimy*, 16.

[548] Nowosielski, *Stepy*, 190.

[549] I.I.Kazas, "O merakh dla podderzhaniya Chufut-Kale" [On the measures for supporting Çufut-Qalé], *ITUAK* 10 (1890): 70.

[550] A.Markevich, *Tavricheskaya guberniya vo vremia Krymskoy voiny* [Taurian "guberniya" at the time of the Crimean War] (Simferopol', 1994), 11-12.

[551] As quoted in Pojata [H.Skirmuntowa], "Szkice z Krymu," *Tygodnik Ilustrowany* 8: 201 (1871): 219, 222. Highly interesting accounts of the French travelers who visited Çufut-Qalé at the time of the Crimean War were explored in Trevisan Semi, "Crimean Karaites in the French Jewish Press," 9-16; Gammer, "Karaites."

[552] Berg, *Bakhchisaray*, 19.

Melitopol', &c.). These emigrants left Çufut-Qalé in 1856-1857, leaving the town even more desolate and decayed than before.[553]

As might be expected, this gradual decline ultimately ended in abandonment. According to the official, government survey of 1857, there were only 30, poor families living in Çufut-Qalé.[554] S.Beim wrote that, by 1862, the population of Çufut-Qalé was reduced to only twelve families.[555] In the account of E.Markov (the 1860s), Çufut-Qalé was depicted as an abandoned, mystical town inhabited only by a few families under the guidance of Avraham Firkovich. Markov also mentioned Firkovich's intentions to revive community life in Çufut-Qalé by resettling Polish Karaites there.[556]

H.Skirmuntowa (Pojata), who paid a visit to Çufut-Qalé in 1869-1870 and called the town "a peaceful republic of Hebrews" or a "Zion of Taurida Israelites". She described the settlement as completely abandoned, haunted by wild dogs, and inhabited only by Firkovich's family. Recalling her entrance to Çufut-Qalé, Skirmuntowa records asking:

> "Maybe all the population is praying in the synagogue? Or everybody is sleeping? Or dead? Or left their Çufut-Qalé to the power of eternity and decay?"

Soon, she found an answer to her rhetorical questions. "Çufut-Qalé... has gone!", explained Firkovich's daughter to Pojata, "Only my father keeps it. Except us, nobody lives here, everybody has left it."[557] F.Remy (1871) mentioned the young Rabbi *Juda Jeruh* [Yehudah Yeru(shalmi)], who entertained him during Firkovich's absence, as the only inhabitant of the town.[558]

It seems that Çufut-Qalé was abandoned entirely after the death of A.Firkovich. L.Hlebnicki-Józefowicz, who visited the town in 1877 (*i.e.* three years after Firkovich's death), left it even more

---

[553] Pigit, *Iggeret Niḏhei Shemu'el*, 2, 10, 12. The author is greatful to Dr. Philip Miller for his help with this highly interesting Karaite source. Dr. Miller also prepared, based on archival sources, an article dedicated to the Crimean War and its consequences for the Karaite community (Philip Miller, "The Crimean Karaites and the Crimean War" (in print)).

[554] Qazas, "O merakh dla podderzhaniya Chufut-Kale," 71.

[555] Beim, *Pamiat'*, 26.

[556] Markov, *Ocherki*, 454-461. This was, undoubtedly, a reference to Avraham Firkovich's project for the resettlment of the Karaites of Luck to Çufut-Qalé.

[557] Pojata [H.Skirmuntowa], "Szkice z Krymu," *Tygodnik Ilustrowany* 8:201 (1871): 222.

[558] Remy, *Krim*, 91-95.

dissatisfied. He wrote, "I left this bare rock with an unpleasant feeling in my soul: it was empty, sorrowful, and wild; only precipices and ruins were before my eyes, a real Dante's place." At the time of his visit, the only inhabitants of Çufut-Qalé were remote relatives of Firkovich from Vilno.[559] Brothers Yakov [Ya'aqov] and Iosif [Yosef] Pigit, who lived there until the well-known events of 1917-1924, are often called the last keepers and inhabitants of the fortress.[560] According to S.Szyszman, they refused to leave the abandoned town, lived in a half-ruined house, and managed to survive by descending to Bakhçeseray to sell the milk of ewes and cows, which were their only property in the ruined fortress.[561]

At the end of the eighteenth – beginning of the nineteenth century, Çufut-Qalé lost not only its administrative and military significance, but also its importance as a center of trade and arts. For a short period, mostly due to the self-sacrificing activity of such leaders of the Karaite enlightenment as Shelomoh Beim and Avraham Firkovich, Çufut-Qalé maintained, at least symbolically, its stature as the center of Karaite lore and culture. However, even their desperate efforts could not stem the abandonment of the town. Thus, by the third quarter of the nineteenth century, there was no stable population in the territory of Çufut-Qalé. Only the keepers of the fortress remained, its last inhabitants, the Karaite last of the Mohicans.

---

[559] [L.Hlebnicki-Józefowicz], "Wspomnienia," 165.
[560] Simon Szyszman, "Les inscriptions funeraires découvertes par Abraham Firkowicz," *Journal Asiatique* (1975): 235.
[561] Simon Szyszman, "Les passionants manuscrits d'Abraham Firkowicz," *Archeologia. Trésor des Ages* 78 (Janvier 1975): 67.

The Karaite last of the Mohicans: brothers Yakov [Yaʻaqov] and Iosif [Yosef] Pigit, the last inhabitants of Çufut-Qalé.

4.1.2. Karaite monuments and topography of Çufut-Qalé.

"Dschouffut-Kale... absolutely does not resemble any other town, village, or settlement which might be normally seen in Europe. If beavers could make their dwellings of stone, on the top of high rocky mountains, only in this case you could imagine something similar to this beaver-town."
(Kohl, *Reisen*, vol.1, 236)

Necropolis in the Valley of Yehoshafat.[562]

The *Beit HeḤayyim* (a Hebrew euphemism for "cemetery", lit. "house of the living" or "the house of life"), situated in the adjacent valley of Yehoshafat, attracted much of the travelers' attention. Given its large, mystic setting in a quiet valley, its attraction is easy to

---

[562] Some aspects of this subchapter have been discussed in Mikhail Kizilov, "Karaimskie necropoli Chufut-Kale i Mangupa po opisaniyam puteshestvennikov 18 – 19 vekov" [Karaite cemeteries of Çufut-Qalé and Mangoup according to description of the eighteenth – nineteenth century travelers], in *Materialy Vos'moy Mezhdunarodnoy Konferentsii po Iudaike* (Moscow, 2002), 191-205.

understand. According to some estimates, there are more than 7,000 graves scattered about the valley floor.[563] Several travelers left important information about the dating of the cemetery: the amount of the gravestones there, and many other interesting and important details.

Travelers' data is extremely important in providing an understanding of how the Karaites of Çufut-Qalé viewed their cemetery. Moreover, these accounts reveal that travelers Jean de Reuilly, Ebenezer Henderson, and Dubois de Montpereux were pioneers in the academic investigation of the cemetery, in the period preceding A.Firkovich and D.Chwolson.

The travel notes of P.S.Pallas (1793-1794) are the earliest source we currently have that mention the "Yehoshafat Valley" by name.[564] Thus, the local Karaites of the second half of the nineteenth century were wrong thinking that this name was given to the valley by A.Firkovich after his visit to the Holy Land in 1830.[565] Much more interesting is the remark of S.Beim, who mentioned that the valley near Çufut-Qalé was named after the Yehoshafat Valley in the Holy Land in memory of a certain Karaite family from Jerusalem, which had been buried in the valley near Çufut-Qalé.[566]

E.Markov (1860s) left the following picturesque description of the similarity between the Yehoshafat Valley in Çufut-Qalé and the Yehoshafat Valley in the vicinity of Jerusalem:

> A real valley of Yehoshafat, a valley of the resurrection of the dead. Graves, mountains, ruins on the top of the mountains, everything indeed smells like Jerusalem... My memory revived all the poetical pictures of Jerusalem's landscapes...[567]

According to S.Beim, Çufut-Qalé was similar to the vicinity of Jerusalem: the mount of Meydan-Dağ ("mountain of the open space") reminded him the mount of Moriah, whereas Beşik-Dağ ("cradle mountain"), situated opposite Çufut-Qalé, the Mount of Olives.[568] A very late Karaite legend, dedicated to Beshik-Tau (Beşik-

---

[563] A.G.Gertsen, "Arkheologicheskie issledovaniya karaimskikh pamiatnikov v Krymu" [Archæological investigation of the Karaite monuments in the Crimea], *MAIET* 6 (1998): 747.

[564] Pallas, *Travels*, 35; the same, *Bemerkungen*, 35.

[565] See the full account of Firkovich's visit to the Holy Land in 1830 together with S.Babovich in A.S.Firkovich, "Palomnichestvo," transl. B.Y.Kokenai, ed. M.Eizeri, *Leningradskiy evreiskiy almanakh* 2 (1986).

[566] Beim, *Pamiat'*, 41.

[567] Markov, *Ocherki*, 89.

[568] Beim, *Pamiat'*, 40-41; see also S.Weissenberg, "Istoricheskie gnezda Kryma i

Dağ), preserved some bits of the original Karaite traditions relating to this place. According to this legend, once on the Beşik-Dağ a wooden cradle was hidden, which belonged to one of the first Karaite pilgrims to Jerusalem. As the Mount of Olives near Jerusalem is said to reveal the Ark of the Covenant, hidden there by the prophet Yirmiyahu, in the future, Beşik-Dağ is said to house the cradle that will hold the newborn Savior of world (*i.e.* Messiah) in it.[569]

Marshall Marmont, who visited Palestine a short while before his visit to the Crimea, compared "la vallée de Josaphat" with Qidron Valley.[570] According to A.Gertsen and Y.Mogarichev, the decorative round tower built on the Southern flank of the Eastern defensive wall of Çufut-Qalé, was also supposed to imitate the monument in the Jerusalem Yehoshafat Valley, known as *"Yad Avshalom"* (Avshalom's monument).[571]

The Eastern Wall of Çufut-Qalé. According to A.Gertsen and Y.Mogarichev, the decorative round tower built on the Southern flank was supposed to imitate "Yad Avshalom" (Avshalom's monument) in Jerusalem. (photo by M.Kizilov)

Kavkaza" [Historical nests of the Crimea and Caucasus], *Evreiskaya Starina* 6:1 (1913): 67.

[569] Unfortunately, some parts of this interesting legend were undoubtedly transformed by the influence of the Karaite-Khazar theory. This legend was narrated to A.Szyszman by T.S.Levi-Babovich: *MS LLAS*. F.143-1531,3r-4v.

[570] Marmont, *Voyage*, 297.

[571] Gertsen, Mogarichev, *Krepost'*, 86.

Visiting the cemetery became an obligatory part of undertaking a voyage to the Crimea.[572] The travelers usually remarked that the magnificent scenery of the place engrossed them in a pious contemplation regarding the vanity of earthly life. E.Clarke (1799) mentioned that a visit to the "field of the dead" was the only exercise of the Karaite women.[573] Edmund Spenser (1836) found the cemetery filled with pious Karaite mourners: "Here, the mourner was sorrowing over the loss of a dear relative; there, adorning the tomb with flowers, or some other memorial affection."[574]

The impression produced by the magnificent scenery of the ancient Hebrew cemetery upon the travelers became even stronger in the second half of the nineteenth century, when the necropolis grew in size and started looking even more forlorn and mystical:

> Thousands of tombstones, with two horns, or with one, or without, they, like a thick harvest, went to the mouth of the valley, being pale as crowds of the dead...[575]

The travelers rarely attempted to determine the number of the tombstones situated in the valley. J.Kohl wrote that graves "are standing as close to each other as ears in a field."[576] S.Beim, who guided O.Shishkina to the cemetery in 1845, told her that more than 40,000 people had been buried there.[577] The same overestimated number was delivered by Beim to A.Koshliakov in 1847.[578] A.Demidov was much closer to reality when he noted about 4,000 graves in 1837.[579] As noted, according to some estimates, there are more than 7,000 graves in the territory of this cemetery at present.[580]

In addition to observations of a general character, the travelers left a number of more detailed notes. Some scholars and travelers of the first half of the nineteenth century tried to classify tombstones and gather information about their dating. The Karaite "Rabbi" (most likely

---

[572] Even the Russian emperor Nicholas I visited the cemetery in 1837 (Safonov, *Opisanie*, 19-20).
[573] Clarke, *Travels*, 189.
[574] Spenser, *Travels*, vol.1, 375.
[575] Markov, *Ocherki*, 89. The "horns" he refers to are the vertical stones at the head and foot of the grave resembling the headboard and footboard of a bed [*ed*].
[576] Kohl, *Reisen*, vol.1, 239.
[577] Shishkina, *Zametki*, 109.
[578] [A.Koshliakov], *Desiatidnevnaya poezdka*, 40.
[579] Demidov, *Voyage*, vol.1, 372; the same, *Travels*, 38.
[580] Gertsen, "Arkheologicheskie issledovaniya," 747.

Yiṣḥaq Ben-Shelomoh), who accompanied French traveler Jean de Reuilly in his trip to the Yehoshafat Valley (1803), considered the grave from 5204 (*i.e.* 1444 c.e.) to be the most ancient one. M.Fazzardi, the traveler's translator, managed to decipher only a few words from the epitaph. Of interest, also, is the fact the Karaite guide told de Reuilly: that he was the first traveler who showed an interest in the dating of the cemetery, and, consequently, the first to see its most ancient tomb.[581]

E.Henderson (1821), who should be remembered as the pioneer of the academic investigation of the cemetery, wrote down the inscription from the oldest grave that was shown to him, and attributed it to 5004 (=1244 c.e.). According to the words of his Karaite guide, the members of the community held this grave in great respect. Nevertheless, Henderson was mistaken when he thought that 5004 (=1244 c.e.) of the Hebrew calendar corresponded to 1364 c.e.; moreover, several mistakes made by him when interpreting the tombstone inscriptions cast doubt on his competency as a specialist in Hebrew.[582]

Other nineteenth century travelers left information about the dating of the most ancient tombstones of the cemetery. K.Kaczkowski (1825) mentioned that the "oldest tombstone of their (*i.e.* Karaite) cemetery belongs to 1400".[583] The Karaite sage Mordekhai Sultanski informed P.I.Koeppen that the oldest graves of the necropolis dated back to 5009 (1249 c.e.) and 5013 (1253 c.e.). Sultanski also mentioned to Koeppen that, in his opinion, there might be more ancient graves in the cemetery, whose inscriptions, unfortunately, had already been too effaced to be deciphered.[584]

As has been mentioned, in the 1840s, A.Firkovich created a completely new theory, according to which the earliest graves of the cemetery belonged to the first centuries C.E. This pseudo-historical concept was reflected in many of his writings, first of all *Avnei Zikkaron* (Vilna, 1872). Thus, starting from the 1840s, most of the

---

[581] The only words which the traveler managed to decipher were:
"Cecy ...... Joseph, fils de Schabatai
Le Tombeau .... 5204"
(Jean De Reuilly, *Voyage en Crimée et sur les bords de la Mer Noire, pendant l'année 1803* (Paris 1806), 133).

[582] Henderson erroneously considered "*daot*" to be a female form of "*dalet*" (?!); moreover, his reconstruction of the beginning of the epitaph ("*Shema'* [Yisra'el]") also looks rather improbable (Henderson, *Researches*, 313-314). The author is greatful to A.Fedorchouk for his assistance with this source.

[583] Kaczkowski, *Dziennik*, 92.

[584] Koeppen, *Sbornik*, 29.

travelers received information from their Karaite guides that stated a much earlier dating of the cemetery's tombstones than the travelers of earlier periods. O.Shishkina (1845) mentioned that S.Beim was proud that A.Firkovich found the grave of the legendary Yiṣḥaq Sangari, who "died more than a thousand years ago and, according to legend, converted the *Kozars*, who at that moment ruled Taurida, to the Jewish law".[585] Beim also informed A.Koshliakov (1847) that the earliest dates of the tombstones corresponded to the first and second centuries C.E.[586] Ukrainian historian N.I.Kostomarov, who visited Çufut-Qalé in 1861 while the *Even Reshef* was absent, was informed by Gavri'el Firkovich, Firkovich's son-in-law, that "one of the monuments had been placed in the year of the birth of Jesus Christ."[587] Equally ecstatic about Firkovich's discoveries was E.Markov. "This scholar excavated an ancient grave... going back to the earliest years of our era, maybe even to the 6th year A.D."[588]

Travelers' notes represent an absolutely unique source, which allows us to get acquainted with those whose hands were engaged in the process of carving numerous tombstone inscriptions in the cemetery. A.Demidov (1837) described in detail his conversation with "the artist of death," the old Karaite Yehudah Qazas-Mıysız, who spent all his life engraving inscriptions on the tombstones of the cemetery:

> ...we caught sight of a little old man, hidden among the brushwood... The costume of this white-bearded sculptor was of the most grotesque character. On his head was an enormous blue balloon-shaped cap; his eyes were protected from the dust and the glare of the sun by a pair of large round spectacles,

---

[585] Shishkina, *Zametki*, 109. The veracity of the grave of Yiṣḥaq Sangari, allegedly found by A.Firkovich in 1839 and later lost or destroyed, engendered a hot discussion, which has not ceased. A.Harkavy mentioned that, according to Firkovich's own words, the locating of Sangari's tomb was one of the most important tasks of his scholarly mission of 1839. Firkovich also mentioned the existence of some pseudo-ancient Karaite legends about the location of Sangari's burial in Chersonese (Sevastopol') (A.Harkavy, "Po voprosu ob iudeiskikh drevnostiakh, naidennykh Firkovichem v Krymu" [On the Hebrew antiquities found by Firkovich in the Crimea], *ZhMNP* 192 (1877): 111-113). A very serious argument against the reliability of Sangari's grave might be found in the testimony of N.Murzakevich (May, 1841), who had seen the grave soon after its supposed discovery, and was sure its tombstone inscription looked too fresh and well-preserved to be genuine, without traces of moss or decay (Karaulov, "Chufut-Kale i Evrei-Karaimy", 97).

[586] [A.Koshliakov], *Desiatidnevnaya poezdka*, 40.

[587] Kostomarov, *Avtobiographiya*, 291.

[588] Markov, *Ocherki*, 431. Probably, the traveler had seen the grave of Buki attributed by Firkovich to this year (Harkavy, "Po voprosu ob iudeiskikh drevnostiakh," 110).

fastened behind his head with a piece of string; and a painter's parasol shaded the little, shriveled individual, crouched at the foot of the monument upon which he exercised his art [...] "For forty years," he said, "there has not been a gravestone set up here but my chisel has carved the epitaph upon it... I knew, and loved, the greater part of those who sleep here, ere I engraved their names in the great stone book of Jehoshaphat...[589]

Auguste Raffet, who accompanied Demidov during his travels in Southern Russia, left a wonderful drawing depicting the aforementioned carver in the process of making an epitaph.

The drawing of Auguste Raffet (1837) depicting a Karaite carver Yehudah Qazas-Mıysız. Note the carver's instruments lying nearby. Archival documents testify us that it was Yehudah Qazas that was hired by Firkovich for making copies of tombstone inscriptions which had been sawn off by the latter and sent to St.Petersburg

H.Skirmuntowa (Pojata) described in detail her conversation with the Karaite sculptors she met near the

---

[589] Demidov, *Travels*, 38-39; French original in: the same, *Voyage*, vol.1, 372-373.

cemetery in 1870. Skirmuntowa was quite surprised to see what she described as their unsolemn attitude towards the graves of their ancestors:

> "Why does your town look so empty and forlorn?" – we ask the younger [carver], because the older, it seemed, was hardly able to understand us.
> "E-eh, what might be done about it?" – answered he, indifferently shaking his head and shrugging his shoulders.
> "It's a pity, my dear; it is your capital, and it is in such a decay."
> "E-eh?" The Karaite even more indifferently interrupted us, waved his hand, and stepped with one of his feet on a grave, which is a sign of terrible irreverence among the Jews.

Upon Skirmuntowa's request, the carvers led her to the graves of the Sangari family. The tombs of Sangari and his wife, situated close to each other, astonished Pojata by their enormous size. When leaving the place, Pojata put "a last farewell glance upon the sorrowful Çufut-Qalé of living, and even more sorrowful Çufut-Qalé of the dead."[590]

D.Chwolson mentioned that, while working in the territory of the cemetery in 1878, he was often visited by Karaites, Rabbanites, military officers, Tatars, and numerous travelers. The scholar was quite surprised to find that the Karaites who visited the place did not show much interest in the cemetery and could not show him where the oldest graves were located. Chwolson also mentioned the existence of certain superstitious beliefs related to the supposed grave of Yiṣḥaq Sangari and other large tombstones.[591]

Interestingly, S.Beim mentioned that the cemetery had been used as a burial-place not only for human beings, but also for holy books, *i.e.* a kind of *genizah* under the open sky.[592]

To sum up, in spite of the lack of exact information regarding the foundation of both burial grounds, almost all Karaite informants of the early nineteenth century dated the oldest tombstones to the

---

[590] Pojata [H.Skirmuntowa], "Szkice z Krymu," *Tygodnik Ilustrowany* 8: 201 (1871): 222-223.
[591] Chwolson, *Corpus*, 17-18.
[592] Beim, *Pamiat'*, 42. According to the Karaite and Rabbanite religious tradition, all books containing the name of God, must to be placed in *genizot* (special keeping places for worn-out books) or buried in the cemetery like human beings.

thirteenth/fourteenth centuries.[593] The idea that the cemetery goes back to the first centuries c.e., and Khazar times appeared in Karaite society only in the 1840s, as a consequence of A.Firkovich's propagandistic activity.

The view of the cemetery in the Yehoshafat Valley during the winter (photo by M.Kizilov)

---

[593] The hot and rather impolite discussion between the proponents and opponents of Firkovich's theory is beyond the scope of this book. However, most of the unprejudiced and objective scholars are inclined to date the foundation of the cemetery to not earlier than the thirteenth/fourteenth centuries. See on this, and many other problems related to the dating of the Karaite cemeteries in the Crimea, *Studies in a Karaite Community: The Report of the Epigraphic Expedition of the Ben-Zvi Institute to the Jewish-Karaite Cemetery of Chufut-Qal'eh, the Crimea*, ed. *Dan Shapira, Ben-Zvi Foundation, Jerusalem, 2002* (450pp., Hebrew, in print).

Batei Keneset (synagogues, kenesalar).[594]

Present day view of the larger Karaite synagogue (Beit Keneset, Keneae) in Çufut-Qalé.
(photo by M.Kizilov)

---

[594] Practically all Karaite sources, written in Hebrew, used the traditional Hebrew term *"Beit Keneset"* to designate the Karaite houses of prayer (translated into English as "synagogue" – *e.g.* Yosef Shelomoh Lucki's chronicle (1827): Miller, *Separatism,* 88-93). However, in 1911 the Karaite *Ḥakham* S.M.Pampulov suggested substituting *"Beit Keneset"* with the word *"kenesa"* or *"kenasa"* (sing.; pl. *"kenesalar"*; "O naimenovanii 'kennasa'"[On the term "kennasa"] *KZh* 1 (1911), 109). From this moment on, the word "synagogue" was banned from the writings of East European Karaites; moreover, the term *"kenesa/kenasa"* is usually used in academic literature in Russian, Polish, and Lithuanian. A.Gertsen suggested that the essentially late term *"kenasa"* was documented for the first time as late as 1910 (Gertsen, Mogarichev, *Krepost',* 96). There is no doubt, however, that the term *"kenesa"* goes to earlier periods of Karaite history in Eastern Europe. On the basis of nineteenth/early (before 1911) twentieth century testimonies about the usage of the term *"kenesa"* among the East European Karaites, we may suppose that this term was often used in the Tatar and Karaim languages as a substitute for the official, and literary *"Beit Keneset."* According to Dr. D.Shapira, the word *"kenesa",* and its more literary equivalent *"kenasa",* were borrowed by the Turkic languages of the East European Karaites from Arabic. Arabic, in its turn, borrowed it from the Aramaic (private communication). To my knowledge, the earliest usage of the term "Kenissiah" for the designation of the Karaite house of prayer is to be found in an essay on the Karaites of the German Protestant theologian Friedrich Albert Augusti in his *Gründliche Nachrichten von denen Karaiten* (Erfurt, 1752), 33.

182

The fountain for ablution at the entrance to the larger synagogue (kenesa) in Çufut-Qalé, which had been seen by James Webster in 1828. (photo by M.Kizilov)

Interior of the larger synagogue of Çufut-Qalé. (19th century photo)

Parts of the Heikhal from the larger synagogue of Çufut-Qalé. (photo by Leonid Berestovskiy)

184

In general, the concentration of Jewish quarters around their synagogues may be noted in the social as well as in the material life of the Jews in the Middle Ages, and Early Modern period. The two Karaite synagogues of Çufut-Qalé always attracted the attention of travelers, scholars, and tourists by their interesting architectural design and exotic, Oriental appearance. Until recently, both synagogues – in spite of their state, worn-out by the hand of time, and lack of restoration – had been preserved in their entirety, and could be easily seen while visiting Çufut-Qalé. However, recent (2001-2002) "restoration", carried out by the hands of ignorant and careless workers, has destroyed the wooden inner furnishings of the larger synagogue. It seems that the same fate is awaiting the smaller synagogue.[595]

The large synagogue was built in the seventeenth century, presumably on the place of the earlier one.[596] A specific feature of this, and other Karaite synagogues, is its southern orientation.[597] As is known, the Karaites do not recognize the Rabbanite rite of *miqweh* (ritual bath). A stone reservoir in front of the large synagogue is a witness of another Karaite religious tradition according to which hands and feet must be washed before entering the synagogue. J.Webster (1828) suggested that this tradition arose from Muslim influence;[598] however, in fact, this practice stems from a literal interpretation of the Bible.[599]

---

[595] The same "specialists" that destroyed inner furnishings attempted to make a replica of the beautiful wooden Heikhal part of the synagogue; however, while doing this, they "forgot" to restore Hebrew inscriptions, which once had been painted there. Unfortunately, none of my appeals could solve the situation. See my article in the local Crimean newspaper: Mikhail Kizilov, "Merzost' zapusteniya v chufutkalskom khrame" [Abomination of desolation in the Çufut-Qalé shrine], *Khaverim* 50 (2002),:8-9.

[596] Gertsen, Mogarichev, *Krepost'*, 96.

[597] This is because of literal interpretation of the words of Shelomoh [Solomon] in Melakhim Alef [I Kings] 8:44, 8:48; Divrei HaYamim Beit [II Chronicles] 6:34, 6:38, and of the prophet Dani'el 6:10.

[598] Webster, *Travels*, 81-82 [see more in §3.2.1].

[599] [*ed.* Anyone who comes to a Karaite *Beit Keneset* must be *tahor* (ritually pure). In coming to the *Beit Keneset*, however, one may get dirt or fœces on their hands or feet from the street. This is why they are washed before entering, to ensure that the entire body is *tahor* and clean. As it says in Tehilim [Psalms] 26:6 and 73:13, prayer being the substitute for the sacrifices in the Temple, one who prays must be *tahor* and clean, just like the Kohanim who offered the sacrifices on the altar of the Temple [see Shemot (Exodus) 30:18-21 and 40:30:32]. The purpose of a *miqweh* is to treat the *tahorah* of the entire body. Washing the hands and feet just addresses the cleanlines of the hands and feet; it assumes that the rest of the body is already *tahor*. *Beit Keneset* 'Anan in Jerusalem has a laver in its foyer, at the base of the stairs; and the Karaite synagogue in Daly City, CA has bathrooms located in the foyer of its

The smaller synagogue was built later, at the end of the eighteenth century, after the expulsion of the Karaite community from Mangoup; some equipment for this synagogue was also brought from Mangoup.[600] Karaite sources often called this building *Beit HaQodesh* (Hebrew "house of holiness").[601] According to Shelomoh Beim, it was built to receive the surplus congregation when the larger synagogue was overfilled, and to perform special religious ceremonies which were not allowed in the larger synagogue.[602] Its inner and outer design and decorations are much more modest than those of the larger one. It seems that the smaller synagogue was built after 1793-1794: P.S.Pallas who visited Çufut-Qalé in this period mentioned the existence of only one synagogue, undoubtedly, the larger one.[603] In the second half of the nineteenth century, when the local Karaite community considerably decreased, religious services took place only in the larger building, whereas the smaller one was used as a storage facility for the manuscripts gathered by A.Firkovich in his travels in the Crimea, Caucasus, and Orient.[604]

Already in 1799, when the building of the second synagogue had evidently been completed, Vladimir Izmailov pathetically cried, "Oh, miracle!... On the terrible cliff I find the abode of the posterity of ancient Israel; under the clouds I found its temples, condemned by the laws of mortals, but spared by the heavenly thunder...[605]

E.Markov (1860s) described the larger synagogue in the following way:

> The synagogue looks like a real monastery; it is surrounded by reliable walls and is completely hidden in the yard... Its cleanliness is very remarkable. In the first part, where shoes are to be taken off, stand benches, and there are no chairs further on; there are numerous lamps of a very quaint form, which are hung on wooden triangles, as in mosques. There is

---

Beit keneset, where hands and feet may be washed before entering the sanctuary... The *Batei Keneset* in Ramlah, Ofaqim, Be'ershva', Ranen, Maṣlia'ḥ, and Ashdod also have washing stations outside the sanctuary, as does the *Beit Keneset* in Istanbul, and as did the *Batei Keneset* in Cairo.]

[600] T.S.Levi-Babovich, *Ocherk vozniknoveniya karaimizma* [Sketch of emergence of Karaism], (Sevastopol', 1913), 39.

[601] Beim, *Pamiat'*, 50.

[602] *ibid.* 50.

[603] Pallas, *Bemerkungen*, 35; the same, *Travels*, 35.

[604] See descriptions of Markov, *Ocherki*, 456; Pojata [H.Skirmuntowa], "Szkice z Krymu," *Tygodnik Ilustrowany* 8: 201 (1871), 222.

[605] Izmailov, *Puteshestvie*, 141.

a kind of lectern, instead of an altar, and there is a very beautifully decorated Pentateuch of great antiquity. In general, it is very simple, narrow, and poor...[606]

Various objects, from the visits paid to the synagogues by the Russian royal family, were held in special respect.[607] On May 15th, 1847, queen-mother Alexandra Theodorovna donated a precious silver chalice to the Karaite community of Çufut-Qalé, together with an annual fund of fifty rubles for the upkeep of the local school.[608] This chalice, which was put on an honorable place close to the altar, was seen by F.Remy (1871) and A.Daab (1896).[609]

According to some nineteenth century sources, there were two ostrich eggs that hung between the lanterns in the altar part of the larger synagogue. S.Beim, in the mid-1850s, remarked, "they should help the faithful during prayers to elevate their thoughts to God, just like the ostrich looks at its own eggs impassively until they hatch."[610]

Similar information, supplied by S.Beim in 1847, surprised A.Koshliakov and his companions:

The Rabbi explained to us that, according to Karaite tradition, the hen of an ostrich, when having a premonition of the birth of its chick, stands over the course of more than twenty hours without motion, fixing its eye on the egg... thus, we [Karaites], when in God's temple, also should with great attention think about the moment when our soul will leave its shell, and be reborn for a new life. A very poetic and elevated thought...[611]

E.Deinard explained this Karaite tradition as a local superstition, the result of Muslim influence.[612] Beim's eagerness is

---

[606] Markov, *Ocherki*, 87.
[607] Henderson, *Researches*, 311; Lyall, *Travels*, 268.
[608] Szapszal, "Akchokrakly," 21.
[609] Remy, *Krim*, 94; Adolf Daab, *W Warszawie i na Krymie* (Warsaw, 1996), 94.
[610] Trevisan Semi, "Crimean Karaites in the French Jewish Press," 11; Beim, *Pamiat'*, 47.
[611] [A.Koshliakov], *Desiatidnevnaya poezdka*, 37-38.
[612] Deinard, *Sefer Massa Krim*, 92. This interesting local Çufut-Qalé tradition indeed might be explained by Muslim influence. A similar locating of "ostrich eggs" used as an object for concentration of believers was documented in the Khan-Cami (cathedral mosque) in Bakhçeseray (Dombrovskiy, *Dvorets krymskich khanov*, 49). Alternatively, it maybe interpreted using the symbolism of the egg in Hebrew culture, where it is understood as a reference to eternity and bereavment, a reminder of the saddest events in the history of Judaism (*i.e.* destruction of Temple, but also

documented in several sources that explain the use of these eggs; this suggests that it might have been Beim himself who introduced this tradition.

One of these ostrich eggs, originally hanging in the Çufut-Qalé *kenesa* (according to Szapszal's own assertions), was always worn by the last Eastern European Karaite *Ḥakham*, S.Szapszal, as a kind of personal talisman. The *Ḥakham* (or "*Ḥakhan*", as he called himself) wore it on his shoulder, in a special leather cover.[613] In one of his archival papers, Szapszal gives the following explanation for the presence of ostrich eggs in the Çufut-Qalé *Beit Keneset*:

> It is quite probable that the egg – symbol of life – could have been allowed by the spiritual authorities in the Karaite and Muslim temples as a symbol of life/existence and, in addition, to remind that "omne vivum ex ovo..."[614]

After being acquainted with the synagogues' interior and exterior, the travelers' were usually shown manuscript copies of the Bible.[615] E.Henderson, who was especially interested in analyzing *targumim* in the Karaite language, mentioned that one such *targum* had been purchased for 200 rubles by his colleague, Doctor Pinkerton, who had visited Çufut-Qalé in 1816. Henderson attached a detailed analysis of this manuscript to his travel description of Çufut-Qalé and Luck, adding with regret that he had not been able to purchase any of the *targumim* because of their high price.[616] "Younger Firkowitch", who accompanied F.Remy during his visit to Çufut-Qalé, showed Remy one of these rare manuscripts, and mentioned that they had refused to sell this manuscript to Rothschild, who had offered them one-thousand rubles.[617]

---

the hope of final reconstruction with the coming of the Messiah).

[613] This is according to Szapszal's grandson, V.Ormeli: "Vstrechi s dedushkoi" [Meetings with grandfather], *KV* 3 (55) (2000). At the present moment, this egg is kept in the Szapszal collection of the Lithuanian National museum in Vilnius (Lithuania).

[614] It is evident that Szapszal did not have exact information on the origin of this interesting tradition. According to Szapszal, he had seen ostrich eggs in Aya-Sofiya in Istanbul, in a mosque in Saraevo, and (with reference to another traveler) in the Armenian church in Jerusalem ("Nauchnyi obzor predmetov material'noy kultury," MS LLAS, F.143-859: 20-22). [ed. it is obvious that this was a late innovation since according to the Torah ostrich eggs are *tame'* [ritually impure] and impart *tum'ah* [ritual impurity] to anything or anyone that comes in contact with them.]

[615] Lyall, *Travels*, 267; Clarke, *Travels*, 192-193.

[616] Henderson, *Researches*, 310, 332-339.

[617] Remy, *Krim*, 94.

One particular manuscript treasure, from one of the Çufut-Qalé synagogues – a beautiful Torah scroll, written on high-quality parchment, in a case trimmed with velvet and silver – is being kept in the Bakhçeseray historical-architectural museum. Most likely, this Torah scroll was shown in 1820 to I.M.Muraviev-Apostol, who described it in the following way, "written on a parchment, in bookcase trimmed with black velvet, with silver decorations."[618]

Torah scroll, a copy of Avnei Zikkaron, and rare prints from the Çufut-Qalé printing press kept in the Bakhçeseray museum. (photo by M.Kizilov)

---

[618] Muraviev-Apostol, *Puteshestvie*, 123.

Other monuments.

There are other important historical monuments of Çufut-Qalé that are directly related to the history of the Karaite community of the town.

As has been mentioned, from the end of the fifteenth century, Tatar officials often used Çufut-Qalé as a place for housing important prisoners. Among the "reluctant travelers" imprisoned in Çufut-Qalé were such famous persons as the Prince of Transylvania, Janos Kemeny (1657), Polish hetmans Potocki and Kalinowski (1648), Russian boyar Vasiliy Sheremetev (1660-1681), and ambassadors V.Aitemirov (1692-1695) and A.Romodanovski (1681). [619] Moreover, the sources testify that practically all members of the Polish and Russian embassies, of the first half of the seventeenth century, were unable to avoid the very doubtful "honor" of spending some time in Çufut-Qalé's imprisonment.[620] Vasiliy Sheremetev, who spent about twenty-one years in Çufut-Qalé, wrote to Tsar Alexis in despair about the terrible conditions of his imprisonment:

> I wear chains which are heavier than a half-*pood*;[621] I have been closed in a chamber for four years; the windows are blocked with stones, so that only one window remains. I have not been outside of the house for six years, and I satisfy all my necessities right inside of the house... my teeth have fallen out because of scurvy; and from headaches I can hardly see; and from the chains I almost lost my legs, and I suffer from hunger...[622]

It is difficult to hazard the location of the seventeenth century prison;[623] however, in the second half of the eighteenth century, it was

---

[619] The ambassador Vasiliy Tiapkin, who was sent there for signing a peace treaty with the Crimean Khanate in 1680, wrote about the release of two Russian nobles (*boyars*), Vasiliy Sheremetev and Andrey Romodanovskiy from the prison of *Zhidovskiy Gorodok*. He also mentioned that the members of his embassy stayed in "zhidovskie doma" (Jewish houses) of Chufut-Kale: "Stateinyi spisok," 616.

[620] Podhorodecki, *Chanat Krymski*, 75; Novoselski, *Bor'ba*, 120, 128, 194.

[621] *I.e.* more than 8 kg.

[622] As quoted in Gertsen, Mogarichev, *Krepost'*, 92 (translation from Russian is mine – M.K.).

[623] A.G.Gertsen located this prison in one of the cave-dungeons situated on the Southern slope of Çufut-Qalé (Gertsen, Mogarichev, *Krepost'*, 92-93). In our view, however, this cave-prison was used only for those prisoners whose conduct evoked the wrath of the Tatar officials, whereas other, more respected, prisoners were located in regular stone buildings.

located in the house of the Karaite "*Aaron-Kochesh-Balbush*."[624] When taking into account that quite a number of prisoners were located in Çufut-Qalé at the same time, it is possible conclude that there were several buildings used for keeping prisoners. Moreover, it is very likely that there was a small Tatar garrison in the fortress for this purpose, whose presence was not reflected in written sources.

Çufut-Qalé was not only the most important seat of the largest Karaite community in the Crimea, but also the center of Karaite-Jewish culture and learning. It was the Karaites (not Rabbanites, Christians, or Muslims) who introduced the world of printing to the Crimean peninsula: the first printing press in the Crimea was a Karaite one. It was established in Çufut-Qalé in the beginning of the 1730s, under the auspices of Yiṣḥaq Ben-Mosheh Sinan-Çelebi. Moreover, this, and the later Gözlöw *Beit Defus* (Hebrew "printing press"), were the only independent Karaite printing presses in the world! For an unknown reason, in 1741, after the publication of several Karaite and liturgical books (and one Qrımçaq-Rabbanite book), the press ceased to exist. Its activity was, for a short time, revived in 1804 under the guidance of Binyamin Ben-Shemu'el Ağa. Soon after this, the press was transferred to Gözlöw (Evpatoria).[625]

A.Nowosielski (1850), noting Fr.Dombrovski as the source of his data, supplies a number of legends about the printing press in Çufut-Qalé. According to his Karaite informants, the press was established by *Izaak Czelebi* [Yiṣḥaq Çelebi], the son of a Persian Karaite *Moszesinan* [Mosheh Sinan]. Yiṣḥaq went to Constantinople, where a Karaite printing press already existed. There, he bought typesetting materials, and hired several experienced printers. At the time of Nowosielski's visit, the Karaites still remembered the names of the printers hired by Yiṣḥaq from Constantinople. The name of *Mosze Pasza* [Mosheh Paşa] was especially venerated. He was a printer and excellent poet, who could not walk, and described his sufferings in poems.[626] Yiṣḥaq, as well as other wealthy Karaites, donated a lot of money in order to support the printing press. During Nowosielski's

---

[624] In 1777, Selim Shah Murza and two other Tatar dignitaries ('Azaryah Ben-Eliyah, "Sobytiya," 74-75) were imprisoned there. [*ed.* the name is obviously corrupted, perhaps from Aharon Qoyçu Ba'al-HaBayit (*i.e.* Aharon Qoyçu the landlord).]

[625] See details in Philip Miller, "Prayer Book Politics," 15-26; Philip Miller, "Agenda in Karaite Printing," 82-88.

[626] It seems that this poet and printer, Mosheh Paşa, is identical with Mosheh Paşa Ben-Eliyah Paşa. MSs of some of his writings might be found among the other valuable Karaite documents recently acquired by Makhon Ben-Zvi (Jerusalem, Israel) (nr 86). See a survey of this collection in Dan Shapira, "Osef Ḥadash BeMakhon Ben-Ṣevi Shel Mismakhim Qara'im MiMizraḥ Eropah," *Pe'amim* 90 (2002): 155-172.

visit to Çufut-Qalé, a list with the names of those who donated money for the press was still hanging in the main synagogue of the town.[627] T.Czacki mentioned that – in the beginning of the nineteenth century, during the second period of the press' operation – the duties of the printer were fulfilled by a Karaite hired from Volhynia.[628]

O.Aqçoqraqlı was the first who tried to find the exact location of the press.[629] Hebrew type-blocks, found by M.Y.Çoref [Şoref] on the slope under the synagogues in 1987, prompted A.G.Gertsen to suggest that the press was situated close to these two buildings.[630] A remark of S.Szapszal,[631] however, establishes the exact location of the press in the quarter of the town adjoining the synagogues from the northern side.

From written sources, we know about the functioning of several Karaite schools (*Batei Midrash*) in Çufut-Qalé. It is known that, in 1751-1766, the teacher in the local *Beit Midrash* was Simḥah Yiṣḥaq Ben-Mosheh Lucki .[632] In 1852-1857, S.Beim tried to establish a kind of Karaite college in Çufut-Qalé. The young *Ḥazzan* decided to use his house for this purpose. Beim attempted to introduce innovations in education, making it less conservative than it was formerly in Karaite circles.[633] *Popechitel' okruga* (Russ. "a trustee of district") Pirogov (25.05.1857) described this Karaite "college" very darkly:

> It is located near the house belonging to Beim, in some sort of kennel, in a room not larger than two *sazhen*,[634] without a fire-place, with two holes covered with paper instead of windows. In this room, four benches are situated...[635]

Moreover, the report of June 19th, 1857 notes that in all of Çufut-Qalé, "there is no single house suitable for placing the college there.... because most of the houses represented heaps of ruins".[636] In

---

[627] Nowosielski, *Stepy*, 213-214.
[628] Czacki, *Rozprawa*, 1835, 141.
[629] Akchokrakly, "Novoe," 159-160.
[630] Gertsen, Mogarichev, *Krepost'*, 112. In February, 2002, I was given the honor to have a look at these type blocks, in the private collection of M.M.Çoref and his late father M.Y.Çoref.
[631] S.Szapszal, " Akchokrakly," 39.
[632] Schur, *Encyclopedia*, 189.
[633] S.Pigit wrote about the striking differences in the manner of teaching peculiar to his grandfather, Mosheh Qoylu, and that of Beim (Pigit, *Iggeret Nidḥhei Shemu'el*, 2).
[634] Russian measure of lenth equal to 2.13 meters.
[635] Kazas, "O merah dla podderzhaniya Chufut-Kale," 71.
[636] *ibid.* 72.

the 1860s, the *Beit Midrash* was closed due to the lack of pupils, and the existence of two, similar Karaite schools in Bakhçeseray.[637] A schematic plan of Çufut-Qalé, made in 1927 by O.Akchokrakly and B.Jepparov located the school in the quarter between Middle and Burunçaq streets, not far from the synagogues.[638] According to M.M.Çoref, however, the *Beit Midrash* was situated a bit closer, right opposite the larger synagogue (private communication).

Signs of Büyük Qapı

Of great interest also are epigraphic signs carved (or, rather, scratched) on the marble plate of Büyük Qapı (Turk. "Great Gate"), on the Eastern defensive wall of Çufut-Qalé. Paradoxically, these two signs played an important role in the formation of Karaite ethnic symbolism. S.Beim was one of the first to pay attention to these signs (stirrups, pitchfork, and a bullet); he interpreted them as symbols of the military victories of the forty Karaite families who had fought together with Toqtamış and Mengli Giray.[639]

In the twentieth century, these signs became even more important. The Karaite community of Wilno/Vilna placed these two symbols in the center of the community's official seal.[640] In the 1920s, S.Szapszal interpreted these signs as the symbols of Karaite-Turkic clans. In his opinion, the fork-shaped sign, which he called "*Sınaq Tamgha*" (Turk. "pitchfork sign"), was a kind of Karaite military weapon-bicorn, whereas the heart-shaped sign, called by him "*Qalkan Tamgha*" (Turk. "shield sign"), was a depiction of the shield.[641] During the ceremony of his inauguration to the political post of the Polish-Lithuanian *Ḥakham*, Szapszal was given a scepter with these two symbols. Moreover, he replaced the traditional *Magen Dawid* (Shield/Star of David), situated on the entrance gate to the Troki

---

[637] *ibid.* 71-72. E.Markov, however, who visited Çufut-Qalé in the 1860s, described the building of the local Karaite school arranged with "sacred order and cleanliness" (Markov, *Ocherki*, 86-87). Traveler's data seem to be in utter dissonance with the administrative documents quoted above. In our opinion, either the traveler was mistaken or the *midrash* was entirely repaired and rennovated by the time of his visit.

[638] Akchokrakly, "Novoe," 161. Unfortunately, the plan is too imprecise in order to establish exactly in which house of the town the *beit midrash* was located.

[639] Beim, *Pamiat'*, 37. Some nineteenth century authors interpreted these signs as the initial letters of the placename "*Sela' HaYehudim*" – "*samekh*" and "*yod*" or "*Sela' Ha'Ivrim*" – "*samekh*" and "'*ayin*."

[640] See Vilno community documents from *AAN MWRiOP*, 1466, p.166-186.

[641] Tadeusz Kowalski, "Turecka monografja o Karaimach krymskich," *MK* 2:2 (1929): 6.

193

synagogue, with these two symbols.[642] Later, these symbols, when depicted above the symbolic depiction of the Eastern wall of Çufut-Qalé, became a coat of arms for East European Karaites.[643]

However, according to A.G.Gertsen and Y.M.Mogarichev, these symbols could hardly have any relationship to the Karaite community. Most likely, they were the symbols of the Yaşlov Bey clan, who possessed Çufut-Qalé in the seventeenth/eighteenth centuries.[644] A strong argument in favor of this hypothesis is the presence of exactly the same signs on the Middle Gate ("Orta Qapı") of Çufut-Qalé. The middle gate most likely belongs to the fourteenth/fifteenth centuries. This was a time when the Karaite community of Çufut-Qalé was not very numerous, and hardly influential enough to put its putative community signs at the central gate of the Muslim town. Moreover, it is very unlikely that the Karaites, skillful carvers and sculptors, would engrave such a simple, rough emblem, without Biblical allusions and ornate carving.

Variant of the Karaite emblem placed by Seraya Szapszal at the entrance of the Karaite Beit Keneset (kenesa) in Troki in the 1930s. (photo by M.Kizilov)

---

[642] I.Cohen, in 1932, still could see, and even take a picture of, this gate with the Star of David: Israel Cohen, *Vilna* (Philadelphia, 1943), the picture is between page 452 and 453; however, Nazi scholar P.-H.Seraphim during his visit to Troki, in 1938, with satisfaction, could take a picture of strange pagan symbols: Seraphim, Peter-Heinz, *Das Judentum im osteuropaeischen Raum*, 1938, pict.126; see also Freund, *Karaites and Dejudaization*, 129.

[643] See *MK* 2:3-4 (1931), ill.5-6. [*ed.* according to personal conversations with Warren Green, the walls are those of the fortress of Troki.]

[644] Gertsen, Mogarichev, *Krepost'*, 75-77.

194

Signs of the Tatar clans on the Middle Gate ("Orta Qapı"). (photo by M.Kizilov)

Signs on the Büyük Qapı. (from Karamskaya Entsiklopediya, vol.6 (Moscow, 2000)).

Underground well

A late Karaite legend mentions a hidden, underground corridor that led from the Southern gate to a well allegedly situated nearby.[645] To the great astonishment of all skeptics, the legend turned out to be partially true: excavations of 2000-2002 revealed the well, and the lengthy underground corridors connected to it. Of great interest are a number of Hebrew graffiti markings found on the corridor's ceiling, most of them Karaite names and surnames, supposedly of the seventeenth/eighteenth (and maybe even early nineteenth) centuries.[646] At the time of this writing, when the excavations are just completed and not yet published, it is difficult to come to comprehensive conclusions about this mysterious artifact of the Crimean Middle Ages. However, most likely, the well was built around the sixth-tenth centuries, at the time of Byzantine influence in the Western Crimea, and functioned until the end of the eighteenth century. In late mediæval and early modern times, it was used for the needs of the Christian, Muslim, and Jewish communities of Çufut-Qalé; however, it seems that, from the seventeenth century, it stopped being used to supply water.[647] Further investigation will provide more information on the complex, and its significance for the town's history.[648]

---

[645] Beim, *Pamiat'*, 43; M.Y.Firkovich, *Starinnyi karaimskiy gorodok Kale, nazyvaemyi nyne "Chufut-Kale"* [Ancient Karaite town of Kale (Qale'), at present called "Çufut-Qalé"] (Wilno, 1907), 26; Szapszal, *Karaimy*, 22; Kondaraki, *Opisanie*, pt.1, 66.

[646] Among the numerous inscriptions in Hebrew, there are also two in Latin, "Mayja" (perhaps, a corruption of "Marja") and "Zofja"; the names are frequent also among Polish-Lithuanian Karaites. Could they had been left by the Polish Karaite visitors to the fortress? See more details in Mikhail Kizilov, "Podzemnaia taina Chufut-Kale" [Çufut-Qalé's underground mystery], in Simferopol' newspaper *Khaverim* 36 (10) (2001): 18-19.

[647] Evliya Çelebi mentioned that, in the seventeenth century, all water reservoirs of the fortress were broken (Evliya Çelebi, *Kniga*, 94).

[648] The author is greatful to A.F.Kozlov, the director of the speleological center "Onix" (Simferopol', Crimea), for making it possible for me to visit the complex and observe the excavations of the well.

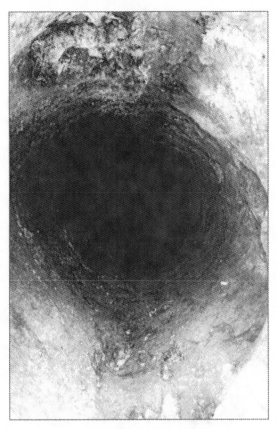

A well found near the Southern gate of Çufut-Qalé, and connected to the underground corridor. (photo by Mikhail Kizilov)

Seventeenth-eighteenth century Hebrew graffiti markings on the well's vault: names of Shemu'el Çınaq and Yiṣḥaq Ben-Eliyah Yeru(shalmi).

These are some of the most important problems related to the history of the Karaite community of Çufut-Qalé. It is very likely that with the discovery of new archæological or written data, future students of its history will face additional historical mysteries or, on the contrary, will find a key for the solution of older ones. Undoubtedly, a comprehensive study of the epigraphic monuments of the necropolis in the Yehoshafat Valley is a necessary factor for filling in numerous gaps in the history of the Karaite community of Çufut-Qalé.

4.2. "Father Mountain" [Baba-Qaya]: Mangoup-Qalé (Theodoro)
4.2.1. Outline of its history

> *"Beautiful Mangoup, known and unknown, keeping silence in*
> *his pretty dialect, mighty by the destruction of power – ruins, strong by*
> *the extirpation of life – remembrances..."*
> (Pojata [H.Skirmuntowa], "Szkice z Krymu. Wycieczka na
> Mangub-Kale," *Kłosy* 17: 433 (1873): 251)

The ruins of the town of Mangoup are situated on the top of a mountain belonging to the southwestern part of the inner chain of the Crimean mountains. Its ravines distinguish four distinct capes on the Mangoup plateau: *Çamlu-Burun* ("Pine Cape"), *Çufut-Çağırgan-Burun* ("Cape of Calling for the Jews"), *Yelli-Burun* ("Windy Cape"), and *Teşikli-Burun* ("Cape with Holes"). In the seventeenth century, the local Tatar population started calling this mountain "Baba" or "Baba-qaya" – "Father cliff".[649] In the Middle Ages (as well as today) it was possible to access the inhabited area of the plateau using paths coming through the ravines of *Tabana-Dere* ("Ravine of Tanners"[650]), *Hamam-Dere* ("Bath Ravine"), and the mediæval road of *Qapı-Dere* ("Gate Ravine").

The natural fortification of this place is extraordinary: the plateau is surrounded almost from all sides by precipices, exceeding, in some places, seventy meters in height. Evliya Çelebi wrote that these precipices resembled "the abyss of Hell," adding that, "Allah created this rock with the purpose that it would serve as a fortress."[651] Another important detail regarding the natural conditions of this place was its good water supply. There are more than nine springs in the territory of the settlement at the present time.[652] This detail was very important for a mediæval castle, especially during a siege. This explains why many travelers of the sixteenth/seventeenth centuries wrote about the good water supply and springs of Mangoup.[653]

---

[649] The name usually given to the highest and largest mountain in a region. See Beauplan, *Opys Ukrainy*, vol.2, 32; vol.1, 51; Kondaraki, "Mangoup-Kale," 419.

[650] [*ed.* While the Russians mistranslated the name as "Valley/ravine of tanners" because of the tanning vats there, it actually means "the valey directly opposite". See footnote 389 on pp.117f. above.]

[651] Evliya Çelebi, *Kniga*, 89.

[652] Gertsen, "Krepostnoy ansambl'," 105.

[653] See Broniovius, *Tartariae Descriptio*, 7; Evliya Çelebi, *Kniga*, 89; Eszer, "Beschreibung," 236.

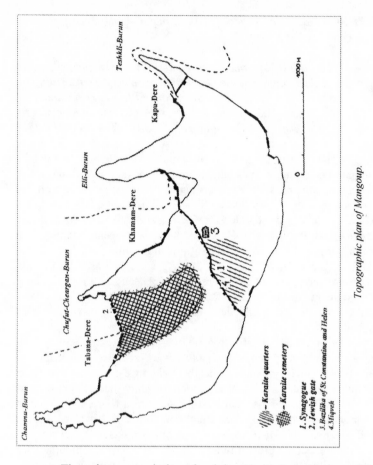

Topographic plan of Mangoup.

1. Synagogue
2. Jewish gate
3. Basilika of St. Constantine and Helen
4. Miqveh

- Karaite quarters
- Karaite cemetery

There is no unanimity of opinion about the meaning of the toponym *Mangoup*. Evliya Çelebi (1665-1666) translated it as "ill-fated," because of the fact that the Turkish commander Gedik Ahmet Paşa lost so many soldiers when seizing the town.[654] Dubois de Montpereux considered it a distorted form of *Mangothia*;[655] A.Demidov supposed that the town's name reflected the presence of the Goths and called it "Mangoute-Kale," *i.e.* "the Goths' Castle."[656] Some scholars

---

[654] Evliya Çelebi, *Kniga*, 92. It is very likely that Beauplan called Mangoup "*meschant chasteau*" [French "wicked" or "evil castle"] taking into consideration this interpretation of the town's name (Beauplan, *Opys Ukrainy*, vol.2, 32; vol.1, 51).

[655] See de Montpereux's contemplations regarding the meaning of this placename in his *Voyage*, 286.

[656] Demidov, *Voyage*, vol.2, 585.

believe that it comes from the Arab *manqub* ("full of caves").[657] The variants of the transcription of this placename, which one comes across in the maps and testimonies of the sixteenth-eighteenth century travelers, also differ: *Manguthia, Mancopa, Mancupra, Mancopia, Makupa,* and even *Oknam* (*i.e.* "*Manko*" written back to front).[658]

Traditionally, scholars consider that the earliest written reference to the usage of this name (in the distorted form *Mank-t*) was found in the letter of the Khazar Khaqan Yosef to Ḥisdai ibn Shaprut (the middle of the tenth century).[659] For a certain period of time this toponym was used simultaneously with the Greek name *Theodoro,* until the Ottoman conquest of 1475, when *Mangoup* replaced the latter. Some later travelers were very impressed by the fact that this town was once inhabited by the Goths, and called it *Kastron Gothias* [Goths' Castle].[660]

Construction of the first fortifications in the territory of the Mangoup plateau date back to the period of Justinian I (527-565).[661] In the eighth century, the town was captured by the Khazars, who left Mangoup in the tenth century. In the ninth century, in spite of the emergence of the independent Gothic diocese with its center in Mangoup (called in the Byzantine sources of the period also *Doros* and *Dorant*), the town was in a state of decline. The renaissance of Mangoup came in the thirteenth century, when the town became the capital of the Greek/Gothic principality of Theodoro. The principality reached the climax of its power and might during the rule of prince Alexis (1405-1444/47). Then, the principality's lands stretched from Chersonesos and Calamita (the region of present-day Sevastopol' and Inkerman) in the West, up to Aluston and Phouna (present-day Alushta and Luchistoe) in the East; moreover, local princes often manifested their claims concerning the southern Crimean lands, which formally belonged to the Genoese administration.[662]

By 1475, the principality of Theodoro represented a strong

---

[657] See the commentaries to Ewlija Czelebi, *Księga*, 264.
[658] Eszer, "Beschreibung," 231, 236; W. Brussius Scotus, *De Tartaris Diarium* (Francofurti, 1598), 6; V.Kordt, *Materialy po istorii russkoy kartografii* [Materials on the history of the Russian cartography] vol.1 (Kiev, 1899), t.11, 22-23, 25.
[659] Gertsen, "Krepostnoi ansambl," 137. It is, however, rather questionable whether this "Mank-t" mentioned in kagan's letter should be identified with "Mangoup."
[660] Guthrie, *Tour*, 68.
[661] According to Procopius, the Goths inhabited this country; on its territory Justinian built "long walls" (Procopius, *Collected Works in Seven Volumes*, vol. 7: *Buildings*, trans. H. B. Dewing (Cambridge, MA-London, 1971), 215-217).
[662] E.V.Veimarn, "O dvukh neiasnykh voprosakh srednevekovia Yugo-Zapadnogo Kryma" [Two unclear questions concerning the Middle Ages in South-Western Crimea], in *AISK* (Kiev, 1968), 79.

political and administrative entity, which included a number of fortified settlements, with the town of Mangoup as its capital. According to information from Italian sources, in the entire principality of Theodoro there were around 30,000 houses (families).[663] According to Jorg of Nuremberg, the number of town defenders locked up there during the siege in 1475 was around fifteen thousand.[664]

However, in spite of its power and influence, the principality could not endure the attack of the Ottoman Empire; and, in December, 1475, after a six-month siege, the town was conquered by the Ottoman army under the command of Gedik Ahmet Paşa.[665] Mangoup did not lose its administrative significance after the Ottoman conquest; it became the center of *qadılıq*, formed predominantly from the lands of the former principality of Theodoro. Unlike Çufut-Qalé, which was in the ownership of the Crimean Khans after 1475, Mangoup and the *qadılıq* were under the jurisdiction of the Ottoman administration.[666] Soon after the Turkish conquest, the defensive fortifications of Mangoup were rebuilt. There is an inscription with the name of governor Tsula (1503)[667] and a letter of the Khan Mengli Giray to Ivan IV (1504)[668] relating this.

In the first half of the sixteenth century, the Ottoman sultans used the descendants of the family of the princes of Mangoup as ambassadors to Russia. In 1514, Kamal (*Kemalbey*), and in 1522, Alexander (*Skinder*) were sent there.[669] According to information from

[663] L.P.Kolly, "Istoricheskie dokumenty o padenii Kaffy" [Historical documents on the fall of Kaffa], *ITUAK* 45 (1911): 17.

[664] Jorg of Nuremberg, *Geschichte von der Turkey*, B as quoted in Vasiliev, *Goths*, 251. Both numerals, however, considerably overestimate the real number of inhabitants of the principality.

[665] The siege of Mangoup became one of the most difficult and prolonged military campaigns of the Ottoman Empire in the fifteenth/sixteenth centuries. See Gertsen, "Krepostnoi ansambl'," 148-154; Vasiliev, *Goths*, 249-266.

[666] *Qadılıq* – an administrative unit in the Ottoman Empire. According to Peyssonel, the Mangoup *qadılıq* consisted of seventy-four villages (Peyssonel, *Traite*, vol.1, 24). Traveler's data correspond to the official Ottoman data of the first half of the sixteenth century, according to which the Mangoup *qadılıq* included 72 villages (Gilles Veinstein, "La Population du Sud de la Crimée," in *Memorial Omer Lufti Barkan* (1992), 229). Evliya Çelebi supplies almost two times exaggerated number of villages of the *qadılıq*: 150 (Evliya Çelebi c *Kniga*, 89).

[667] Vasiliev, *Goths*, 267.

[668] A.Malinovskiy, "Istoricheskoe i diplomaticheskoe sobranie del proiskhodivshikh mezhdu Rossiyskimi velikimi kniaziami i byvshimi v Krymu tatarskimi tsariami s 1462 po 1533 [Historical and diplomatic collection of affairs which took place between the Russian Grand Dukes and the Crimean-Tatar Tsars from 1462 to 1533], *ZOOID* 5 (1863): 400.

[669] N.M.Karamzin, *Istoriya Gosudarstva Rossiyskogo* [The History of the Russian State], vol. II, book 7 (Moscow, 1852; repr., Moscow, 1989), 70, ft. 105.

Evliya Çelebi, Mangoup housed a judge (*qadi*), the Ottoman commandant of a castle (*dizdar*), and a garrison of fifteen soldiers.[670] The Muslim administration stayed there until 1774, when, according to the conditions of Küçük-Kaynarcı peace treaty, Turkey had to withdraw its military forces from the Crimea.

After the Ottoman massacre of the Christian population of the town,[671] the number of inhabitants began to decrease. Martinus Broniovius, who visited the town in 1578 (only a century after the Ottoman conquest), found in Mangoup only one Greek, a few *Judaei* (*i.e.* undoubtedly, Karaites) and Ottomans, and the whole town in ruins.[672] Due to the fact that Mangoup was included in the Ottoman part of the Crimea, there is exact statistical data regarding the number of Karaite households in the Ottoman defters of the sixteenth/seventeenth centuries. There was one Karaite district with forty-eight households in the second quarter of the sixteenth century, thirty-five households in 1542-1543, seventy-six households in 1638, sixty-eight in 1649, and fifty-one in 1662.[673] Numerical data, which was provided by de Beauplan in the seventeenth century, records sixty households. This data is very similar to that of the defters.[674] The density of the population, in all probability, did not change in the eighteenth century. The Ottoman source of 1740 mentioned the presence of sixty houses within the town.[675] Evliya Çelebi records seven districts, 1000 houses and eighty shops; this is certainly considerably exaggerated.[676]

Unfortunately, current, available historical data is insufficient for the establishment of the *terminus ante quem* for Karaites settlement in the territory of Mangoup. The only available sources are very late, and have a rather legendary character. One of them, a Hebrew colophon written around 1700, and preserved in a nineteenth Polish

---

[670] Evliya Çelebi, *Kniga*, 89.

[671] Testimonies from written sources about this massacre can be verified by the data from the archæological excavations of the main Mangoup basilica, where a number of skeletons with traces of mortal wounds or decapitation was found (Gertsen, "Krepostnoi ansambl'," 154).

[672] "Presbyter Graecus unicus, Turcae et Iudaei aliquot ibi habitant, caetera in ruinas, vastitatem, et omnem fere oblivionem versa sunt" (Broniovius, *Tartariae Descriptio*, 7).

[673] Veinstein, "Population," 242; Alan Fisher, " Ottoman Crimea," 221.

[674] Beauplan, *Opys Ukrainy*, vol.2, 32; vol.1, 51. According to the opinion of the editor of Beauplan's book, the average family in the eighteenth century Crimea consisted of appr. 7-10 persons (*ibid.* vol.1, 173). According to O.Halenko, however, this estimation is exaggerated; in his opinion, the average family of that period consisted of appr. 5 persons per household in Kaffa (Halenko, "Iudejski gromady", 49).

[675] Gertsen, "Krepostnoi ansambl," 90.

[676] Evliya Çelebi, *Kniga*, 90.

translation, mentioned the presence of the Karaite community in Mangoup already in the mid-thirteenth century. Another one, an oral tradition narrated to Mordekhai Sultanski by three Mangoup elders, notes that Mangoup was inhabited by Karaites from the Crimean settlements of Eski-Krym and Taş-Cargan soon after the Tatar conquest of the peninsula in the thirteenth century.[677] As has been mentioned, however, both sources are very late and have an unreliable character.

D.Shapira contends that the Karaite community appeared in Mangoup much later, around the mid-fifteenth century, and, initially, consisted mostly of immigrants from Byzantium, fleeing from the Empire after its conquest by the Ottomans.[678] In all probability, only a careful and accurate examination of the tombstone inscriptions from the Karaite cemetery in Tabana Dere can cast a light on this problem.[679] Some data (e.g. the existence of the Qrımçaq surname "Mangupli", i.e. "from Mangoup") suggests that, in addition to the Mangoup Karaite community, there was also a Rabbanite (Qrımçaq) one – whose existence, however, was not reflected in written sources.

In addition to written and epigraphic sources, the presence of the Karaite population is also reflected in the Tatar toponymy of the place. The valley, once occupied by the Karaites, is still called *the Ravine of the Tanners* (Tabana-Dere)[680], while the adjacent cape is called *the Cape of the Calling for the Jews* (Çufut-Çağırgan-Burun). The first placename is a reference to the main occupation of the Karaites; the etymology of the second is, however, unclear. While describing the Karaite monuments of Mangoup, H.Skirmuntowa (Pojata) mentioned "the Hebrew cemetery of the Karaites" and explained the etymology of the placename *Tabana dere* ("the Valley of Tanners," the ravine where the cemetery is situated) by the profession of the Karaites: "Those Protestant-Israelites, with the diligence peculiar to their tribe, ventured to use ancient caves and establish a tannery there." At the time of her travel (1869-1870), all remains of the former splendor of the town disappeared and its magnificent towers "defended only emptiness and miserable Karaite ruins."[681]

---

677 Jaroslav Stepaniv [Daszkiewicz J], "L'époque de Danylo Romanovyc d'après une source Karaïte," *HUS* 3:2 (1978): 335; Koeppen, *Sbornik*, 289-290.

678 Dan Shapira, "A Karaim Poem in Crimean-Tatar from Mangup (Judeo-Turcica III)," in *Turkish-Jewish Encounters*, ed.M.Tütüncü (Haarlem, 2001), 87.

679 Preliminary results of the examination of the cemetery allow one to suppose that the Karaite community appeared there later than in Çufut-Qalé, in the mid-fifteenth century [see below].

680 [ed. See footnote 389.]

681 Pojata [H.Skirmuntowa], "Szkice z Krymu. Wycieczka na Mangub-Kale," *Kłosy*

Unfortunately, written sources did not leave much information on the Karaites of Mangoup. According to the description of Evliya Çelebi (1665-1666), the Mangoup Karaite community appears to be much poorer than that of Çufut-Qalé:

> There are seven Jewish quarters, around a thousand of ill-fated Jewish houses covered with tiles, dirty and lousy, and eighty shops of tanners... All these Jews are of the Karaite denomination. Other Jews dislike the Jews of this confession. They do not know what is forbidden and what is allowed in food... These Jews are indeed Israelites and followers of Moses... They do not know the language of the Jews at all, and speak only Tatar.[682]

According to Evliya, local Karaite tanners were famous in the whole Crimea for the "thick mangoubi hides" they produced.[683] His information is corroborated by de Peyssonel, who mentioned that Mangoup is famous for the woolen and leather goods produced there.[684] Similar information comes from the account of Emidio Portelli D'Ascoli, who mentions that the main inhabitants of Mangoup were the Jews whose occupation was the tanning of hides.[685]

It seems that, in the seventeenth century, Mangoup did not loose its importance as a mighty fortress. Giovanni da Lucca (around 1630) described Mangoup as an impregnable town, with the Jews (*i.e.* the Karaites) as its main inhabitants. Moreover, the traveler also

---

17: 433 (1873): 250.

[682] Evliya Çelebi, *Kniga*, 90. The picture, created by Evliya, of the Mangoup Karaite community as absolutely uneducated and illiterate in terms of religious law seems to be a result of his conversations with the Crimean Rabbanites, who undoubtedly characterized the Karaites in most dark colors. Mr. Mikha'el 'Ezer (Israel), who found a number of manuscript and epigraphic sources testifying to the quite considerable knowledge of Hebrew lore and religion among the community members, is now working on a publication that would disprove the aforementioned "dark" perception of the community (Mikha'el 'Ezer, a paper read during the XIIIth World Congress in Jewish Studies (Jerusalem, August, 2001)).

[683] Of interest is the fact that certain fragments of Evliya's travelogue, which negatively characterize the Mangoup Karaite community, were dropped by the Polish translators, the Karaites A.Zajączkowski, Z.Abrahamowicz, and A. Dubiński (Evliya Çelebi, *Księga*, 262). A similar "censored" variant of Evliya's narration was published by Seraya Szapszal: "Evliya Çelebi Seyahatnamesi (Recenzja)," *MK* 2:3-4 (1931), 67. For a full and unabridged translation see Evliya Çelebi, *Kniga puteshestviya* [The book of travel], transl. Y.Bakhrevskiy (Simferopol', 2000), 34.

[684] Peyssonel, *Traite*, vol.1, 259.

[685] Eszer, "Beschreibung," 236. There are many references to tanning as the main buisness of the Karaites of Mangoup in the centuries to follow.

205

mentions that, in the territory of the town, considerable valuables belonging to the Crimean Khans were kept there. The Khans often found in Mangoup a reliable shelter during the internal wars in the Khanate.[686] Most likely, it was these valuables that attracted the attention of the Zaporozhian Cossacks who sacked the town in the course of sudden attack in 1629.[687] The testimony of da Lucca concerning the military importance of Mangoup as a fortified fortress is corroborated by the information of Karaite chronicler Ya'aqov Ben-Mordekhai, who wrote that – in 1684, in the course of forty days (from June 3rd until July 11th) – Mangoup was besieged by the army of Devlet Giray who wanted to capture Haci Giray II there.[688]

In the sixteenth/seventeenth centuries, in the territory of Mangoup (as well as in Çufut-Qalé), there was a prison for important prisoners of war.[689] It seems that the Karaites fulfilled "supplementary" functions at the prison (i.e. the lending of money and providing of victuals to prisoners). One of the Dominican friars who was imprisoned there in 1663, mentioned that he and his companions had received some help from the merciful Jewish women of Mangoup.[690]

Apart from epigraphic and archæological data, we do not have many sources providing information on the history of Mangoup in the eighteenth century. However, the silence of the sources suggests that the town was in a state of decline[691] and, as well as Çufut-Qalé, fulfilled the role of a ghetto for the Karaite population. The end of the eighteenth century was marked by drastic events such as the removal of the remains of the Ottoman garrison – the fight of the Russian

---

[686] Lucca, "Fatta da me," 56.
[687] See the the chronicles of Portelli D'Ascoli and Xačatur in Eszer, "Beschreibung," 236; Schutz, "Armenische Chronik," 148.
[688] "Neskolko istoricheskikh zametok napisannykh Ravvi Iakovom, synom Ravvi Mordukhaia v kontse knigi Igeret-Gavi-Kuvakh" [Some historical notes written by Rabbi Ya'aqov, the son of the Rabbi Mordekhai, at the end of the book "Igeret-Gavi-Kuvakh], *Vremennik Imperatorskogo Moskovskogo Obshtchestva Istorii i Drevnostey Rossiyskikh* 24 (1854): 132. Several other Karaite chronicles of the seventeenth/eighteenth centuries are now being edited and prepared for publication by Golda Akhiezer (Israel). She holds that the composition of historical works of this type was typical only of the Crimean Karaites, and was not done by their Polish-Lithuanian brethren (private communication).
[689] Among the most important prisoners of the Mangoup prison were such famous Russians as Afanasi Nagoi and Vassili Griaznoi (both – sixteenth century), the highest officials of Tsar Ivan IV "the Terrible". See also Broniovius, *Descriptio*, 7.
[690] Eszer, "Neue Forschungen," 227.
[691] Alan Fisher supposed that one of the main reasons for the worsening of the demographic and œconomic situation in seventeenth century Mangoup (and the whole Crimea in general) was the frequent, devastating raids of the Don and Zaporozhian Cossacks (Fisher, "Ottoman Crimea," 216, 221).

detachments against the Tatar rebels, who found a refuge in the fortress[692] – and a complete abandonment of the town, soon forsaken by its last inhabitants, the Karaites.

St.Siestrzencewicz de Bohusz was, probably, the last visitor to see the town still peopled, when he visited during the last quarter of the eighteenth century.[693] In a later edition of his memoirs, Siestrzencewicz added, "Ils (*i.e.* the inhabitants of Mangoup) se sont transportés à Tschefout-Kalé."[694] This remark of St.Siestrzencewicz records the fact of the migration of the Karaite community of Mangoup to Çufut-Qalé, which took place in the beginning of the last decade of the eighteenth century.

The problem of establishing the exact date and reasons for the emigration of the Mangoup community is very complicated. Mangoup was completely abandoned by the Karaites soon after the Russian annexation of the Crimea. In 1833, M.Sultanski, who had interviewed three Karaites previously from Mangoup (Yiṣḥaq Qırğıy, Yosef Dani, and Shabbetai Qoyçu), reported to P.I.Koeppen that, by 1783, there were about seventy families in Mangoup that left the town about a decade later, in 1791.[695] T.S.Levi-Babovich, with reference to the colophon on one of the Torah scrolls of the Perekop synagogue (or, rather, that of Armianskiy Bazar), mentioned that Mangoup was left by the Karaites in 5552 (=1792 c.e.).[696] At the time of P.S.Pallas's journey (1793-1794), the town was entirely forsaken and visited only in the summer by "Jewish couriers of Dschufut-Kale."[697]

The sources testify that the emigration of the Karaites from Mangoup happened very fast, and without any special reason. In spite of a general fading of the town, there were still remains of the population (around seventy families, *i.e.* circa 300-400 persons), houses, and a functioning synagogue. The situation may be clarified by a poem in Crimean Tatar entitled "Mangup Türküsi" (The Song of Mangup). Its author, an old Karaite named Simḥah, laments that he had to leave the town in 5553 (=1793 c.e.), and demands punishment for the enemies that forced the Karaites to abandon Mangoup:

---

[692] See Thomas Milner, *The Crimea, Its Ancient and Modern History* (London, 1855), 46-48; Neilson, *Crimea*, 81-82.

[693] According to our estimates, the metropolitan's travel took place somewhere about the time of the Russian annexation of the Crimea, most probably in 1783-1785.

[694] St.Siestrzencewicz de Bohusz, *Histoire de la Tauride* (the 1800 and 1824 editions), cited by McDonald Stearns, "Crimean Gothic. Analysis and Etymology of the Corpus," *Studia Linguistica et Philologica*, vol.6 (1978), 21.

[695] P.Koeppen, *Sbornik*, 290.

[696] Levi-Babovich, *Ocherk*, 39.

[697] Pallas, *Travels*, 122; the same, *Bemerkungen*, 122.

207

1. O Teacher, Teacher! O mountains of snow!
   One separated from [his] homeland is weeping.
   The fire fell inside me,
   I am separated, burned, I am weeping.
2. One left each other
   Even the reason did not remain in the head
   In the year 5553 (=1793 c.e.)
   It was destroyed; burned, I am weeping.
3. Passing, I crossed its valley
   I went, I fell into the hand of the enemy
   I gave up my property
   I am going away, burned, I am weeping.
4. "A bud," they say, "is not from a rose" [?].
   My soul will never separate from thee
   with God's help, it will be restored soon,
   I am coming back; burned, I am weeping
5. Its ways are impassable because of stones
   The tears of my eye[s] come down
   From [my] inseparable friends and fellows
   I am separated; burned, I am weeping
6. Its water and its fruits are on high places
   Those who have heard thus say:
   "Mangup became destroyed," they say
   It is destroyed, burned, I am weeping
7. O high mountains that I remembered!
   My face is smiling, my heart is weeping
   O places where I worshipped!
   [They] are destroyed; burned, I am weeping
8. O high mountains that I remembered!
   My face is smiling, my heart is weeping
   "Mangup became destroyed," they say
   It is destroyed; burned, I am weeping
9. This is my supplication to Thee every day:
   "Let my enemies be punished!"
   They call me "the sad Simḥah"
   Until I die, burned, I am weeping.[698]

---

[698] Shapira, "Karaim Poem," 84-85. A special word of thanks goes to Dr. D.Shapira for his persmission to place the English translation of the poem, in full, in this book. Dr. Shapira is also preparing two other variants of this poem for publication in *Vestnik EUM* (2003) (forthcoming).

D.Shapira, the publisher and translator of the poem, believes that the "enemies" Simḥah was referring to are the members of the Russian administration.[699] In my opinion, however, it was the new owner of the lands of the former Mangoup *qadılıq*, the Tatar landlord Adil Bey Balatuqov, who decided to expel the Karaites.[700] As a consequence, in the 1790s, part of the lands of the former Mangoup *qadılıq*, which included the mountain of Baba-Qaya (Mangoup), Haci-Sala village, and the Qaralez Valley, became the property of the Tatar clan of the Balatuqovlar. Some sources directly mention the fact that it was Tatar oppression that forced the Karaites to leave Mangoup.[701] The Çufut-Qalé elders, with whom A.Firkovich socialized in 1839, directly accused Adil Bey Balatuqov not only of expelling the Karaites from Mangoup, but also of desecrating of their cemetery.[702] Nevertheless, the exact reasons for and circumstances under which this action took place are still unclear.

Thus, the history of the Karaite community in Mangoup, and simultaneously the history of Mangoup as an inhabited place, was closed in 1792-1793. Most of the last Karaite inhabitants of the town emigrated to Çufut-Qalé. References to the presence of the surname "Mangoubi" in the nineteenth/twentieth century Karaite communities of Odessa, Moscow, St.Petersbutg, Istanbul, Cairo, and even Chicago testify to the resettlement of the former Mangoupians far beyond the borders of the Crimea.

4.2.2. Monuments

> *"There is nothing, in any part of Europe, which can surpass the tremendous grandeur of the scenery."*
> (Clarke, *Travels* , 280)

When describing Mangoup, the travelers left many valuable notes about its defensive fortifications, religious buildings, caves, and monuments related to the history of the Karaites. The view of this magnificent stronghold nestled on the top of a high mountain usually produced a strong impression on the travelers. The monk Matthew, at

---

[699] Shapira, "Karaim Poem," 91-92
[700] For more details, see in Mikhail Kizilov, "K istorii karaimskoi obshtchiny Mangupa" [On the History of the Karaite Community of Mangoup], *Vestnik EUM* (2003) (forthcoming).
[701] Deinard, *Massa Qrim*, 16.
[702] Firkovich, *Avne Zikaron*, 7.

209

the end of the fourteenth century, expressed his impression of the view of the town in the following way, "...an awe-inspiring and extraordinary marvel, unheard of and almost unbelievable;" standing in the plain, "like a six-cornered table, and its walls seemed made by heaven but not by the hands of men."[703] Touched by the deplorable state of the monuments of the town, the Marquise de Castelnau expressively wrote, "Misfortunate place! I cry about your destruction..."[704] I.M.Muraviev-Apostol had similar feelings. He mentioned, while leaving Mangoup, "What is Mangoup? My despair..."[705]

The mediæval citadel of Mangoup. After the Ottoman conquest of 1475 it has been used as an arsenal and a prison. One of the Dominican friars imprisoned there in 1663 mentioned the help of the merciful Jewish (i.e. Karaite) women which helped him to survive there. (photo by Mikhail Kizilov)

Dwelling quarters

In the Late Middle Ages, both in European and Islamic societies, ethnic zoning was a very important feature for a settlement. Men regarded themselves as citizens of the quarters in which they had separated themselves with their own kind. It seems that quarters' gates

---

[703] See the translation of the fragments of the work of Matthew in Vasiliev, *Goths*, 189.
[704] Castelnau, *Essai*, 191.
[705] Muraviev-Apostol, *Puteshestvie*, 189.

also played significant role in this separation, as symbolic barriers distinguishing one ethnic district from another.[706]

The Karaite district of Mangoup was situated in the territory of Tabana-Dere – starting from the lower defensive wall, to the upper reaches of the valley [see the map of Mangoup]. In the Mangoupian *"Juderia"*, there were Karaite houses, shops, baths for tanning hides, a cemetery, a school (*beit midrash*), and a *beit keneset*. According to Evliya Çelebi, the central gate was used mostly by Muslims, while the smaller gate, "which even a loaded horse can hardly pass through," was used by the Jewish population.[707] The central gate has not survived; however, the Jewish one is still in a very good state. Evliya Çelebi found not only a considerable number of homes, but also numerous tanners, two meat shops, and a tavern in the Karaite quarter of Mangoup.[708] According to estimates, based on a personal observation of the site, the Karaite quarter of Mangoup consisted of approximately sixty-eighty houses.

Cemetery

"Jewish cemetery. It would not be bad to decipher the inscriptions."
(Griboedov, *Sochineniya*, 440.)

The cemetery in Tabana-Dere is considerably smaller than that in the Yehoshafat Valley, consisting of approximately one thousand graves. Already in the beginning of the twentieth century, the necropolis was in a ruinous state. Its former owners, the Tatar Balatuqovlar, treated the tombs as if they were nothing more than stones, and used them for the construction works on the reservoir in the valley of Qoruv-Dere ("valley of hoar frost"), near Mangoup.[709]

The problem of dating the tombstone inscriptions in this cemetery, similar to the situation with the tombstones from Çufut-

---

[706] *E.g.* are cases concerning the right of passage through the gates of the Karaite and Rabbanite communities of mediæval Cairo (Goitein, *Mediterranean Society*, 14-15, 40).

[707] Evliya Çelebi, *Kniga*, 90.

[708] "...around a thousand of misfortunate houses... eighty shops of tanners... two meat shops and one tavern selling *buza*" [an alcoholic beverage derived from malted millet] (Evliya Çelebi, *Kniga*, 90).

[709] S.M.Dubnov, "Istoricheskaia taina Kryma" [Historical mystery of the Crimea], *Evreiskaia Starina* 7:1 (1914): 12. Plans to excavate the site of this reservoir, discovered in the course of an archæological field-survey carried out in summer 2002, are slated for the near future.

Qalé, is far from being solved.[710] Avraham Firkovich, who investigated the necropolis in the nineteenth century, came to the conclusion that the earliest tombstone inscriptions go back to the period of Khazar dominance in the Crimea. According to some reports, archæological excavations in the territory of the cemetery were carried out by Karaites from Feodosia [Kaffa] and Simferopol' in 1890.[711] In 1912-1914, an archæological investigation of the historical monuments of Mangoup (including the synagogue and the cemetery) was undertaken by R.H.Loeper, who dated its existence to the ninth/tenth centuries, and was of the opinion that the necropolis belonged to the Qrımçaq Jews.[712] The Karaite sage M.Sultanski informed P.Koeppen that the grave of Yiṣḥaq Ben-Mosheh goes back to 5034 (=1274 c.e.).[713] The famous Jewish scholar, S.Dubnov, dated one of the earliest tombs of the cemetery, the grave of Euphrosinia Bat-Yosef, to 1387.[714] However, the date of the tomb can be quite distinctively read "הרטזו", *i.e.* 5216 (=1455/1456 c.e.).[715] If we accept Dan Shapira's suggestion that the establishment of the Karaite community in Mangoup goes back to the mid-fifteenth century, the earliest Karaite graves in the territory of the settlement, also could not belong to the earlier periods.[716]

    Unfortunately, the cemetery in Tabana-Dere (Mangoup) did not attract much of the travelers' attention. Most of them simply mentioned the fact that the tombs of the cemetery were similar to those situated in the Yehoshafat Valley.[717] Of interest is a brief note by the famous Russian writer Alexander Griboedov, who, as early as 1825,

---

[710] The monograph of M.Ezer (Israel) and N.Kashovskaia (St.Petersburg), based on many years of their work with the monuments of the cemetery, provide a comprehensive chronology and profound analysis of the tombstone inscriptions of the cemetery (in progress).

[711] Gertsen, "Arkheologicheskie issledovaniya," 745.

[712] Dubnov, "Istoricheskaia taina," 11-12.

[713] Koeppen, *Sbornik*, 29, 269, ft.397. Unfortunantely, this tomb has never been found.

[714] Dubnov, "Istoricheskaia taina," 13-14. Dubnov have not seen the original of the inscription, only a blurred and unclear estampage.

[715] This conclusion is based on my own investigation of the monument *de visu*. T.S.Levi-Babovich, in the beginning of the twentieth century, similarly, dated the tomb of Euphrosinia to 1455 (Levi-Babovich, *Ocherk*, 39).

[716] Cf. N.V.Kashovskaya and A.G.Gertsen, who stated that the cemetery began functioning no earlier than the mid-fifteenth century (A.G.Gertsen, "Arkheologicheskie issledovaniya karaimskikh pamiatnikov v Krymu" [Archæological investigation of the Karaite monuments in the Crimea], *MAIET* 6 (1998): 747).

[717] Markov, *Ocherki*, 425-426; Remy, *Krim*, 109; Pallas, *Travels*, 122; the same, *Bemerkungen*, 122; Clarke, *Travels*, 277; Oliphant, *Russian Shores*, 303; Muraviev-Apostol, *Puteshestvie*, 123, etc.

mentioned the necessity of deciphering the Hebrew inscriptions of the cemetery.[718]

Karaite tombstone inscription from Mangoup. (photo by Leonid Berestovskiy)

Beit HaKeneset (the synagogue)

"Poor and simple edifice fortified with clay; windows and ornaments...
are not to be found"
(Alexander Berthier-Delagarde, "Kalamita i Feodoro" (Calamita and
Theodoro), *ITUAK* 55 (1918): 29)

As has been mentioned, in the beginning of the 1790s, with the expulsion of the community, the Mangoup synagogue was partially

---

[718] Griboedov, *Sochineniya*, 440.

destroyed, and some of its contents transferred to Çufut-Qalé. Some travelers remarked on its presence, but rarely supplied additional details.[719] L.Oliphant, who was awaiting the end of a sudden shower under the cover of the tower in Tabana-dere, brought "the ruins of the synagogue into the corner of the picture."[720] A.Berthier-Delagarde, who saw it in the beginning of the twentieth century, described the synagogue as a small, simple, poor edifice, surrounded by a wall, without windows or ornamentation.[721] The synagogue is a building of 10.5x16m, which is oriented to the South-East. Coins, found during the archæological investigations of the synagogue in 1997 (carried out by A.G.Gertsen and O.B.Belyi), suggest that the building functioned from the first half of the fifteenth century up to the last quarter of the eighteenth century. Of great interest also is a large and precious silver finger-ring with the name of Shabbetai Ben-Barukh found during the excavations.[722] At the present moment, only the ruins of the synagogue remain.

Present-day view of the ruins of the Karaite synagogue of Mangoup. The remains of the Heikhal part still might be seen. (photo by M.Kizilov)

[719] Neilson, *Crimea*, 81; Remy, *Krim*, 110; Castelnau, *Essai*, 191.

[720] Oliphant, *Russian Shores*, 305.

[721] Alexander Berthier-Delagarde, "Kalamita i Feodoro" (Calamita and Theodoro), *ITUAK* 55 (1918): 29.

[722] A.G.Gertsen, a paper read during the 7th International Conference in Jewish Studies in Korolevo (01.02.2000).

Cave-miqweh

The presence of a cave, which some scholars consider to be a *miqweh*, situated 30m West of the synagogue, suggests either that this synagogue was at some point in the possession of the Rabbanite community, or that during a certain period it was attended by both Jewish communities (Karaite and Rabbanite). However, there is also a possibility that there was another synagogue in the town which has not survived. Of interest is the Hebrew graffito on the wall of southern gallery of the church of St.Constantine and Helena[723] which gave some scholars grounds to suggest that, after 1475, it was also used as a synagogue.[724] The first excavations of the synagogue, which were started by R.Loeper and A.Gidalevich as early as in 1912, engendered a hot and rather impolite discussion between the members of the Karaite and Qrımçaq communities, with regard to the problem of which community possessed the synagogue.[725] However, the silence of written sources on this point, together with the fragmentary character of the archæological data, have not given an answer to the question. It seems that this riddle will only be solved by further archæological investigation of the areas adjacent to the cave-*miqweh*, or by some new, written sources related to the Jewish community of Mangoup.

---

[723] The graffito reads, ה ק ק ק ("*qof-qof-qof-hey*"), which might be read as the abbreviation for, 'ה קדש קדש קדש ("*Qadosh Qadosh Qadosh HaShem*") reading of Mrs. Darya Vassiutinskaia (St.Petersburg).

[724] *Evrei v Krymu*, 21.

[725] See survey of this discussion in Levi-Babovich, *Ocherk*, 35-66.

Cave in Mangoup supposedly used as a miqweh. (photo by M.Kizilov)

4.3. Karaite quarters in the Crimean towns.

4.3.1. Staryi Krym (Sulkhat, Eski-Qırım) and Feodosia (Kaffa).

In all probability, the earliest Karaite enclaves settled in Staryi Krym (Sulkhat, Eski-Qırım) and Feodosia (Kaffa). The Tatars, who appeared in the Crimea in 1223, made the town of Sulkhat (or Qırım) the first capital of the Khanate, in the second half of the thirteenth century.[726] It seems that the first Karaite settlers could have migrated to the Crimea with the Tatar invaders, around the mid-thirteenth century. Late Karaite legends about their arrival to the Crimea with the Tatar Khans,[727] and the references to Sulkhat as the first seat of the Karaite community, also testify in favor of this hypothesis.

---

[726] Bakhrushin, "Osnovnye momenty," 323.
[727] See Haxthausen, *Studien*, 399; Kohl, *Reisen*, vol.2, 258.

216

The earliest known reference to the existence of the Karaite community in Staryi Krym, and the Crimea in general, is from 1279.[728] One source – of rather suspicious origin, a Hebrew colophon written around 1700 and preserved in a nineteenth century Polish translation – mentioned the presence of a large Karaite community in Sulkhat and Kaffa already in the mid-thirteenth century.[729] Some later, and rather unreliable, Karaite traditions, retold by E.Deinard, also speak about the community of Sulkhat as the largest and earliest Crimean Karaite community.[730] The Armenian traveler Minas Bzhishkian (1820s) thought that the Karaite community of Sulkhat was established in Genoese times, which is "testified [to] by their memorial notes and graves".[731]

An interesting source on the history of Sulkhat and its Karaite community is a marble slab kept in the Crimean Museum of Local Lore in Simferopol'(КП-15558, А-20750). Its front contains an Arab inscription with the date of 1309 (*i.e.* one of the most ancient Arab inscriptions in the Crimea!), whereas on its back side one may see the Hebrew tombstone inscription of Mordekhai Ben-Mordekhai (d.1517). The fact that the "*ra'aya*" Karaites dared to take the slab from the Muslim mosque, and use it as a gravestone, undoubtedly testifies to the decline of the Muslim community of Sulkhat, in the beginning of the sixteenth century.[732]

It seems that the first Karaite settlers appeared in Kaffa approximately at the same time as in Sulkhat, in the second half of the thirteenth century. Local Crimean historian V.Ch.Kondaraki mentioned that one of the girders of the Kaffa Karaite synagogue contained the date of its foundation, 5052 (=1292 c.e.).[733] It seems that the inscription from Kaffa of 1404, which records a considerable donation made to the local Karaite synagogue, is also related to this *Beit Keneset*.[734] Johann Schiltberger (1500s) reported that there were

---

[728] The Karaite scholar Aharon Ben-Yosef HaRofe' mentioned the calendar dispute between the Rabbanites and Karaites of Sulkhat that happened in this year (Danon, "Karaites," 294; Ankori, *Karaites*, 60).

[729] Stepaniv, "L'époque de Danylo Romanovyc," 371-373.

[730] Deinard, *Sefer Massa' Qerim*, 13-14, 64-65.

[731] M.Bzhishkian, "Keozlev ili Evpatoria" [Közlöw or Evpatoria], *Surb-Khach* 2 (1996): 36, ft.17.

[732] This marble slab can be seen at the entrance to the aforementioned museum in Simferopol'.

[733] Kondaraki, *Universalnoe opisanie*, pt.15, 133.

[734] D.G.Maggid, "Evrei v Krymu" [Jews in the Crimea], in *Istoriya evreiskogo naroda*, vol.12 (Moscow, 1921), 104. It seems that the drawing placed by E. de Villeneuve in his *Album historique et pittoresque de la Tauride* (Paris, 1853) is the only surviving depiction of this synagogue; of special interest is the stone reservoir for ablution, an

two synagogues ("*zwoe sinagog*") within the quarters of the Rabbanite and Karaite communities of Kaffa.[735] E.Portelli D'Ascoli also mentioned that – in Kaffa, in the seventeenth century – there were two synagogues for the representatives of the different religious trends within Judaism.[736] The presence of Karaite settlers in Kaffa in the first half of the fifteenth century is also testified to by the names of the Karaites who migrated from the Crimea to Constantinople after 1453.[737]

According to data from the Turkish *defterler* of the Kaffa *eyalet* of the sixteenth century, there were ninety-one Karaite households in Kaffa in 1520 (*defter* TT 370), and 124 in 1542 (TT 214). According to the estimations of O.Halenko, this would be equal to around 442 – 480 members of the community during those years.[738] Halenko also came to the conclusion that the Karaite *jemaat* [cemaat] (community) was the main Jewish community of Kaffa, with *papas* Avraham as its head. The *defter* of 1542 mentions six female slaves (*esir*) belonging to the members of the community.[739]

The famous seventeenth century German Hebraist Johann Buxtorf wrote about 1200 Karaites living in Feodosia, and reading the Torah in a Turkic translation.[740] The coexistence of Rabbanites and Karaites within the territory of Feodosia (Kaffa) continued during the nineteenth century as well. According to information from Reginald Heber (1800s), the Karaite quarter was located in the northern part of

---

exact copy of the reservoir in front of the large synagogue of Çufut-Qalé. See Szyszman, "Les passionants Manuscrits," 69. Also of interest is the fact that, in the beginning of the twentieth century, the Karaites tried to seize the old synagogue in Staryi Krym; however, the Rabbanites managed to defend their right of possessing the building on the basis of the presence of the *miqweh* there. A similar conflict was taking place at approximately the same time in Feodosia (Weissenberg, "Istoricheskie gnezda," 65).

[735] Schiltberger, *Reisebuch*, 63.

[736] Eszer, "Beschreibung," 232.

[737] Danon, "Karaites," 299.

[738] Halenko, "Iudejski gromady", 50. It must be said, however, that the estimations of the scholar must be put to question.

[739] Halenko, "Iudejski gromady", 59. On the role of the Jewish population in the Crimean slave trade see Mikhail Kizilov, "Jewish Population and the Trade in Slaves and Captives in the Crimean Khanate in the XVIIth century" (to be published in the Proceedings of the Thirteenth World Congress of Jewish Studies).

[740] As quoted in Zajączkowski, *Karaims*, 43. It seems that Buxtorf borrowed this data from Antoine Leger of Geneva, who had undertaken a trip to Constantinople in 1622-1631, with the aim of studying the life of local Karaites (Szyszman, "Gustaf Peringers Mission," 215). This numerical data, too large for the Feodosian community, seem to reflect the number of all Karaites (including those of Kaffa) living in the Crimea in the first half of the seventeenth century.

Feodosia near the Oriental market (*bazar*). In Heber's opinion, the Karaite quarter was one of the most populous parts of the town, while many other sections were "entirely waste and ruinous."[741] J.Kohl (1838) supposed that there were only ten Karaite families (*i.e.* around fifty-sixty persons) living in the town during his visit.[742]

A description of Feodosia's Karaite synagogue, and the house of a rich broker *Mardochai-Mosche* (*i.e.* Mordekhai Mosheh), was left by August von Haxthausen (1843). The traveler described the house as Oriental, however, with some European elements; Haxthausen was also honored with an opportunity to see the daughter-in-law of Mardochai dressed in festive clothing. Later, he visited the Karaite synagogue, where he was met by *Jeschuah Dawidowitch Koen* [Yeshu'ah Ben-Dawid Kohen], a local "Rabbi," who informed him that there were around three hundred Karaite males in Feodosia in the first half of the nineteenth century. The "Rabbi" also made a special prayer for the Russian Emperor, and the traveler, so that the latter "would be able to find what he was looking for." When parting, the "Rabbi" gave Haxthausen leaves from "*einer Handschrift der Mischora*" (a corruption of "Masorah", *i.e.* "a Masoretic manuscript"), which had been found, according to his words, eight hundred years ago in the vicinity of the synagogue.

The traveler also remarked on the indignation and jealousy of the local Rabbanites, when they discovered that the Karaite synagogue had been visited earlier than their own. This story received further development, when, on the request of the Rabbanites, Haxthausen visited their synagogue, and found in its *genizah* heaps of various Hebrew manuscripts. Moreover, the traveler was of the opinion that he found the manuscript source for some of the pages that had been donated to him by the Karaite "Rabbi".[743]

A.Demidov (1837) mentioned that the Armenian and Karaite merchants of Feodosia had a reputation as the most trustworthy and

---

[741] Unfortunately, I was not able to find the original manuscript of this interesting account, once kept in the Crimean library "Tavrica", whose traces seem to disappear after World War II. I used extensive quotations placed in Clarke's travelogue (Clarke, *Travels*, 130-131).

[742] Kohl, *Reisen*, vol.2, 260.

[743] Haxthausen, *Empire*, 102-103; Haxthausen, *Studien*, 390-393, 407. If the last statement is correct, it would mean that the Karaites somehow managed to access and partially acquire some of the Rabbanites' manuscripts. Now, we can only regret that Firkovich could not empty the *genizah* of this synagogue, as he did in Qarasubazar. These manuscript treasures, as well as the building of the synagogue, which was, probably, one the oldest synagogues of the former USSR, disappeared in the flames of World War II.

generous traders in the region. In addition, it was Feodosia where Demidov's companion, Auguste Raffet, made one of his most impressive drawings, depicting local Karaites portrayed against the picturesque walls of old Feodosia.[744]

At the present moment, the so called "*Karaimskaya slobodka*" (Russ., "a Karaite quarter") – once inhabited by the Karaite and Qrımçaq communities, with the eighteenth/nineteenth century houses, and the half-demolished cemetery situated nearby – is located in one of the districts of Feodosia, in the region of Armianskaya (Timiriazeva), Zheliabova (Turetskaya), and Karaimskaya (Furmanova) streets.[745]

The View of the "Karaimskaya slobodka" ("a Karaite quarter") in Feodosia. (photo by M.Kizilov)

---

[744] Demidov, *Voyage*, vol.1, 509. See illustration.

[745] For more about the topography of the "Karaite quarter" and some other aspects of the nineteenth/twentieth century history of the Karaite community of the town, see (with some caution) in D.Losev, "*Sled malogo, no gordogo naroda*" [The trace of the small, but proud people], in *Krymskiy Albom* (Feodosia-Moscow, 1996), 103-120.

4.3.2. Evpatoria (Gözlöw).[746]

The beautiful nineteenth century facade of the synagogue courtyard. (photo by M.Kizilov)

Present day view of the vandalized Evpatoria Karaite cemetery. (photo by M.Kizilov)

---

[746] See also Mikhail Kizilov, "Karaimskaya obshtchina g.Gezleva (Evpatoria) v 18 – 19 vv. po opisaniyam ochevidstev" [Karaite community of Gezlev (Evpatoriya) according to descriptions of eyewitnesses], in *Tirosh. Trudy po Iudaike 5* (Moscow, 2002), 245-256. The author is greatful to Yevgeniy and Liudmila Nikiforov, a wonderful family of Euvpatorians, whose hospitality I enjoyed during my field trips to the town in 2000 and 2002.

The earliest travel descriptions of the Karaite community of Gözlöw appeared quite late, in the eighteenth/nineteenth centuries. According to A.Firkovich, however, the earliest tombstone inscription from the Evpatorian cemetery goes to 1593.[747] In spite of the fact that Evliya Çelebi's description of Gözlöw (1665-1666) is very detailed, he left no information about the Karaite and Rabbanite populations of the town.[748]

The first testimonies to supply us some details on the history of the Karaite community of Gözlöve date to the beginning of the eighteenth century. One of the documents of the Gözlöw Rabbanite (Qrımçaq) community, dating to 1705, was directed to Mosheh Ben-Sinani, the head of the Karaite community of Gözlöw. It is an appeal for help in the construction of the two synagogues in the town.[749] In 1711, de la Motray also mentioned the presence of the Jewish (i.e. most likely, Karaite) population in the town, in whose possession there was a synagogue.[750] According to Peyssonel (1753), by the middle of the eighteenth century, the Karaites played an important role in the population of Gözlöw, which amounted, at that time, to around six to seven thousand people.[751]

At the end of the eighteenth/beginning of the nineteenth century, when it was enlarged by the masses of the Karaites who left the mediæval settlements of Mangoup and Çufut-Qalé, the Karaite community of Gözlöw became the most numerous and influential Crimean Karaite community.[752] The wealth, prosperity and respectable status of the Karaites of Gözlöw were noted by many travelers of the nineteenth century.[753] As a symbolic reflection of the aforementioned changes, the Karaite press at Çufut-Qalé was moved to Gözlöw in 1833, where a number of very important and significant books written by Karaite authors of various lands and periods were published. The quality of these books, in contrast to the poor quality of those

---

[747] Philip Miller also considered that the time of the establishment of the Karaite community in Gözlöw dates to the sixteenth century (Miller, *Separatism*, 15). During the visit to the half-demolished Evpatoria Karaite cemetery situated on the outskirts of the city, near the road leading to Simferopol' (September, 2000), the author of this book could not find tombstone inscriptions earlier than 1740.
[748] Evliya Çelebi, *Kniga*, 68-75.
[749] Achkinazi, *Krymchaki*, 160, nr32.
[750] Motray, *Travels*, 23.
[751] Peyssonel, *Traite*, vol.1, 16.
[752] On the rivalry and struggle for dominance between the communities of Gözlöw and Çufut-Qalé, see Miller, "Spiritual and Political Leadership," 1-8.
[753] Holderness, *Journey*, 178; Demidov, *Voyage*, vol.1, 477; Demidov, *Travels*, 153, 156.

published in Çufut-Qalé, rival the best examples of Rabbanite publishing.[754]

Travelers' data traces the rapid growth of the Karaite community of Gözlöw in the nineteenth century, which can be explained by emigration from other communities (first of all, from the dying Mangoup and Çufut-Qalé, and from Lithuania and Volhynia (esp. from Luck) as well), and high birth rate due to the prosperous conditions of the community. P.S.Pallas (1794), without specifying whether it was a Karaite or Rabbanite population, mentioned that there were 695 Jews in the town (he called it "Koslof" or "Güsl-Öwe"), who had in their possession one synagogue, two schools and 240 houses.[755] According to the Armenian traveler Bzhishkian (1820s), the Karaite community of Gözlöw was located in the Western part of the town and consisted of 800 houses.[756] J.Kohl (1838) wrote that the Karaite population of Gözlöw consisted of 800 people.[757] E.Chojecki mentioned that, at the time of his travel (1843), the Karaite population consisted of 1200 Karaites.[758] F.Remy, who referred to the census of 1866, recorded that there were 1525 Karaites in Gözlöw.[759]

Of great interest are the travelers' testimonies of the contacts between the Evpatoria Karaites and the representatives of the Rabbinic and Karaite communities of Poland and Lithuania. The travel diary of the Crimean Karaite Binyamin Ben-Eliyah Douvan [Duvan] who, together with five other Karaites, ventured to undertake a pilgrimage to the Holy Land in 1785, mentioned a Troki Karaite, Zeraḥ Ben-Avraham, as a member of his group.[760]

However, it seems that the Karaites also maintained trading contacts with the European Rabbanites. The Marquis de Castelnau (1820s) noted that the local Karaites, using the sympathy they gained from the Crimean Tatars, by their knowledge of the Tatar language and

---

[754] See details in Miller, "Prayer Book Politics," 15-26; Miller, "Agenda in Karaite Printing," 82-88. According to information from old local inhabitants, the printing press was situated in the narrow avenue in the town's center, present-day *Tipographskiy pereulok* (avenue).

[755] Pallas, *Bemerkungen*, 502.

[756] M.Bzhishkian, "Keozlev ili Euvpatoria," 35-36. Bzhishkian's data seem to be rather exaggerated (cf. testimonies of other travelers).

[757] Kohl, *Reisen*, vol.2, 260.

[758] Chojecki, *Wspomnienia*, 217. This numerical estimation appears very correct, unlike the exaggerated data of Kaczkowski and Nowosielski. According to the census of 1866, there were 1525 Karaites and 325 Jews in Evpatoria (Remy, *Krim*, 5).

[759] Remy, *Krim*, 5-6.

[760] The nineteenth century translation of the travel diary to Karaim was published in 'Ananiasz Zajączkowski, "Opis podróży do Ziemi Świętej," *MK* 2:3-4 (1931), 26-42.

223

their similarity in customs, used to buy large quantities of goods from them, and then sell them to the Polish (*i.e.* Ashkenazic) Jews.[761]

Gözlöw (Evpatoria), one of the most important Crimean ports in the nineteenth century, was frequently described by the travelers as the settlement with the largest Karaite community in the Crimea. Important data concerning the internal life and general atmosphere within the Karaite community of Gözlöw is in the travel diary of the Karaite embassy to St.Petersburg in 1827, which was written by Yosef Shelomoh Lucki .[762] K.Kaczkowski, who visited Evpatoria in 1825, mentioned that the Tatars called the city "*Guzlewe*", Russian and Poles "*Kozlow*", whereas the official title was "*Eupatorja*". The traveler estimated its population at 5000 inhabitants, mostly Tatars and Karaites. Kaczkowski, who happened to visit Gözlöw on Saturday, noticed that, "all the streets were filled with the Karaites, because it was *szabas*" (*i.e.* Shabbat [the traveler, being from Poland, pronounced the word like the Ashkenazi Rabbanites of Poland do]). The houses of the Tatars and Karaites, built in Oriental style, with the windows directed to the inner courts of the buildings,[763] rather depressed him, "it seems that there were as many isolated dwellings of madmen as houses."[764]

Marshal Auguste Frederic Louis de Marmont visited Evpatoria (Kosloff) on July 3rd – 4th, 1834. His general impression from his visit to the Karaite community of the town seems very positive. On the outskirts of Gözlöw, he was met by a deputation of wealthy Karaites, who were singing a special hymn (probably, in Hebrew) in his honor. Marshal spent the night in the "charming" house of the "principal Karaite" Simḥah Babovich, where, according to his own words, he was "surrounded by care and reverence." On the next morning, in the company of count M.S.Vorontsov, the governor of the Taurida province, he visited the local Karaite synagogue, where a special prayer for the successful continuation of his journey was recited.[765] However, according to the memoirs of Avraham Firkovich, Marshal's visit was a complete disaster for the community. The

---

[761] Castelnau, *Essai*, 304-305.

[762] Miller, *Separatism*, 74-94.

[763] Typical eighteenth/nineteenth century Karaite houses were surrounded by the blind wall so that the unsolemn eyes of strangers could not disturb the serene Oriental intimacy of its inhabitants. They usually were two-storey houses, with windows and balconies directed into the inner court of the building; the master of the house lived in the upper part of the building, whereas the lower one was often used as a stable. See also Szapszal, *Karaimy i Chufut-Kale*, 21.

[764] Kaczkowski, *Dziennik*, 38-40.

[765] See Marmont, *Voyage*, 294-297.

Karaite sages, when asked about the history of their origin, were unable to supply Marshal with any exact information. Firkovich wrote that, while hearing the awkward silence he received in response to his historical inquiries, "Marshal smiled and remarked, 'Amazing, you do not know anything about your past. You do not even know about events which happened just three hundred years ago.' "[766]

The description of Gözlöw left by A.Nowosielski (1850) is of special significance. Reading it is like entering a time machine, so comprehensive is the picture he paints of the life of this city in the nineteenth century. Whilst reading Nowosielski's memoirs, one can easily visualize a large Crimean port during the hot summer, its crooked narrow streets and dirty houses, the patchwork of various ethnic groups, the crossbreeding of Oriental and European cultures, the Karaites, Tatars, and Greeks sitting in silence in their coffee houses, smoking long tobacco pipes, and drinking coffee.

In Nowosielski's opinion, "*Gozlewe*," the Tatar name of the city, should be translated as "caves", or "underground hollows", because under the Turkic and Tatar dominion, when representatives of non-Muslim denominations did not have the right of erecting houses of prayer on the ground, the Karaite population of the town established their synagogues in underground caves. In all probability, this "underground" etymology of the city's name is a reference to the existence of the real underground Karaite synagogue in Gözlöw, which functioned during the period of the Crimean Khanate.[767]

One of the most important Karaite synagogues, the so-called synagogue of 'Anan Ben-Dawid in Jerusalem, was also built underground. It is very likely, that the early Crimean Karaite synagogues might have been intended to imitate the synagogue of 'Anan. [*ed.* More likely, it was done as a defense against attack.] It is

---

[766] Vikhnovich, *Firkovich*, 91.

[767] Nowosielski, *Stepy*, 27, 36. The traveler also maintained that, in Evpatoria, according to local tradition, there were many caves concealed under the houses and connected one to another; he also mentioned that one of these underground synagogues existed until 1803. In our opinion, this data may reflect the fact that, during some period of time, the Gözlöw Karaite synagogue was made to function cladestinely, because of Muslim persecutions (cf. similar situation that was taking place in Constantinople at the end of the eighteenth century, when the local Karaites had to pray in secrecy, because of persecution by the local authorities: Mann, *Texts*, 319). During my visit to Evpatoria in September, 2000, the local inhabitants informed me that the town, indeed, has a number of still unexplored underground corridors and basements covered by the houses of the old part of the town. [*ed.* Göz/Köz means "eye" and also a "hole in a rock" [like the "eyes" of a potato in English. Gözlöw is the adjectival form and means "possessing eyes" (holes in the rock), *i.e.* caves.]

225

very interesting to mention in this regard that the French travelers, who visited Evpatoria in 1854-1855, recorded a local tradition that stated that the Evpatoria synagogue had been founded by a lineal descendant of 'Anan Ben-Dawid in the eleventh century. Moreover, according to the local Karaites, the "eighth century" Torah kept in the synagogue, also belonged to 'Anan Ben-Dawid.[768]

Nowosielski estimated that the Karaite community of Gözlöw amounted to 500 families, so that, "the population of Evpatoria consisted mainly of the Karaites."[769]

Greatly impressed by the large Karaite synagogue, built in the beginning of the nineteenth century, Nowosielski dedicated several pages of his travelogue to its splendor, paying special attention to the description of its inner courts, marble monuments with Hebrew inscriptions, and other details. The astonished traveler wrote:

> This view, ancient Hebrew letters on the monuments and tombstones, seemed to be so unusual for me that I got an impression as if I were somewhere in Palestine, at the time of the existence of the kingdom of Israel...

While coming out of the synagogue, Nowosielski's interest was attracted by a monument, with an inscription in Russian, dedicated to the exemption of the Karaites from military conscription.[770]

A.Nowosielski also left a very detailed description of his meeting with the members of the Babovich family, whom he had met while traveling on a steamboat to Sevastopol'.[771] He left brief remarks about a few other outstanding Karaites, as well. He wrote about his visit to a Tatar coffee house where, with air of importance, "a Karaite with two golden medals on his neck was sitting and smoking pipe; he was the head of the city." This person might be identified as Mosheh Tongur, who fulfilled the duties of the mayor of Evpatoria until 1855/1856.[772]

In 1854, a short while before the seizure of Evpatoria, during the Crimean War (called by English sources, "the War in the East"), about 500 Karaite families left the town, afraid of the possible

---

[768] See the French newspaper *Moniteur* (28.01.1855) as translated in Rule, *History*, 193.
[769] Nowosielski, *Stepy*, 42.
[770] Nowosielski, *Stepy*, 36-40. The abovementioned monument, with inscription in Russian, was preserved until our days and might be seen on the place where it was noticed by the traveler: on the left from the central entrance to the large synagogue.
[771] See details in 2.4.4.
[772] Nowosielski, *Stepy*, 29. The author of the article is grateful to Dr. Philip E. Miller for his help and advice in this and many other problems this book deals with.

consequences of the military events. [773] Unfortunately, we do not have many sources at our disposal related to the destiny of the Karaite families during the seizure of Evpatoria in 1854-1856, apart from the tombstone inscriptions gathered by Ya'aqov Ben-'Ezra Babacan. These highly important documents – depicting the sufferings and sorrows of the exiled Karaites, which are kept in the collection of the Jewish manuscripts of the Institute of Oriental Studies in St.Petersburg – are being prepared for the publication by Philip Miller. [774]

One of the French reporters who visited Evpatoria in 1854-1855 paid attention to the local Karaite cemetery and called it the finest Israelite cemetery in the whole world: "It contains... a countless multitude of monolith tombs of marble, granite, or other hard stone, of monumental form, and covered with very curious inscriptions." Among the tombs of the cemetery the traveler noticed one belonging, in his opinion, to the end of the sixteenth century. It contained an epitaph dedicated to a Karaite scribe, who died at the age of nearly a hundred years. [775] Unfortunately, not much of the cemetery's splendor has remained since the time of the French visitor: practically all the costly and beautiful nineteenth century monuments of the cemetery have been stolen or destroyed by vandals during the Soviet and "Perestroika" times. [776] Only a few have been preserved by the community; they are kept in the courtyard of the local synagogue.

K.Kessler – who visited Evpatoria after the end of the war, in 1858 – left a detailed description of the Karaite religious school, which was located near the synagogues, and had about 250 pupils:

> Every teacher leads the pupils given to his care throughout the whole educational course in the school... all pupils of a given teacher, young and adult, are gathered together in one chamber... Parents have the right to choose a teacher for their children... The salary of each teacher corresponds to the number of his pupils... [777]

In 1913, the leading institution of Karaite education was *Alexandrovskoe karaimskoe dukhovnoe uchilische* (Alexander's

[773] Markevich, *Tavricheskaya guberniya*, 11-12.
[774] Philip Miller, "The Crimean Karaites and the Crimean War" (forthcoming).
[775] As quoted in Rule, *History*, 194.
[776] The destiny of many Jewish cemeteries in Eastern Europe. In Simferopol', for example, there is a large complex, consisting of a public bath, night club, and kind of parking place, built mostly from the tombs of the local nineteenth century Orthodox and Jewish cemeteries.
[777] Kessler, *Puteshestvie*, 136-137.

Karaite religious college), founded by the *Ḥakham* S.Pampulov, and enlightenment thinker I.I.Qazas.[778]

A contemporary tourist or scholar wishing to visit Evpatoria would be astonished to see the abundant architectural monuments of the eighteenth/nineteenth centuries related to the history of the local Karaite community. Numerous luxurious villas and houses of the Karaite aristocracy, the monument erected by the community in honor of the Russian soldiers killed during the Crimean War – the atmosphere of the old part of town, whose narrow and crooked streets had once been inhabited by the Karaites, Rabbanite Qrımçaqlar, Greeks, Armenians, Tatars, and Gypsies – all these convey to the visitor an unforgettable feeling of infiltration into the history of one of the most important seats of the Crimean Karaites. Of special interest are monuments such as the half-demolished Karaite cemetery, the house of S.Babovich (53 Karaimskaia street), the building where the Karaite library *"Karay Bitikliği"* was once situated (13 Yefet street), et al. The beautiful nineteenth century building of the larger Evpatorian Karaite synagogue (as well as many other interesting Karaite monuments) situated on Karaimskaya str. 68 is now open for visitors. It was restored by the local Karaite community (now consisting of app. 100 members),[779] in 1999; religious services were resumed in the smaller synagogue, furnished with the altar from the Halicz Karaite *Beit Keneset.*[780]

4.3.3. Qarasubazar(Belogorsk).

The first information from travelers about the Karaite community of *Qarasubazar* (Belogorsk) dates to the second half of the seventeenth century. According to Evliya Çelebi (1665-1666), there were three hundred Karaite males in Qarasubazar; they had to pay *kharadj* (=land-tax), and wear yellow signs on their caps.[781]

---

[778] The building of the *"uchilische"* is preserved today.

[779] According to other sources, the community consists of appr. 260 people (Alexander Mashtchenko, "Edinstvennaia v SNG deistvuiushtchaya kenasa" [The only functioning *kenasa* of the CIS], *Krymskoe vremia*. February 8th, 2001.

[780] The Halicz Karaite synagogue (kenesa) was entirely destroyed as late as 1985, in the beginning of *Perestroika*. The *Heikhal*, which was miraculously saved, was, for a long time, hidden in one of the local Karaite houses, and in 1994 was delivered to Evpatoria. See more details about it in the article of the present day *Ḥazzan* of the local community: Viktor Zakharievich Tiriyaki, "Sokhranenie religioznykh traditsiy karaimov Galicha na rubezhe XX-XXIvv." [Preservation of the religious traditions of the Halicz Karaites on the juncture of the XX-XXIst centuries, in *Karayimy Halycha: Istoriya ta Kul'tura/The Halych Karaims: History and Culture* (Lwow-Halicz, 2002), 76-83].

[781] Evliya Çelebi, *Kniga*, 131-132.

228

A.Demidov, who visited "Kara-Sou-Bazar" in 1837, praised the multicultural atmosphere of the town, whose various ethnic groups used to spend their time in coffee houses "in silence, whilst smoking long tobacco-pipes." Local Karaites attracted travelers by their manly, noble appearance and habit to wear large, precious finger-rings.[782]

It seems that, by the nineteenth century, the Karaite community of Qarasubazar had become considerably smaller: F.Remy, with reference to the census of 1866, mentioned that there were, "2000 Juden" (i.e. most likely, Qrımçaqlar and Ashkenazim) and "50 Karaim."[783] The paradoxical co-existence of these three different sub-ethnic groups of Jewish believers continued further on: the census of 1897 reported that there were forty-seven Karaites still living in the town.[784] In spite of its small number, the Karaite community continued to play an important role in the life of the town. In the beginning of the twentieth century, the Karaites I.B.Szyszman and B.E.Babovich were elected as town mayors.[785]

4.3.4. Bakhçeseray.[786]

A Karaite community appeared in Bakhçeseray after the annexation of the Crimea to Russian Empire in 1783, and the liquidation of the prescriptions of the Tatar administration, which prohibited the Karaites from staying in the town overnight. However, in spite of this ban, at least from the seventeenth century, the Karaites owned a number of shops in Bakhçeseray, at that time the capital of the Crimean Khanate. P.Sumarokov, who visited the town in 1799, mentioned that the Karaites were, "the first merchants of the town, they trade in the best *Tsaregrad* [Constantinople] goods; some of them engaged in various crafts."[787]

---

[782] Demidov, *Voyage*, vol.1, 498-499. The traveler was right when he divided the town's name into three separate Turkic words: Qara ("black"), Su ("water"), and Bazar ("market"), which alltogether mean the "Market on the Black Water." Qara-Su ("Black Water") is the name of the small river coming through the center of the town. Paradoxically, the Soviet authorities renamed the town to Belogorsk (Белогорск – "[town near] white mountains" – a reference to the Aq-Qaya ["White Cliffs"] situated nearby), *i.e.*. a toponym with opposite meaning and color.

[783] Remy, *Krim*, 190.

[784] "Karasubazar," *EJ* 10, 785-786.

[785] *KZh* 1 (1911): 125-126.

[786] "Bakhçeseray" means the "palace of gardens" (from Tatar "Bakhçe" (garden) and "saray" (palace). It was decided to use the transcription "Bakhçeseray", becase it is closer to the original Turkic name of the town, which was in use until the end of the nineteenth century, instead of the present day Russ. Бахчисарай (Bakhçesaray).

[787] Sumarokov, *Puteshestvie*, 141.

229

L.Oliphant (1852) was astonished to see the beauty of the "lovely Jewesses", Karaite maidens of Bakhçeseray, "congregated under an old archway, and laughingly criticizing the strangers."[788]

N.Berg (1854), who witnessed the life of the town during the events of the Crimean War, wrote about the loyalty and fidelity showed by the local Karaites to the Russian government. He estimated the Karaite population of the town at seventy families (*i.e.* around 420 people), mostly emigrants from Çufut-Qalé. He believed that the Karaites were far more successful merchants than the Tatars; the traveler located the Karaite quarters of Bakhçeseray in the center of town, "on the right from the entrance [to the town]." Berg mentioned that the part of the street with the Karaite shops was called *базырянсурасы* ("*bazyriansurasy*" [Bazıryansurası]), *i.e.* "merchants' row, the best row of stalls [Russ. "*krasnyi riad*"], the shops of real merchants".[789] F.Remy, with reference to the census of 1866, mentioned that there were 489 Karaites in the town.[790] At present, the available data numbers the Karaite community of Bakhçeseray at fifty people.[791] The once splendid, and beautifully decorated Karaite synagogue of Bakhçeseray (Lenina street) is now in a very deplorable state, having been "given" to some post Soviet institution; it's state is worsening with every year, not to say with every minute.

---

[788] Oliphant, *Russian Shores*, 277.

[789] Berg, *Bakhchisaray*, 7, 19.

[790] Remy, *Krim*, 64.

[791] O.B.Belyi, "Iz istorii karaimskoi obshtchiny Bakhchisaraya" [From the history of the Karaite community of Bakhçeseray], *Nomos (Kwartalnik Religioznawczy)* 28/29 (1999/2000): 153-165.

Present day view of the Bakhçesaray Karaite synagogue (kenesa). (photo by M.Kizilov)

4.3.5. Other towns.

At the end of the eighteenth/beginning of the nineteenth centuries, after the removal of oppressive Tatar legislation, the Karaite communities, attracted most likely by the new trading opportunities of the developing Crimean œconomy, started to appear in practically every large town of the peninsula. O.Belyi found a number of archival documents, the earliest of which dates to the 1830s, related to the Karaite community of Kerch, another important Crimean port, situated in the Eastern part of the peninsula.[792] Some nineteenth century sources briefly remark on Karaite communities of the northern Crimea, which appeared in Perekop (or in its suburb known as *Armianskiy Bazar* [Russ. Армянский Базар, at present Armiansk]) soon after the Russian

---

[792] O.B.Belyi, "Iz istorii kerchenskoi karaimskoi obshtchiny" [From the history of the Karaite community of Kerch], in *IV Dmitrievskie Chteniya* (Yalta, 2000), 56-60.

annexation of the peninsula in 1783.[793] According to the census of 1897, there were 320 Karaites in Armianskiy Bazar.[794] Nineteenth century travelers left brief remarks about the Karaite communities of Simferopol'[795] and Sevastopol',[796] however, without providing any substantial information. According to S.Szapszal, in addition to the urban communities, there were also rural settlements, in the villages of: Çabaq ("fish), Köksu ("Blue Water"), Taş-Cargan ("Stone-?", Yağmurçuq ("Light Rain"), Otuz ("Thirty"), and Büyük-Özenbaş ("Great Stream Head").[797]

---

[793] Levi-Babovich, Ocherk, 39.

[794] L.P.Kruzhko, *Armiansk. Stranitsy istorii* [Armiansk. Pages of its history] (Kiev, 1999), 43, 68-69.

[795] Both communities were formed at the end of the eighteenth/beginning of the nineteenth centuries. Visitors still can see the beautiful Karaite synagogue of Simferopol', sitiated very close to Lenin's square, on the Karaimskaia street. Built in 1891-1896, during Soviet times, the synagogue was given to the local radio-committee. This synagogue is a highly curious and, perhaps, unique example of the idiocy of the Communist regime: In order to carry their atheistic propaganda, the Soviets put a five-cornered red star right on the place of the six-cornered Star of David! What is funny, is that the silouette of the Jewish star can still clearly be seen behind the outline of the Soviet one. This building is known for this nonsense to, perhaps, all inhabitants of Simferopol'.

[796] See Remy, *Krim*, 184; Neilson, *Crimea*, 66-67. One of the first references to the Karaite community of Sevastopol' goes to 1829, when the local Karaites, unlike Rabbanite Jews, were allowed to live in the city and own property there and its suburbs (I.A.Diakonova, "Naselenie Sevastopol' a v kontse XVIII – pervoy polovine XIX veka" [Population of Sevastopol' at the end of the eighteenth/first half of the ninteenthth century], in *IV Dmitrievskie Chteniya* (Yalta, 2000), 23). Sevastopol's beautiful nineteenth century Karaite synagogue, situated on Bolshaia Morskaia street, the most central street of the city, is now functioning as a sportive complex "*Spartak*." Situated on the "Rudolfova gora" the Sevastopol' Karaite cemetery, as well as several other Crimean Karaite cemeteries of the nineteenth-twentieth centuries, is in a very deplorable half-ruined and vandalized state.

[797] Чабак, Коксю, Таш-Джарган, Ягмурчук, Отуз, Биюк-Озенбаш (Szapszal, *Karaimy*, 7). It is very likely that he borrowed this data from Firkovich's *Avnei Zikkaron*.

232

The present-day view of the Karaite synagogue in Simferopol'. Note the star of David peeping beyond the five-corner Communist star. (photo by M.Kizilov)

4.3.6. Yaşlov, Taş-Cargan, and Tepe-Kermen ("Hill Castle").

In addition to the aforementioned Crimean towns and settlements, where the presence of the Karaite communities is well established, there are also several settlements where one can cautiously suppose the existence of a Karaite population as well. The data detailing the existence of these communities, it should be noted, is late, and comes from somewhat unreliable sources.

A very late nineteenth century Karaite tradition documented by Koeppen and the travel account of E.Chojecki (1845) mention the presence of a Karaite population in Taş-Cargan, a small Tatar settlement close to the former Aq-Meçıt (Simferopol').[798] As noted, S.Szapszal included Taş-Cargan in his list of Karaite settlements.[799]

---

[798] Koeppen, *Sbornik*, 289-290; Chojecki, *Wspomnienia*, 233.
[799] Szapszal, *Karaimy*, 7.

A sixteenth century document, a letter from Polish ambassador M.Broniewski to King Stefan Batory (1.01.1579), might shed some light on the veracity of this claim. The letter was sent from "Tassarlagano [undoubtedly, a Latinized corruption of "Taş-Cargan"] pago Tartarico", where Broniewski was probably kept in kind of "mild imprisonment".[800] Taking into account the aforementioned nineteenth century data, and the fact that in all settlements (Çufut-Qalé, Yaşlov, Mangoup) where the members of the foreign embassies were housed there was, necessarily, a Jewish population, it can be very cautiously supposed that – in Taş-Cargan, in the sixteenth/seventeenth centuries – there was also a Jewish (most likely, Karaite) population that fulfilled "supplementary" functions to prisoners (i.e. money lending and providing victuals).

Sometimes foreign embassies stayed in Yaşlov [Yaşlovü], a small settlement of the clan of Yaşlov Beys [Yaşlov Beyler] between Aq-Meçıt (Simferopol') and Bakhçeseray. One of the seventeenth century sources mentioned that there were Jewish merchants who had financial affairs with members of the embassies: Andrey Nepeitsyn (1634) remarked that he had stored some of his goods at the place of "the Jew Ezra of Yaşlov".[801] Again, with great caution, taking into consideration the fact that, in the two adjacent settlements (Mangoup and Çufut-Qalé, the latter also being a possession of Yaşlov Beys), these Jewish merchants were Karaite, it is possible to suppose that Jewish merchants of Yaşlov were also Karaite.

The interpretation of several Hebrew epigraphic inscriptions found in Tepe-Kermen,[802] a mediæval cave-town situated close to Çufut-Qalé, represent a problem that has been discussed by scholars since the beginning of the twentieth century.[803] On the basis of my personal acquaintance with the aforementioned inscriptions, I came to the conclusion that one of them should be read as מרדכי בן־משה "Mordekhai Ben-Mosheh" (according to Kokovtsov, who had not seen the inscription de visu, "Mordekhai Ben-Buta"). The other, which is hardly readable, according to M.Ezer should be read as נחמו ("Naḥamu") – a name common for both local Karaites and

---

[800] Broniovius, *Tartariae Descriptio*, introduction to the work, no page numbers.
[801] "Skazanie sviashtchennika Iakova," 686.
[802] Tepe-Kermen – "the castle on the hilltop" (from Tatar "tepe" [hilltop] and "kermen" [castle]).
[803] N.A.Borovko, *Tepe-Kermen* (Simferopol', 1913), 24-25, 32, 38-39; A.Gidalevich, "Peshtchernyi gorod Tepe-Kermen i ego drevnee evreiskoe kladbishtche" [Cave town Tepe Kermen and its ancient Jewish cemetery], *Evreiskaia starina* 2 (1914): 198-205; D.Maggid, "K nadpisiam v Tepe-Kermene" [On the inscriptions in Tepe-Kermen], *Evreiskaia starina* 3 (1914): 490-491.

Rabbanites.[804] The third inscription, which is undoubtedly the date, was interpreted by Gidalevich to הרפח (5288=1528 c.e.), whereas, according to our opinion, it should be read as התפח (5488=1728 c.e.).

Unfortunately, both mediæval and later sources are silent concerning the history of the settlement and its inhabitants. The only data relevant to this problem might be found in the late nineteenth century travel account of F.Remy (1871), who mentioned that Tepe-Kermen, as well as Mangoup had once been inhabited by the Karaites, who left the settlement a long time before the abandonment of Çufut-Qalé.[805] It seems that Tepe-Kermen, which is mentioned as a part of the agricultural grounds of the Çufut-Qalé community, starting from the seventeenth century,[806] could have been used as a temporary shelter by Karaite shepherds.

---

[804] Michael Ezer, "Ktuvot Tepe-Kermen: Mordekhay Ben-Butai" in *Studies in a Karaite Community*, ed. Dan Shapira (in print).
[805] Remy, *Krim*, 97, 106.
[806] See *Sbornik*, 78-83.

CHAPTER 5
CONCLUSION

5.1. Travel accounts as important written source on the ethnic history of the Karaites.

Travel accounts, and their interpretation, are valuable sources for understanding the history of the Crimean Karaites, as has been clearly shown. There are common topics and patterns in the descriptions of the Crimean Karaites in travelers' journals that describe different aspects of Karaite cultural, religious, administrative, and social life. Travelers' accounts also reveal the common perception of what Europeans of the time viewed as a "peculiar and remarkable" ethnic group: The Karaites.

Most of the known accounts of European travelers who left notes on the Crimean Karaites from the fifteenth to the nineteenth century were collected and analyzed here. They can be roughly divided into three groups, which differ not only in their historical content, but also in the style and manner of their writing: accounts of the late mediæval and Renaissance period (fifteenth-sixteenth centuries), accounts before the Russian annexation (seventeenth century to 1783), and those written after this event (1783 to the second half of the nineteenth century).

The "Crimean parts" of the travelogues examined consisted mainly of ethnographic information (*i.e.* the descriptions of various ethnic groups inhabiting the Crimea during this period) and the descriptions of the largest Crimean towns, their architectural monuments, and fortifications. The aforementioned travel accounts represent an idiosyncratic and highly interesting type of written source, which conveys rare and detailed information regarding the history, ethnography, linguistics, toponymy, and archæology of the Karaites of Eastern Europe and their settlements. The data provided by the travel accounts, when compared to that collected from other sources (archæological, ethnographic, epigraphic, archival etc.), enables the integrative reconstruction of the history of the Karaites in Eastern Europe and the Crimea.

The travel accounts, moreover, delight their readers in conjuring up a colorful world. This type of written source has an unofficial, personal character. Travelers' notes are, as rule, distinguished by their profound infiltration into the historical reality described by their authors, supplying a number of peculiar and unusual details, sincere emotionalism and expression. Paradoxically, travelers' notes, as "external observers" who are not integrated into Karaite

237

society, supply us more cultural and historical details about the everyday life of the Crimean Karaites, than, say, writings of the "internal observers," the Karaites themselves, such as 'Azaryah Ben-Eliyah, and Yosef Shelomoh Lucki , who tended to concentrate, rather, on internal community matters.

Certain data, usually related to the travelers' evaluation of moral precepts and other ethical stereotypes, should be treated very carefully. Moreover, when analyzing travelers' data, one should always take into consideration the psychology of each author, his/her level of education, knowledge of foreign languages, nationality, confessional affiliation, personal biases and prejudices, ability to make in-depth conclusions, tendency to exaggerate facts and data, etc. In the case of the Crimean Karaites, the idealized depiction of their moral qualities was largely influenced by the general anti-Talmudic predisposition of the travelers and by the scholarly authority of the early reports by T.Czacki and E.Clarke [see more below].

Despite the lengthy research involved in the compilation of this volume, there is no doubt that some new travel accounts that would enable us to create a more accurate, in-depth picture of the life and history of the Crimean Karaites may be discovered. Moreover, similar comparative studies may be carried out with the regard to the history of other dispersed Karaite communities of the world: there is no doubt that most of the travelers who visited, say, Cairo, Constantinople, Troki, Halicz, Luck, or Jerusalem in the fifteenth - nineteenth centuries left some valuable notes on the history of local Karaite communities.[807]

And, finally, the last (but not the least) observation that should be made: because of the subjective and ambivalent character of the sources used in this study, it is highly probable that some readers will not agree with the interpretation of the travelers' data herein proposed. While being aware of this danger, an attempt was made to be

---

[807] I intend to carry out another research project of similar content and methodology, which will be dedicated to the general image of the Polish-Lithuanian Karaites as reflected in travel accounts of the fifteenth – ninteenth centuries. See Guillebert de Lannoy, *Oeuvres de Ghillebert de Lannoy,* ed. Ch.Potvin (Louvain, 1878), 40-41; Gustav Peringer, *Epistola de Karaitorum Rebus in Lithuania* (1691); Friedrich Albert Augusti, *Gründliche Nachrichten von denen Karaiten* (Erfurt, 1752); Balthasar Hacquet, *Hacquet's neueste physikalisch-politische Reisen in den Jahren 1788. und 1789. durch die Dacischen und Sarmatischen oder Nördlichen Karpathen,* pt.1 (Nürnberg, 1790), 198; Joseph Rohrer, *Versuch über die jüdischen Bewohner der österreichischen Monarchie,* pt.3 (Vienna, 1804), 145-149; Wincenty Smokowski, "Wspomnienia Trok w 1822 r.," *Athenaeum* 5 (1841): 157-183; Syrokomla, *Wycieczki*; Teodor Tripplin, *Dziennik podróży po Litwie i Żmudzi odbytej w 1856 roku,* vol.1 (Wilno 1856); Cohen, *Vilna,* et alia.

as objective as possible. It is hoped that, despite all possible shortcomings and infelicities, the attention of the academic (and non-academic) audience was attracted to this hitherto undeservably under-investigated source on the history of the Karaites, thus providing new, valuable, and important data to the field of Karaite Studies.

5.2. Overall image of the Crimean Karaites in the travelers' portrayal.

On the basis of this in-depth analysis of the travel accounts, it is possible to come to certain conclusions regarding the overall image of the Karaites in the portrayal of the eighteenth/nineteenth century travelers (earlier accounts seem to be too scattered and too brief to allow such conclusions).[808] The most noticeable feature of the travel writings of this period is their excessive stress upon the good nature and general (moral and physical) purity and cleanliness of the Karaites. As a rule, the Karaites were looked upon as a tidy, clean, industrious, and wealthy ethnic group with a mild, hospitable character (which was always rewarded and distinguished by the governments of the countries where they lived), and an equivocal, enigmatic past and origin. Travelers often remarked that the Karaites were free from many superstitions of the Rabbanites, and were not corrupted by the "vicious" teaching of the Talmud.[809]

The solid reputation and proverbial honesty of the Karaites, known everywhere in the Crimea, both in professional and private relations, was considered another distinctive they possessed.[810] Some

---

[808] The travelers of the late Middle Ages and Early Modern period (fifteenth-eighteenth centuries) did not pay much attention to the Karaites, and hardly differentiated them from the Rabbanites.

[809] "...unshackled by the trammels of the Talmud, their minds are not circumscribed by the puerile sophistries of the Rabbins..." (Extract of a Letter from the Rev. Drs. Paterson and Henderson," *JEx* 6 (1821): 470); "Zealous in preservation of the Bible and observing its corruption performed by the Rabbanites by the means of the Talmud and Commentaries, they had full rights to consider them to be apostates... Their natural simplemindedness shuddered witnessing the swindle, which they correctly ascribed to the corruption of the Divine Law by the Talmud" (Syrokomla, *Wycieczki*, 67-68); "the Karaites had not been witnesses of the religious revolution effected by Jesus in Palestine, nor had they become acquainted with the Christians until a later period: they entertained therefore no hereditary animosity against Christianity" (Haxthausen, *Empire*, 111); "In this struggle smarter, educated and untiring Talmudists always gained the upper hand over simple... [and] more primitive Karaites..." (Kohl, *Reisen*, vol.2, 259). Similar phrases might be found in Henderson, *Researches*, 322; Teodor Tripplin, *Dziennik podróży po Litwie i Żmudzi odbytej w 1856 roku*, vol.1 (Wilno 1856), 107, 111; Guthrie, *Tour*, 83; Nowosielski, *Stepy*, 206; and many other travel accounts.

[810] Clarke, *Travels*, 193; Henderson, *Researches*, 323; Demidov, *Voyage*, vol.1, 371; Demidov, *Travels*, 36; Bonar, McCheyne, *Narrative*, 441.

travelers even testified that the Karaites in Poland, Lithuania and Crimea were such loyal and faithful citizens of their countries that none of them had ever committed a criminal deed, and had never been taken to court in the course of several centuries.[811] A.Haxthausen mentioned that, because of such exemplary behavior, the Karaites were relieved of the double poll-tax imposed upon the Rabbanites.[812]

It is worth reflecting upon the reasons for such idealization, in my opinion, of the Karaites as portrayed by the travelers. One of the main reasons for such a favorable evaluation of the moral and physical qualities of the Karaites, was, in all probability, the fact that all the travelers were believing Christians, with internalized anti-Semitic pre-conceptions and biases against the Jews, which were commonly held in nineteenth century circles, and, therefore, were quite prejudiced regarding the Rabbanites, who represented, in their eyes, the "typical" form of Judaism. A recurring motif in the travel accounts of the first half of the nineteenth century is the comparison between the "bad Jews" (*i.e.* the Rabbanites, "corrupted" Jews, whose ancestors took part in the Crucifixion, and who since remain enslaved to the vicious and false teachings of the Talmud), and the "good Jews" (*i.e.* the Karaites, "pure" Jews, whose past is not blotted by anti-Christian sentiment and who remained beholden to the Old Testament, uncorrupted by Talmudic ranting).[813] Almost all descriptions of the Crimean Karaites are based on this superimposed dichotomy. Naturally, such comparisons were always slanted in the favor of the Karaites.

Thus, it is possible to suggest that the travel accounts reflect the ideological tendentiousness of their writers who projected a view of the Karaites as "exemplary Jews" in contradistinction to the widespread "Talmudophobia" of Christian Europe of that time.[814]

In addition, there was another factor which contributed to the bias in the travelers' reports, namely, the sheer pressure of the

---

[811] Henderson, *Researches*, 323; the letter of Rzewuski in Szapszal, "Adam Mickiewicz," 5-8; Nowosielski, *Stepy*, 206; Smokowski, "Wspomnienia," 162; Syrokomla, *Wycieczki*, 61-65; and many other travel accounts.

[812] Haxthausen, *Empire*, 112; the same, *Studien*, 408-409.

[813] Especially symptomatical in this respect is the account of E.Henderson, who very favorably referred to the Karaites, and, with strong disapproval and indignation, described the communities of Polish Rabbanites: *Researches*, 306-339, 220-232.

[814] However, the image of the Karaite depicted by Evliya Çelebi, the only Muslim traveler who left some notes on the Crimean Karaites, is not so eulogistic: He finds that some of their houses are rather miserable and dirty, the Karaites are afraid of such nuisances as the thunder of weapons, and they are hated even by their Jewish brethren (Evliya Çelebi, *Kniga*, 90, 94).

authoritative opinions of E.Clarke and T.Czacki, two early scholars who described East European Karaites in the beginning of the nineteenth century. The phrases about exemplary Karaite honesty, which are common place in many a travel account, were cloned from Clarke's, "Their honesty is proverbial in the Crimea; and the word of a Karaite is considered equal to a bond."[815] Another stereotypical phrase, praising the Karaites, is nothing but a repetition of T.Czacki's conclusion that, "archives testify that none of the Karaites of our country (*i.e.* Poland) in the course of the last four centuries has ever been sentenced for committing a crime."[816] This phrase was repeated by practically all authors describing the East European Karaites in the nineteenth/early twentieth centuries,[817] in spite of the fact that archival research does not enforce its veracity; moreover, despite its obvious unfeasibility, this phrase is often repeated by some present-day authors as well!

Taking all this into account, nevertheless, there are many reasons to consider the idealized evaluation of the Karaites in the accounts as a manifestation of an authentic response on the part of the travelers, to a certain extent, quite justifiable. Due to their adoption of the Oriental customs of the Crimean Tatars, and due to their prosperous and stable position in the society, the hygienic conditions distinguished in the Karaites' everyday life were indeed much better than those of the Rabbanite Jews. The highly positive attitude of the Russian government towards the Karaites can also be distinguished as

---

[815] Clarke, *Travels*, 193.

[816] My translation from Czacki, "Rozprawa," 270. This observation seems to be an exaggeration resulting from the aforementioned "idealization" of the Karaites in the eyes of external observers. Criminal deeds committed by the Crimean and Polish Karaites or legal processes against them are often mentioned in primary sources and secondary literature: Mann, *Texts*, 733; Balaban, "Karaici w Polsce," 40, 79-81; Stefan Gąsiarowski, "Karaimi w Kukizowie," in *Żydzi i Judaizm we współczesnych badaniach polskich,* K.Pilarczyk i S.Gąsiarowski (eds), vol.2 (Kraków, 2000), 79; see also numerous cases of this kind in the Archive of the Karaite Spiritual Assembly: *GAARK*, f.241, op.1 and in the pinkas of the Troki community prepared for the publication by Philip Miller: "Lithuanian Karaite Communal Organization after 1793" (in print). The impossibility of this "proverbial" non-criminal nature of the Karaites and the necessity of checking all legal cases accumualted in the course of the last 400 years (a task, perhaps, too difficult to be completed) had been mentioned in the petition of the Troki Rabbanites as early as in 1835 (Gessen, "Bor'ba karaimov g.Trok," 577).

[817] See Henderson, *Researches*, 323; the letter of Rzewuski in Szapszal, "Adam Mickiewicz," 5-8; Nowosielski, *Stepy*, 206; Smokowski, "Wspomnienia," 162; Syrokomla, *Wycieczki*, 61-65; Bohdan Janusz, *Karaici w Polsce* (Krakow, 1927), 5-6; Józef Smoliński, "Karaimi i bożnica ich w Łucku," *Ziemia* 3:7 (1912): 100; Bohdan Janusz, "Karaici i cmentarzysko ich," *Ziemia* 2 (1911): 5, et alia.

another reason for their material and financial prosperity: they were not only exempt from military service, which was compulsory for the Rabbanites, but were also relieved from the double poll tax imposed upon their co-religionists.[818]

5.3. General European tendencies that influenced the process of forming the ethnic self-consciousness and historical views of East European Karaites.

"While taking into account the presence of a certain Semitic element, we deny the Crimean Karaites neither the right of considering themselves a Turkic people, nor demanding from others understanding of this right..."
(Tadeusz Kowalski, "Turecka monografja o Karaimach krymskich," *MK* 2:1 (1929): 8)

"No longer considering themselves Jews, and no longer considered so by the State, they seem to have abandoned or lost that major value which Jews cherished, and which had sustained Judaism during two millennia of exile..."
(Miller, "Agenda in Karaite Printing," 87)

The "Karaite question" appeared as a sort of echo of the "Jewish question" which became a topic for serious debates which were going in many European countries (the Russian Empire prominent among them) at the end of the eighteenth, up through the nineteenth century. To summarize this problem, the European governments of that period wanted to integrate into Christian society the influential and wealthy Jewish communities, which up to that time managed to preserve their "alien" and separated status.

One of the most important factors that hindered the integration of European Jewry into Christian society, in addition to their "alien" language (Yiddish), distinctively different clothing, external appearance, specific culture, &c., was their adherence to Judaism, a religion, which was considered alien and "corrupt". As is known, the Talmud, an important part of the Rabbanite religious creed and tradition, evoked especially hostile and contemptuous reactions

---

[818] Miller, *Separatism*, xvi-xvii. The indigenous Crimean Rabbanite Jews-Qrımçaqlar, as well as Karaites, also tried to use an "Oriental" motif in order to be exempted from anti-semitic Russian laws: They were very similar to the Karaites in their half-Tatar everyday practices. The only difference was their usage of the Talmud; as a consequence, all their pleads were disregarded (Vikhnovich, *Firkovich*, 89).

from Christian thinkers and official governmental authorities of that time.

In this situation the Karaites, who decisively rejected the teaching of the Talmud, and were often seen as prospective targets for Christian missionary activity,[819] became the object of a focused interest by high-ranking anti-Talmudic authorities, as a convenient tool in anti-Rabbanite propaganda. Rapidly growing interest in the Karaites among the nineteenth century Christian scholars and missionaries is one of the evidences of the importance of this propaganda.[820] Its echoes can be traced in the testimonies of the nineteenth century travelers as well [see §5.2 above]. Thus, on the official pretext of their exemplary behavior and beneficial activity for the state, the Karaites were distinguished with a number of privileges and benefits,[821] in contrast to the Rabbanites, who suffered from a number of humiliating and burdensome laws that forced them to pay heavy double taxes, serve in the army, live only within the limits of the pale of settlement, &c.

When contemplating the reasons why the end of the eighteenth/nineteenth century was marked by a new stage in the shaping of the Karaites' national self-identification, it is worth recalling the fact that, in general, the nineteenth century is the age of forming national ideologies: it is in this period that several of the largest European Empires were formed together with unshakable national theories. It is in this time that we first hear such terms as a "nation" and "nationalism," and, finally, the end of the eighteenth/nineteenth century is the time of the Jewish Emancipation. Some of the general features peculiar to the process of forming

---

[819] See "Extract of a Letter from the Rev. Drs. Paterson and Henderson," *JEx* 6 (1821): 470.

[820] See W.Häusler, *Das Galizische Judentum in der Habsburgmonarchie. Im Lichte der Zeitgenossischen Publizistik und Reiseliteratur von 1772-1848* (München, 1979), 35, 74; Green, "Karaite Community," 102; Extract of a Letter from the Rev. Drs. Paterson and Henderson," *JEx* 6 (1821): 469-470; "Interesting Communication of Dr. Pinkerton, Respecting the Jews in Poland," *JEx* 6 (1821): 444-445; "Extract of a Letter from the same [W.Ferd.Becker]," *JEx* 7 (1822): 74.

[821] In 1774 Austrian empress Maria Teresa (1740-1780) granted the Karaites the same rights as other citizens of the Empire (Schur, *Encyclopedia*, 194-195, 36-37). The exact circumstances of this event, the first occasion when the Karaites were differentiated from their Rabbanite brethren, needs to be explored, most likely, in the light of the Austrian archival documents. In 1795, the Russian government exempted them from the double taxation, and, in 1827, from military conscription. See more details in Miller, *Separatism*, 3-67); in addition to these, and some other alleviations in their status, in 1863, they were given the same rights as other Christian citizens of the Russian Empire (V.Smirnov, foreword to *Sbornik*, xviii-xix).

national ideologies allow us to illustrate the process of the forming of the national ideology and self-identification of the East European Karaites.

Together with socio-œconomic and political factors, one of the most important features of the forming of all national ideologies is the so-called process of the "romanticization" of ethnic history, which is first manifested in the appearance of "romantic" mythological concepts, which later usually receive "academic" development and verification. Pseudoscientific, romantic theories and mythological concepts of this type, as a rule, justified a nation's territorial and historical claims, making its history look much more ancient, noble, and autochtonic, strengthening the feeling of common national identity, and promoting the development of patriotic and nationalistic tendencies.[822] On the other hand, there also existed an opposite mythological tendency that, in order to construct a unified and unanimous ideological concept of the past, compelled a nation (or ethnic group) not only to remember, but also to forget. Forget, first of all, about some events that would make this ideological concept look awkward, such as unsuccessful military campaigns, devastating defeats, offences to national pride, etc.

When speaking about the formation of the Karaite national ideology in the eighteenth/nineteenth centuries, it is possible to distinguish the following main factors which influenced its development. It seems that this process might be best observed against the background of A.Toynbee's system of, "challenge-and-response pattern."[823] Thus, the first challenge to the well-being of East European Karaites as an ethnic entity was represented by the edict of Catherine the Great, in 1794, that put them on the same precarious legal level as

---

[822] The Karaites were not unique in such "romanticization" of their history: similar traditions testifying their ancient rights to live on this place since immemorial times had practically every small ethnic community in Europe (on the psychological mechanisms and reasons for this romanticization see Bernard D. Weinryb, "The Beginnings of East-European Jewry in Legend and Historiography," in *Studies and Essays in Honor of Abraham A.Neuman*, ed.Meir Ben-Horin et alia (Leiden, 1962), 445-502). The Karaite case is unique from another standpoint: the Karaites were, perhaps, the only Judaic community which cherished these romantic delusions until the end of the nineteenth century. Moreover, they were the only community which, in the twentieth century, on the grounds of this naive romanticization managed to build the scientific theory proving their non-Jewish, Turkic-Mongol-Ugrian-Khazar origin [see below].

[823] To justify this sort of methodological approach towards the history of the Karaites, see the book of one of the best specialists in this field, Zvi Ankori, who analyzed the early stages of the Karaite history with the usage of Toynbee's methodology: Zvi Ankori, *Karaites*, 8-58.

Rabbanites and jeopardized their prosperous and secure œconomic position in the Crimea and elsewhere in the Russian Empire. Their response was swift, and efficient: a number of petitions and appeals were sent to various official authorities, and a special embassy to solve this problem was sent to her Imperial Majesty, Catherine II in 1795.[824] 1795 might be considered as the starting point for the awakening of Karaite national feelings, peacefully sleeping during the previous centuries. Another challenge, the edict of 1827 about the military conscription of the Jews of the Russian Empire, that again jeopardized Karaite identity, evoked an even stronger reaction: a new, more representative embassy was sent to Nicholas I, with the aim of obtaining special legal status that distinctively differentiated them from other representatives of Jewish population of the Empire. Soon afterwards, Simḥah Babovich, a leader of this successful embassy, who clearly understood the necessity of undertaking more decisive measures securing the position of the Karaites, lobbied for the creation of the Karaite Spiritual Consistory in March, 1837.[825]

However, an even more serious challenge, which compelled the Karaites to start a serious full scale re-construction (or, rather, constructing) of a unified conception of their ethnical past, *i.e.* conception, which would not evoke any further suspicions of official authorities, was the edict of the count M.S.Vorontsov (1839). This was directed to the Karaite leaders, and consisted of a number of questions related to the history of the Karaites, the time of their coming to the Crimea, peculiarities of their religion, etc.[826] In spite of the seemingly superficial inquisitive tone of this edict, its main implication was very clear: the Karaites had to justify their privileged status. In response, in 1839, a historic expedition, headed by Avraham Firkovich, was organized. The expedition, with the help of local officials, sometimes with the application of force, managed to "discover" valuable epigraphic and manuscript data that later resulted in an absolutely new understanding of Karaite history, fully reflected in Firkovich's famous *Avnei Zikkaron*.

According to this concept the Karaites, the only true Biblical Jews, and the descendants of the ancient Judeans, arrived in the Crimea

---

[824] The history and successfully result of this embassy are described in the chronicle of Yiṣḥaq Ben-Shelomoh. See Miller, *Separatism*, 13-17, 215-219.

[825] Miller, "Spiritual and Political Leadership," 3.

[826] The text of the letter of the civil governor of Taurida, M.Muromtsev to the Karaite *Ḥakham* Simḥah Babovich was published by O.Belyi in his "Obzor arhivnykh dokumentov po istorii karaimskoi obshchiny Kryma v pervoi polovine XIX veka" [Survey of the archival documents on the history of the Karaite community of the Crimea in the first half of the nineteenth century], *Krymskiy Muzey* 1995/1996, 114.

as early as in the sixth century B.C.E., *i.e.* much earlier than the Crucifixion of Jesus and composition of the "vicious" Talmud. Moreover, it was Karaite missionaries that converted the nomadic Khazars to Judaism. Unlike the "newcomers" (Talmudic Jews), the Karaites were always honest, and loyal to the governments of the countries where they lived. All this provided grounds for understanding the Karaites as the most ancient part of the Crimean population, loyal to Christianity and faithful to Russian empire [see more in §2.2].

The official government structures also seemed to be satisfied. No other additional inquiries were sent, and, consequently, in 1863, the Karaites were given the same rights as other Christian citizens of the Russian Empire.[827]

Thus, it seems quite evident that these external "challenges" "awakened" the national consciousness of the East European Karaites, and stimulated their interest in studying their own history starting from the late 1830s.

Speaking about the aforementioned processes of "romanticization" and "forgetting" of some episodes of one's past, they also might be found in the process of forming the Karaite national self-identity in Eastern Europe in the nineteenth/twentieth centuries. It was in the nineteenth century when the Karaites started to "forget" the centuries-old cultural ties that bound them to their Rabbanite brethren. In the beginning of the twentieth century, earlier romantic theories about the origin of the Karaites from the Ten Lost Tribes of Israel and/or ancient Judeans were replaced by an equally romantic "Khazar" theory, which soon became the focus of East European Karaite national identity. The postulate concerning the Turkic Khazar origins of the East European Karaites, first mentioned by Russian orientalists V.V.Grigoriev and V.D.Smirnov and later transformed by S.Szapszal into a kind of "scientifically" proved theory was recognized as official Karaite doctrine after the election of S.Szapszal to the post of the Taurida *Ḥakham* in 1915.[828]

The reverse side of the Khazar theory was the necessity to "forget" about the existing bonds and ties that attached the Karaites to

---

[827] V.Smirnov, foreword to *Sbornik*, xviii-xix. About Firkovich's expedition see Vikhnovich, *Firkovich*, 91-107.

[828] Critical analysis of the "Khazar theory", and some other romantic concepts of the appearance of the Karaites in Eastern Europe was made by Zvi Ankori in his *Karaites*, 58-85. Moreover, one should also recall other, similar "romantic" theories concerning the Khazar origins of Crimean Rabbanite-Qrımçaqlar, and the loud book of A.Koestler concerning the Khazar roots of Ashkenazic Jewry (Arthur Koestler, *The Thirteenth Tribe* (London, 1976)).

the Jewish people, thus an obstacle on their way to a secure and flourishing œconomic position in Russia and Poland. This might be an explanation of why and how the East European Karaites accepted a theory which "proved" their independent ethnic and religious origins, first of all their Khazar-Turkic ancestry. Later, it allowed them to form convictions that they were not Jews, but Turkic proselytes who embraced Karaism, a separate religion, which resembles Judaism on the same scale as Christianity and Islam.[829]

It is quite possible that the history of the forming of the Karaite national self-identification was much more complex and intricate than presented by the author of this book (the reader is reminded that the main objective of the book was the analysis of travel accounts).[830] A number of documents testify to the careful preservation of Hebrew traditions by, say, Moscow or Halicz Karaites at least until World War I; moreover, some of the traditional Karaite believers were rather frustrated by the Turkization of their traditions by S.Szapszal. It seems that the process of the loss of Karaite Jewish traditions and self-identification, which was started by the Karaite intellectual and ideological elite in the beginning of the twentieth century, reached wider circles of Karaite believers much later, after World War II, together with their developing integration into Soviet society, and the strengthening of Communist atheistic propaganda.

It seems that an especially strong impact of this process of "exogenous and endogenous dejudaization"[831] was in the Crimea, where some of the Crimean Karaites tend to substitute the religion of their forefathers with pagan practices venerating "sacred" oaks and the cult of Turkic deity Tengri Khan [see §3.2.2].

Paradoxically, it was the Crimean Karaite Alexei/Avraham Kefeli, at present a *Ḥazzan* of the Ashdod (Israel) Karaite community, who composed a leaflet entitled, "*Karaimy. Razjasnitelnaya broshura po istorii karaimov Kryma i osnovam karaimskoi religii*" [Karaites. Explanatory leaflet on the history of the Crimean Karaites and basics of the Karaite confession] (Ashdod, 2002). This publication challenged

---

[829] I have often heard these explanations of the essence of Karaite belief from Polish and Lithuanian Karaites; it seems that the first to express these "ecumenical" views was S.Szapszal. See one of his interviews of 1936 as quoted in Warren Green, "The Karaite Community in Interwar Poland," *Nationalities Papers* 14: 1-2 (1986): 107.

[830] This topic is dealt with in detail in the forthcoming doctoral dissertation of the author; see also Golda Akhiezer, "Tefisot HaZehut HaHistorit Shel HaQara'im BeMizraḥ Eropah BeMme'ot Ha-19 — Ha-20," *Pe'amim* (2003) (forthcoming); Fred Astren, *History, Historicization and Historical Claims in Karaite Jewish Literature* (PhD thesis, University of California 1993).

[831] Term coined by Roman Freund in his *Karaites and Dejudaization*.

247

all the East European Karaites not to believe in theories concerning their Turkic origins and return to their genuine Karaite roots, religious, cultural, and ethnic:

> Return to your roots, to our religion! Do not look for [true] Karaism in the theories of the Turkic origin of the Karaites, which were merely tactics of survival during fascism! And even in the years of the fascist occupation of the Crimea, there were [liturgical] services conducted in Biblical Hebrew!

Not daring to venture to forecast whether Polish-Lithuanian and Crimean Karaites will answer this call, I would like to finish my work with a quotation from Mourad el-Qodsi, a Karaite author who visited the Karaite communities of Eastern Europe in the summer of 1991:

> I feel strongly that there is still much more to know, and to learn about the Karaite communities there. We must try to know what really did happen during the communist regime, and even long before that, what kind of activities they had before and after communism, and above all what kind of future they expect.[832]

This, however, would be a topic for another voluminous book, and another lengthy research.

---

[832] El-Qodsi, *Communities*, 29.

Afterword

Dear reader, we have just finished our virtual journey to the enigmatic realm of the Karaite Crimea. I hope that the road was not too hard and uneven. I hope also that this book would induce at least some of you to undertake your own attempt of exploring this hitherto under-investigated area (both literarily, and in the form of an actual trip to the Crimea) in order to corroborate, or, on the contrary, disprove some of the conclusions made by the author.

" 'Whenever destiny would take you to Çufut-Qalé, do not delay your visit to your old friends.' While saying this the Rabbi, in accordance with oriental customs, puts his hand upon his heart, bows and sees the travelers off beyond the gates of his premises..."

Appendix A: Poem of Shelomoh Beim

112

ГИМНЪ БОГУ.

1.

Во свѣтлости лица Царева жизнь. О Ты, Спаситель, живущій вовѣки, внемля воплю Израиля!

Ниспошли свѣтъ Твой, чудное спасеніе Твое, на славу Царя крѣпкаго и благочестиваго—славы силъ нашихъ!

2.

Призря съ высоты небесъ на народъ Твой, призывающій имя Твое во гласѣ молитвы и моленія своего!

Внемли, Отецъ небесный, молитвамъ его (твоего народа), которыя онъ возноситъ къ тебѣ въ своихъ собраніяхъ!

3.

Ты, Царю вселенной, ниспосылаешь Монархамъ спасеніе, на которое они уповаютъ. Благослови и споспѣшествуй пути Царя правосуднаго, неоцѣненнаго, чтущаго Тебя (Боже), дивный и праведный!

4.

Великій Государь! Крѣпость и утвержденіе наше! Счастіе его постоянно увеличивается; имя его преславно, и какъ благъ совѣтъ его!

113

1.

בְּאוֹר פְּנֵי מֶלֶךְ חַיִּים
שׁוֹכֵן עַד הַגּוֹאֵל ·· פְּנֵה נָא אֵל
שׁוֹעֵת יִשְׂרָאֵל
שְׁלַח אוֹרְךָ ·· הַפְלֵא עֶזְרְךָ
עַל הֲדָר
אַדִּיר מֶלֶךְ ·· יְקָר הִלֵּל
מָאֵין עֻזִּי

2.

הַבֵּט מִשָּׁמַיִם ·· עַל עַמְּךָ
קוֹרְאִים שְׁמֶךָ
בְּקוֹל רִנָּתָם ·· וּבְתַחֲנָתָם
הַקְשֵׁב
לְרֹב שִׂיחָתָם ·· בְּמַקְהֵלוֹתָם
אַתָּה אָבִימוֹ

3.

נוֹתֵן לִמְלָכִים ·· יֵשַׁע חוֹרְכִים
מוֹשִׁיעַ פְּלָכִים
אָנָּא תְבָרֵךְ ·· תַּצְלִיחַ דֶּרֶךְ
תַּמִּים
מֶלֶךְ יְקִירְךָ ·· אֵין לוֹ עֶרֶךְ
אַדִּיר צִדְקוֹ

4.

אַמְפְּרָאטוֹר גָּדוֹל ·· עֹז יִגְמְדְּל
מְבֹל לֹא יֶחְדַּל
מְכִבֵּד שְׁמוֹ ·· וּמַה טּוֹב טַעֲמוֹ

Ч. II

251

— 114 —

Онъ милосердъ, благочестивъ, прекрасенъ, праведенъ и незлобивъ! Онъ вѣнецъ главъ нашихъ!

5.

Кто, будучи подобенъ Богу, въ праведности исправляетъ недостатки, пожигаетъ терніе, изливаетъ щедроты на бѣдствующій, трепещущій и скитающійся народъ? Не узрятъ несчастія тѣ, которые тщательно будутъ исполнять слово Царя нашего.

6.

Родъ Его возвеличенъ, окруженъ всѣми благами. Августѣйшая Его Супруга, первородный Сынъ Его и все Августѣйшее Потомство и блаженное сѣмя Его, избранника Божія, свидѣтельствуютъ о его добродѣтеляхъ.

7.

Да наслаждаются Они долголѣтіемъ безмятежной жизни; да умножится радость Ихъ, да возвеличится благодать Ихъ, да облекутся Они въ блестящую славу, да увеличится счастіе Ихъ, ибо—въ этомъ спасеніе наше!

8.

Всѣ правители, всѣ подданные Его, повинующіеся волѣ его, хранящіе Его велѣнія, да процвѣтаютъ во спасеніи, да освѣщаются свѣ-

— 115 —

רחמן
יקר בנעמו ·· צדיק בתמו
נזר לראשינו

5.
מי כאל צדק ·· תקן בדק
וּבכלה חזק
גמל חסדים ·· לנעים נדים
עם דל
לא יראה אידים ·· כל החרדים
לדבר מלכה.

6.
בית מרום מרעד ·· לטובה עד
ברוב כל מסעד
נית יקרו ·· בנו בכורו
עם כל
ילדי פאר ·· וזרע אשירו
בחיר צורנו.

7.
ימצא. רב חיים ·· לשבעתים
באין ידים
ירבה ששונם ·· ויגל חנם
יעטה.
צבי מאונם ·· וירהב קרנם
כי זה ישיענו.

8.
כל שדיו עבדיו ·· תחת ידו

252

Appendix A: Poem of Shelomoh Beim (continued)

томъ, да будетъ счастливъ путь ихъ во всемъ,
да живутъ въ радости, по волѣ Творца нашего!

9.

Преклонимъ колѣна, простремъ руки наши
къ небесамъ!

10.

Боже невидимый! Споспѣшествуй миру Ца-
реву! Велѣнія властителя нашего блестящи,
какъ сафиръ и алмазъ.

11.

Да преклонятся предъ Нимъ всѣ возстающіе
на Него, да успокоятся и да насладятся миромъ
Его народы. Да исполнитъ Спаситель Его всѣ
Его желанія, да процвѣтаетъ миръ въ Его вопи-
ствѣ, спокойствіе въ предѣлахъ Его государ-
ства, и посреди нашего народа (Евреевъ).

12.

Господи силою Твоею возвеселится Царь и
о спасеніи Твоемъ возрадуется зѣло, сказано въ
Писаніи (а).

(а) Переводъ исправленъ въ С. Петербургѣ, господиномъ
Профессоромъ Левисономъ, и много отъ этого выигралъ.

117

שׁוֹמְרֵי פִּקֻדָיו
יֵשַׁע יִפְרָחוּ ·· בְּאוֹר יִזְרָחוּ
דַרְכָּם

בְּכָל יַצְלִיחוּ · יִחְיוּ. יִשְׂמְחוּ
כִּרְצוֹן קוֹנָם

9.

יִכְרַע עַל בִּרְכַּיִם ·· לִפְנֵי שָׁמַיִם
נִפְרֹשׂ כַּפַּיִם

10.

אֱלֹהֵי עוֹלָם · תְּקַדֵּם הֲלוֹם
פְּנֵי
מֶלֶךְ בְּשָׁלוֹם ·· סַפִּיר יַהֲלוֹם
גְּזֵרַת מַלְכוּ

11.

יִכְרְעוּ. לוֹ קָמָיו ·· יָנוּחוּ עַמָּיו
יִשְׂמַח בְּשְׁלוֹמָיו
יָפִיק גְּאָלוֹ ·· אֶת כָּל מִשְׁאָלוֹ
יִפְרָח
שָׁלוֹם בְּחֵילוֹ ·· שַׁלְוָה בִּגְבוּלוֹ
וּקְהַל עַמּוֹ

12.

כַּכָּתוּב ה בְּעֻזְךָ יִשְׂמַח מֶלֶךְ וּבִישׁוּעָתֶךָ
מַה יָּגֵל מְאֹד

Indices

1. Persons
1.3. Travelers.[833]

Afanasyev-Chuzhbinskiy, A. (Russia, 1863)
Aitemirov, Vasiliy (Russia, 1692-1695)
Basov, Ivan (Russia, 1628)
Beaudoin (France, 1855)
Beauplan, Guilliaume Levasseur de (France, the second quarter of the 17th century)
Berg, Nikolay (Russia, 1854-1856)
Bobrov, S. (Russia, c.1804)
Bonar, Andrew A. (England, 1838)
Broniovius, Martinus (Marcin Broniewski) (Poland, 1578-1579)
Bzhishkian, Minas (Armenian traveler, 1820s)
Castelnau, Gabriel de (France, 1820)
Chevalier, Pierre (France, 1663)
Chojecki, Edmund (Poland, 1843)
Clarke, Edward Daniel (England, 1800)
D'Ascoli, Emidio Portelli (*wrong variant:* Dortelli) (Italy, 1630s)
D.B. [D.N.Bantysh-Kamenskiy?] (Russia, 1816)
Daab, Adolf (Poland, 1896)
Deinard, Ephraim (Russia-USA, 1860s)
Demidov, Anatoli (Russia, 1837)
Evliya Çelebi (Turkey, 1665-1666)
French officer, the author of *Lettres sur la Crimée* (France, 1808)
Hablizl (Hablitzl, Habliz, Russ. Gablits), Carl Ludwig (Russia, 1785)
Griboedov, Alexander Sergeevich (Russia, 1825)
Guthrie, Maria (England, 1795-1796)
Hacquet, Balthasar (Germany?, 1788 – 1789)
Haxthausen, August Franz von (Germany, 1843)
Heber, Reginald (England, 1800s)
Hell, Xavier Hommaire de (France, 1840s)
Henderson, Ebenezer (England, 1821)
Hlebnicki-Józefowicz, L. (Poland, 1877)
Holderness, Mary (England, 1827)
Izmailov, Vladimir (Russia, 1799)
Kaczkowski, Karol (Poland, 1825)
Kemeny, Janos (Hungary, 1657)

---

[833] The data in the brackets designates the country of the traveler's origin and the time of his/her travel to the Crimea (or the time of the first publication of his/her travelogue).

Kessler, Charles (Karl) (Russia, 1858)
Kleeman, Nikolaus Ernest (Austria, 1769)
Kohl, Johann Georg (Germany, 1838)
Koshliakov, A. (Russia, 1847-1848)
Kostomarov, Nikolay (Russia, 1861)
Lannoy, Guillebert de (France, c.1421)
Lucca, Giovanni Giuliani da (*alia:* Jean de Luca) (Italy, 1620s-1630s)
Lyall, Robert (England, 1822)
Markov, Yevgeniy (Evgeni) (Russia, 1860s)
Marmont, Auguste Frederic de (France, 1834)
Matthew (the end of the 14th century)
McCheyne, Robert Murray (England, 1838)
Mickiewicz, Adam (Poland, 1825)
Mikhailovskiy-Danilevskiy, A.I. (Russia, 1818)
Montpereux, Frederic Dubois de (France, 1838)
Mosheh Petahyah of Regensburg (Jewish traveler from Germany, between 1177 – 1187)
Motray, Aubry de la (France, 1711)
Muraviev-Apostol, Ivan Matveevich (Russia, 1820)
Murzakevich, Nikolay (Russia, 1836, 1841)
Neilson, Andrew (England, 1820s)
Nepeitsyn, Andrey (Russia, 1634)
Nikiforov (Russia, 1764)
Nowosielski, Antoni [Antoni Marcinkowski] (Poland, 1850)
Oliphant, Laurence (England, 1852)
Olizar, Gustav (Poland, 1823-1825)
Pallas, Peter Simon (Germany-Russia, 1793-1794)
Peringer, Gustav (Sweden, 1691)
Peyssonel, Claude Charles de (France, 1753)
Pirogov (Russia, 25.05.1857)
Pojata (Helena Skirmuntowa) (Poland-Lithuania, 1870)
Pushkin, Alexander Sergeevich (Russia, 1820s)
Raffet, Auguste (France, 1837)
Remy, F. (Germany, 1871)
Reuilly, Jean De (France, 1803)
Rohrer, Joseph (Austria, 1804)
Rubruquis, William de (1253)
Rzewuski, Henryk (Poland, 1825)
Safonov, S. (Russia, 1837)
Savelov, Petr (Russia, 1628)
Schiltberger, Johann (Germany, 1400s)
Sheremetev, Vasiliy (Russia, 1660-1681)

Shishkina, Olimpiada (Russia, 1845)
Siestrzencewicz de Bohusz, Stanislaw (Poland, c.1783-1785)
Spenser, Edmund (England, 1836)
Sumarokov, Pavel (Russia, 1799, 1803-1805)
Syrokomla, Władysław [Ludwik Kondratowicz] (Poland-Lithuania, 1854)
Tarbeev, Stepan (Russia, 1628)
Tchernichowsky, Sha'ul (Russia-Israel, 1920s)
Theodore (thirteenth century)
Tiapkin, Vasiliy (Russia, 1680-1681)
Tolstoy, Alexey Konstantinovich (Russia, 1856)
Viazemskiy, P.A. (Russia, 1867)
Webster, James (England, 1828)
Zhukov, N. (Russia, c.1858)
Zhukovskiy, Vasiliy Andreevich (Russia, 1837)
Zotov, Nikita (Russia, 1680-1681)
Zuev, Vasiliy (Russia, 1782)

1.2. East European Karaites.[834]

Aharon-Kochesh-Balbush (perhaps a corrupted form of Aharon Qoyçu Ba'al HaBayit [Aharon Qoyçu the landlord]), the owner of the house used as prison (Çufut-Qalé, second half of the 18th century)
Avraham Ben-Yoshiyah, the author of *Emunah Omen* (Çufut-Qalé, 18th century)
Avraham, *papas* (head) of the Kaffa community (16th century)
'Azaryah Ben-Eliyah, chronicler (Çufut-Qalé, 1777)
Babacan, Ya'aqov Ben-'Ezra (emigrant from Evpatoria, second half of the 19th century)
Babovich, B.E., the mayor of Qarasubazar (1900s)
Babovich, Naḥamu Ben-Shelomoh, Taurida *Ḥakham* in 1857-1879 (Evpatoria, 1799-1882)
Babovich, Simḥah Ben-Shelomoh, the first political *Ḥakham* (Evpatoria, 1790-1855)
Beim ('Azarievich [Ben-'Azaryah]), Yevva Moiseevna (Ḥawa Bat-Mosheh), the wife of Shelomoh Beim in 1853-1867 (b.1835-d. Bakhçesaray, 1883)
Beim, Shelomoh Ben-Avraham, *Ḥazzan* in Çufut-Qalé – Bakhçesaray (c.1843-1861) and Odessa (1861-1867), Taurida *Ḥakham* 1855-1857 (b. Çufut-Qalé, 1817- d. St.Petersburg, 1867).

---

[834] The data in the brackets designates the life-time of a person or the time when he/she is mentioned in a source; cursive script points at the corruption of original Hebrew/Turkic names as supplied in a source.

Binyamin Ben-Shemu'el Ağa, master of the Khan's mint (Çufut-Qalé, d.1824)

Binyamin Ben-Eliyah Douvan [Duvan], a traveler to the Holy Land in 1785 (Crimea, b.1747)

Çınaq, Shemu'el, mentioned in a graffito (Çufut-Qalé, 18th (?) century)

Dani, Yosef, emigrant from Mangoup (1833)

Dawid Ağa, the rival of Shemu'el Ben-Avraham Ben-Yoshiyah (Çufut-Qalé, 18th century)

Euphrosinia Bat-Yosef (Mangoup, d.5216 (=1455/1456 c.e.)

Firkovich, Avraham Ben-Shemu'el, collector and scholar (b. Luck, 1787 – d. Çufut-Qalé, 1874)

Firkovich, Gavri'el, son-in-law of Avraham Firkovich, husband of Milka [Malkah] Firkovich (Poland-Crimea) (d.a.1866)

Firkovich, Zaria Avra'amovich (Zerah Ben-Avraham), a son of Avraham Firkovich (Russia)

Younger Firkowitch, a son of Avraham Firkovich? (Çufut-Qalé, 1871)

Yishaq Ben-Mosheh (Mangoup, according to M.Sultanski died in 5034 (=1274 c.e.))

Yishaq Ben-Avraham of Troki, scholar and theologian, author of *Hizzuq Emunah* (c.1533-c.1594)

Yishaq Ben-Shelomoh, the head of Çufut-Qalé community (1754-1826).

Izaak Czelebi (Yishaq Ben-Mosheh Sinan-Çelebi), the founder of the printing press in Çufut-Qalé (c.1696-1756)

Jeschuah Dawidowitch Koen [Yeshu'ah Ben-Dawid Kohen], *Hazzan* in Feodosia in 1843

Jezza Nizanowicz ('Ezra Ben-Nisan HaRofe'), physician and theologian (Troki, 1595-1666)

Yosef Ben-Yeshu'ah HaMashbir, *Hazzan* in Derazhne, imprisoned in Bakchesaray in 1666, stayed in Çufut-Qalé in 1667-1670) (d. Luck (?), 1678)

Yosef Shelomoh Ben-Mosheh Lucki , scholar-emigrant to the Crimea (1777?-1844)

Juda Jeruh [Yehudah Yeru(shalmi), the "young Rabbi" of Çufut-Qalé (1871)

Karaimowicz, Eljasz, a Karaite (?), colonel of the Perejaslaw Cossacks (d.1648)

Qazas-Mıysız , Yehudah, carver of the tombstone inscriptions (Çufut-Qalé, 1837)

Qırğıy, Yishaq, emigrant from Mangoup (1833)

Qoyçu, Shabbetai, emigrant from Mangoup (1833)

Qoylu, Mosheh, *shammash* in Çufut-Qalé in the 1850s, grandfather of Shemu'el Ben-Shemaryah Pigit

Lewi-Babowicz (Levi-Babovich), Tuvyah Ben-Simḥah, *Ḥakham* in Sevastopol' (1910-1930) and Cairo (1934-1956) (Crimea, 1879-Cairo, 1956)

Mangubi, received Nicholas I in his house in Çufut-Qalé (1837)

small Mangub (Mangubi), son of a rich merchant in Odessa (1838)

Mardochai-Mosche [Mordekhai Mosheh], broker (Feodosia, 1843)

Mardochaj-Ben-Berach (Mordekhai Ben-Berakhah), head of Çufut-Qalé community (d. Sakiz (Chios), 1757)

Mordekhai Ben-Mordekhai (Eski-Qırım, d.1517).

Mordekhai Ben-Mosheh (Mordekhai Ben-Buta?), mentioned in graffito in Tepe-Kermen

Mordekhai Ben-Nisan Kukizow, scholar (Poland, d.1709)

Mosheh Ben-Sinani, the head of the Gözlöw community (1705)

Mosze Pasza (Mosheh Paşa Ben-Eliyah Paşa?, 18th century printer in Çufut-Qalé)

Pigit, Iosif [Yosef], last inhabitant of Çufut-Qalé (d. 1920s)

Pigit, Shemu'el Ben-Shemaryah (b. Çufut-Qalé, 1849 – d. Ekaterinoslav, 1911)

Pigit, Yakov [Ya'aqov], last inhabitant of Çufut-Qalé (d. 1920s)

Shemu'el Ben-Avraham Ben-Yoshiyah, master of the Khan's mint, assassinated in 1769 (Çufut-Qalé, 1716-1769)

Shemu'el Ben-Dawid, Crimean pilgrim to the Holy Land in 1641 (d.1673)

Shabbetai Ben-Barukh (Mangoup, 17th century?)

Simḥah Ben-Yosef HaZaqen, a Karaite (?) (late 18th – early 19th centuries?), the owner of the finger ring donated to A.S.Pushkin in the 1820s

Simḥah, the author of *Mangup Türküsi* (1790s-1800s)

Sinan Ben-Yosef (Sinan Çelebi), according to Firkovich arrived in the Crimea in 1501

Sultanski, Mordekhai, the author of *Zekher Ṣaddiqim*, *Ḥazzan* in Çufut-Qalé in 1826 – 1842?, in Evpatoria in 1855-1862 (Luck – Çufut-Qalé – Evpatoria, 1772-1862)

Symche Izaak (Simḥah Yiṣḥaq Ben-Mosheh Lucki), scholar-emigrant to Çufut-Qalé (d.1766)

Szapszal, Seraja (*alia:* Seraya/Sergey Markovich), son of Mordekhai (Mark) Moiseevich [Ben-Mosheh] Szapszal, elected Taurida *Ḥakham* in 1915, East European *Ḥakham* in 1928-1939/1945 (b. Bakhçesaray, 1873 – d. Vilnius, 1961)

Szomoil- Ağa (Shemu'el Ben-Avraham Ben-Yoshiah Yerushalmi Ağa), master of the Khan's mint, assassinated in 1769 (Çufut-Qalé, 1716-1769)

Szomolak Ağa, the rival of Shemu'el Ben-Avraham Ben-Yoshiyah (Çufut-Qalé, 18th century)

Szyszman [Şışman], I.B., the mayor of Qarasubazar (1900s)

Tongur, Mosheh, the mayor of Evpatoria until 1855/1856

Tschausch Awram (Çavuş Avraham Ben-No'aḥ HaKohen) (Çufut-Qalé, 1838)

Ussuff/Youssouf/Yosef, "rabbi" in Çufut-Qalé in the 1830s

Ya'aqov Ben-Mordekhai, chronicler (Mangoup, second half of the 17th century)

Yashish, Nazlı Bat-Berakhah, married to Simḥah Babovich in 1851 (Evpatoria)

Yiṣḥaq Ben-Eliyah Yeru(shalmi), mentioned in a graffito (Çufut-Qalé, 18th (?) century)

Yosef (Yosef Ağa?), the builder of the fountain *Yusuf Çoqraq* (Çufut-Qalé, before 1783)

Zeraḥ Ben-Avraham, a Troki Karaite traveler to the Holy Land in 1785

1.3. Byzantine and Near Eastern Karaite scholars
'Anan Ben-Dawid
Aharon Ben-Eliyahu
Aharon Ben-Yosef
Başyaçı, Mosheh
Beği family
Binyamin Ben-Mosheh al-Nahawendi
Dani'el Ben-Mosheh al-Qumisi
Eliyahu Başyaçı
Kalev Afendopoulo
Ya'aqov Ben-Re'uven
Ya'aqov al-Qirqisani

2. Geographical names[835]
2.1. Settlements
Aq-Meçıt
Armianskiy Bazar (Armiansk)
Ashdod
Bakhçeseray
Balaklava

---

[835] Cursive script points at unconventional and seldom used placenames.

Be'ersheva'
Kaffa (Feodosia)
Cairo
Çufut-Qalé
Constantinople (İstanbul)
Derazhne (Derazno, Derazhno, Derazhnia)
Eski-Qırım (Staryi Krym)
Gevherkerman
Gözlöw (Evpatoria)
Halicz
Hasköy
Hit
Jerusalem
Qalé-i Yahudiyan
Qarasubazar (Belogorsk)
Qaray-Qalé
Kerch
Kukizow
Qirq-Yer (Qirq-Or)
Luck
Lwow
Mangoup (Mangoup-Qalé, Theodoro)
Nowe Miasto
Or (Ferakh-Kerman, Perekop)
Poniewiez (Poniewież)
Poswol
Sela' HaQara'im
Sela' HaYehudim
Sevastopol'
Simferopol'
Taş-Cargan
Tepe-Kermen
Topracala
Troki
Yaşlov

2.2. Placenames
Aşlama-Dere
Baba-Qaya
Balta Tiymez
Burunçaq
Çufut-Çığargan-Burun (Cape of Calling for the Jews)

261

Yehoshafat Valley (Iosofatova dolina, 'Emeq Yehoshafat)
Karaimszczyzna (a Karaite district of Troki)
Maryam-Dere
Tabana-Dere
Yusuf Çoqraq

3. Ethnonyms[836]
Armenians
Black Jews
Bukharian Jews
Çufut (çufutlar)/ Dschufutt
Cossacks
Crimean Goths
Crimean Tatars
Falasha
Genoese
Greeks
Israelites
Karai Yaodi
Karaibes
Khazars
Qrımçaqlar
Melanchleni [Μελανχληνοι]
Mongols
Poles
Russians
Turks
yahudi (yahudiler)

4. Religions and religious movements
'Ananites
Boethusians
Christians
Christianity
Islam
Judaism
Millenarians
Muslims
Pharisees

---

[836] Cursive script points at unconventional or seldom used terms, or at corrupted and pejorative forms.

Protestants
Rabbanites
Sadducees
Samaritans
Shi'ites
Sunnites
Talmudists

Subject Index

H

Halicz, 30, 31, 32, 33, 35, 38, 39,
   129, 228, 238, 247, 261
Hasköy, 27, 64, 261
Helena Skirmuntowa, 93, 256
Henryk Rzewuski, 98
Hit, 29, 261

I

Islam, 26, 66, 76, 102, 103, 105,
   106, 107, 128, 247, 262
Israelites, 35, 67, 70, 81, 91, 171,
   205, 262
Ivan Basov, 134
Ivan Matveevich Muraviev-
   Apostol, 60
Izaak Czelebi, 128, 258

J

J.Kohl, 56
James Webster, 119, 183
Janos Kemeny, 190
Jean de Luca, 256
Jean De Reuilly, 65, 177
Jehosaphath Valley (Iosofatova
   dolina, 'Emeq Yehoshafat), 262
Jerusalem, 17, 20, 23, 27, 28, 29,
   34, 74, 89, 97, 117, 122, 123,
   124, 129, 148, 156, 174, 175,
   181, 185, 188, 191, 205, 225,
   238, 261
Jeschuah Dawidowitch Koen, 67,
   110, 258
Jezza Nizanowicz, 130, 258
Johann Georg Kohl, 61
Johann Schiltberger, 48, 217
Joseph Rohrer, 238
Juda Jeruh, 171, 258
Judaism, 20, 24, 25, 26, 29, 31,
   35, 36, 38, 59, 66, 68, 71, 117,
   126, 187, 218, 240, 242, 246,
   247, 262

K

Kaffa (Feodosia), 148, 261
Kalev Afendopulo, 27, 260
Karai Yaodi, 60, 72, 262
Karaibes, 61, 262
Karaimszczyzna (a Karaite district
   of Troki), 262
Karol Kaczkowski, 54, 116
Kerch, 67, 148, 231, 261
Khazars, 31, 35, 67, 68, 69, 71,
   111, 126, 147, 201, 246, 262
Kukizow, 31, 33, 261

L

Laurence Oliphant, 111, 115
Luck, 261
Ludwik Kondratowicz, 69, 257
Lwow, 261

M

Mangoup (Mangoup- Qalé,
   Theodoro), 261
Mardochai-Mosche, 219, 259
Mardochaj-Ben-Berach, 129, 259
Maria Guthrie, 60, 66, 112
Martinus Broniovius, 48, 203
Mary Holderness, 126, 132
Maryam-Dere, 150, 151, 155, 262
Melanchleni [Μελανχληνοι],
   262
Millenarians, 33, 70, 262
Minas Bzhishkian, 217
Mongols, 51, 67, 262
Mordekhai Ben-Berakhah, 259
Mordekhai Ben-Buta, 235, 259
Mordekhai Ben-Mosheh, 235, 259
Mordekhai Ben-Nisan Kukizow,
   33, 259
Mordekhai Sultanski, 30, 177, 204
Mosheh Ben-Sinani, 222, 259
Mosheh Koilu, 192
Mosheh Tongur, 226
Mosze Pasza, 259

Printed in the United States
117304LV00001B/1/A

9 780970 077561